DISCRETIONARY JUSTICE
A Preliminary Inquiry

DISCRETIONARY JUSTICE

A PRELIMINARY INQUIRY

KENNETH CULP DAVIS

LOUISIANA STATE UNIVERSITY PRESS
BATON ROUGE

Copyright © 1969, by
Louisiana State University Press

Library of Congress Catalog Number 69–12591
Manufactured in the United States of America by
Thos. J. Moran's Sons, Inc.

If all decisions involving justice to individual parties were lined up on a scale, with those governed by precise rules at the extreme left, those involving unfettered discretion at the extreme right, and those based on various mixtures of rules, principles, standards, and discretion in the middle, where on the scale might be the most serious and the most frequent injustice? I believe that officers and judges do reasonably well at the rules end of the scale, because rules make for evenhandedness, because creation of rules usually is relatively unemotional, and because decision-makers seldom err in the direction of excessive rigidity when individualization is needed. And probably injustice is almost as infrequent toward the middle of the scale, where principles or other guides keep discretion limited or controlled. I think the greatest and most frequent injustice occurs at the discretion end of the scale, where rules and principles provide little or no guidance, where emotions of deciding officers may affect what they do, where political or other favoritism may influence decisions, and where the imperfections of human nature are often reflected in the choices made.

The question whether injustice is more common at the discretion end of the scale should be pondered in the light of another significant question: With which portion of the scale is research primarily concerned? This question has an obvious answer. The further we go toward the rules end of the scale, the greater the quantity of useful literature; the further we go toward the discretion end of the scale, the fewer the books and articles. Indeed, I know of no systematic scholarly effort to penetrate discretionary justice.[1] Writers about law and government characteristically recognize the role of discretion and explore all around the perimeter of it but seldom try to penetrate it.

A few oversimplifications about the literature of jurisprudence, of public administration, and of administrative law can quickly sketch the general nature of the inadequacy of those bodies of literature with respect to discretionary justice: Jurisprudence misses many realities about justice because it is too much concerned with judges and legislators and not enough with administrators, executives, police, and prosecutors. Furthermore, jurisprudence acknowledges the law-discretion dichotomy and then spends itself almost entirely on the law half. Public administration writers, instead of observing, describing, and criticizing governmental processes, as I think they should do, hid their heads in the sand for several decades while denying that administration involved policy-making, and then they became preoccupied with trying to construct a value-free science of administration. That focus, happily, may be about to shift, for leaders in the field have asserted in a recent report: "Efforts to make it [public administration] a science have run afoul of reality." [2] The literature of administrative law is likewise singularly unhelpful to a study of discretionary justice, except peripherally here and there. Administrative law literature is devoted mainly to the 10 or 20 percent of administrative action that involves either formal proceedings or judicial review, and it largely neglects the 80 or 90 percent that escapes both formal proceedings and judicial review.

Doing the research needed for a developing legal system may be compared with keeping in repair an old roof of an enormous building. Our scholarly roof in its present condition is strange to behold.

---

1 Writings whose primary focus is substantive policy (e.g., prison administration, regulation of railroads, sentencing) often deal with exercise of discretion and may involve problems of justice. But I think a primary focus on discretionary justice cutting across all kinds of subject matter is altogether different.

2 John C. Honey, "A Report: Higher Education for Public Service," 27 Pub. Ad. Rev. 294, 301 (1967). See also Norton Long, "Politicians for Hire—The Dilemma of Education and the Task of Research," 25 Pub. Ad. Rev. 115, 118 (1965): "The problem of education of public administrators has been clouded by the misconception that only scientific knowledge constituted reliably useful instruction." And see footnote 52 of Chap. 8, below.

Most of it at the rules end is extremely strong, but portions at the discretion end have rotted away, leaving big holes where the water rushes in and does great damage. Only an occasional worker gives attention to the big holes, while the majority of workers swarm over the rules end, stopping or preventing slow leaks, and reinforcing at points where leaks seem impossible. The reinforcements are both excessive and spotty. The roof is a hundred feet thick in some spots, but these are the very spots that attract still more workers. Not much is attempted except patchwork, and that is one reason the workers ignore the big holes, many of which call for structural changes requiring architectural imagination.

For every new book that tries to do something about the big holes in the scholarly roof, a thousand seek to reinforce the portions that are already strong.

Of course, I do not mean to imply that I can repair the holes or even draw the blueprints for doing so. Although this essay does advance a number of proposals designed to improve our system of discretionary justice, I regard such proposals as incidental to my main purposes, which are (1) to dispel the virtually universal impression that discretionary justice is too elusive for study, (2) to open up problems that seem susceptible of further research and thinking, and (3) to formulate a framework for further study.

My hope is that this essay may induce some of the workers who are crowding the rules end of the roof to direct their talents to the areas of discretion that are so urgently in need of repair. The construction work that is needed will require many workers for many decades.

Acknowledgments. To Louisiana State University I am grateful for the gracious invitation to deliver the Edward Douglass White Lectures in April, 1966, and for the cordiality to my wife and me on that occasion from members of the LSU law faculty, including especially Dean and Mrs. Paul M. Hebert, Professor and Mrs. Melvin G. Dakin, and Professor and Mrs. Wex Malone. The lectures were an early version of what has gradually grown into this essay.

For valuable criticisms and suggestions, I am pleased to express my gratitude and my thanks—

To four friends who have read the entire manuscript, Professor Walter Gellhorn of Columbia University, Professor Stanley Kaplan of the University of Chicago, Professor Frank Newman of the University of California (Berkeley), and Professor Victor Rosenblum of Northwestern University, who, when this is published, will have become president of Reed College.

To one friend who read the early version presented in the lectures, Professor Walter Blum of the University of Chicago.

To two friends who have read portions pertaining to criminal processes, Professor Norval Morris and Dr. Hans Mattick, director and associate director of the Center for Studies in Criminal Justice at the University of Chicago.

To five friends who have especially helped on problems of European law and practice, Professor Max Rheinstein of the University of Chicago, Dr. Ernst Pakuscher of the German Supreme Administrative Court, Professor Fritz Scharpf of the University of Constance, Professor Gerhard Casper of the University of Chicago, and Professor Peter Schlechtriem of the Universities of Chicago and Freiburg.

For assistance in summer interviewing in Washington, as well as for ideas and imagination, I am grateful to Professor Daniel Gifford of the State University of New York at Buffalo, Professor Clark Havighurst of Duke University, Professor Norman Abrams of the University of California at Los Angeles, and Professor Gerard Moran of Rutgers University.

For facts, ideas, confidences, and inspiration, I am indebted to innumerable government officers, probably several hundred, who have generously given their time and energy to answer questions and to contribute to my continuing education in the realities of the administrative process.

For financial assistance I am grateful to the Walter E. Meyer Research Institute of Law and to the University of Chicago, and for free office space in Washington, to the Brookings Institution and to the law firm of Arnold and Porter.

K.C.D.

Contents

DISCRETIONARY JUSTICE
A Preliminary Inquiry

The What and the
Why of Discretion

1. *Where law ends.* Engraved in stone on the Department of Justice Building in Washington, on the Pennsylvania Avenue side where swarms of bureaucrats and others pass by, are these five words: "Where law ends tyranny begins." [1]

I think that in our system of government, where law ends tyranny need not begin. Where law ends, discretion begins, and the exercise of discretion may mean either beneficence or tyranny, either justice or injustice, either reasonableness or arbitrariness.

One who enters that Department of Justice Building may quickly find that the workers there who are exercising governmental power are concerned with applying law, with making discretionary determinations, and with various mixtures of law and discretion. They are much more occupied with discretion than with law. Not one of them who understands his job would agree that where law ends tyranny begins. Every conscientious employee of the Department of Justice, from the Attorney General on down, is striving to assure that where law ends, wise and beneficent exercise of discretionary power will begin.

The central inquiry of this essay is what can be done to assure that where law ends tyranny will not begin. More precisely, the central inquiry is what can be done that is not now done to minimize injustice from exercise of discretionary power. The answer is, in broad terms, that we should eliminate much unnecessary discretionary power and that we should do much more than we have been

1 The quotation is from William Pitt.

3

doing to confine, to structure, and to check necessary discretionary power. The goal is not the maximum degree of confining, structuring, and checking; the goal is to find the optimum degree for each power in each set of circumstances.

The two subjects on which the literature of administrative law primarily focuses—trial-type hearings and judicial review—are here de-emphasized, because our main concern is with the vast mass of discretionary justice that is beyond the reach of both judicial review and trial-type hearings.

2. *What is discretion?* A public officer has discretion whenever the effective limits on his power leave him free to make a choice among possible courses of action or inaction.

Some elements of this definition need special emphasis. Especially important is the proposition that discretion is not limited to what is authorized or what is legal but includes all that is within "the *effective* limits" on the officer's power. This phraseology is necessary because a good deal of discretion is illegal or of questionable legality. Another facet of the definition is that a choice to do nothing—or to do nothing now—is definitely included; perhaps inaction decisions are ten or twenty times as frequent as action decisions. Discretion is exercised not merely in final dispositions of cases or problems but in each interim step; and interim choices are far more numerous than the final ones.[2] Discretion is not limited to substantive choices but extends to procedures, methods, forms, timing, degrees of emphasis, and many other subsidiary factors.

An officer who decides what to do or not to do often (1) finds facts, (2) applies law, and (3) decides what is desirable in the circumstances after the facts and the law are known. The third of these three functions is customarily called "the exercise of discretion," and it is the subject of this essay.

Even though no position here taken depends upon further refinement of the meaning of discretion, the full reality about discretion is somewhat more complex. A decision as to what is desirable may include not only weighing desirability but also guessing about unknown facts and making a judgment about doubtful law, and the mind that makes the decision does not necessarily separate facts,

---

2 Sec. 8 of this chapter discusses interim decisions.

law, and discretion. Furthermore, the term "discretion" may or may not include the judgment that goes into finding facts from conflicting evidence and into interpreting unclear law; the usage is divided. And still another complexity must be reckoned with: An officer who exercises discretion needs not only the facts which give rise to the discretionary problem; he may also need facts to guide his exercise of discretion. For instance, the policeman finds facts that the boy has committed a misdemeanor, but his determination whether to lecture and release the boy or whether to arrest him may depend upon his finding facts about the comparative effects on such a boy of either discretionary choice; appraising this second set of facts, or guessing about them, is clearly a part of the exercise of discretion. So the reality may be rather untidy: Exercising discretion may be a part of finding facts and applying law, and finding facts may be a part of exercising discretion.[3]

When we isolate what we regard as the exercise of discretion, we find three principal ingredients—facts, values, and influences. But an officer who is exercising discretion seldom separates these three elements; most discretionary decisions are intuitive, and responses to influences often tend to crowd out thinking about values.[4]

3. *Discretionary justice to individual parties, social justice, and policy-making.* Without trying to draw precise lines, this essay is concerned primarily with a portion of discretionary power and with a portion of justice—with that portion of discretionary power

3 Finding facts may also be a part of determining law. The facts about the parties, to which the law is applied, are called adjudicative facts. The facts that are used for the purpose of determining law or policy or exercising discretion are called legislative facts. See 2 Davis, *Administrative Law Treatise* § 15.03 (1958) .

4 One approach to a study of discretionary justice—not the one here taken— could be to penetrate the mental, psychological, and emotional mechanisms that operate in the making of a determination involving discretionary justice. Perhaps all choices of values are ultimately determined by the emotions, but even if that is true, the intellect may still play a major role. One appealing position is the following: "The great insight of modern philosophy . . . is that ultimate convictions can be based neither on intellectual intuition nor on proofs which must after all depend on premises. . . . That our valuations are tied up with our emotions and not grounded in a rational vision of absolute values is surely right, but we should not ignore the difference between untutored emotion and cultivated emotion. . . . [T]here is a vast difference between an informed and an uninformed choice, a responsible and an irresponsible decision." Walter A. Kaufmann, *Critique of Religion and Philosophy* (1961) , 410.

which pertains to justice, and with that portion of justice which pertains to individual parties.[5]

Important subjects which are excluded from the primary focus of this essay, even though some are inevitably drawn into the discussion, include: (1) Broad policy-making, as distinguished from deciding individual cases; (2) social justice, that is, justice for segments of the population, as distinguished from justice for individual parties; (3) the discretion of a court with respect to making and remaking and applying law;[6] and (4) the discretion of juries.[7]

Although we are concerned with justice to individual parties both in courts and outside courts, instances of administrative discretionary justice to individual parties are probably at least a hundred times as numerous as instances of judicial discretionary justice to individual parties; courts do not usually make discretionary determinations on such questions as whether to initiate, whether to investigate, whether to arrest, whether to prosecute, whether to negotiate, whether to settle, whether to do nothing.

Discretionary justice obviously overlaps with policy-making, because the central part of each is a determination of what is desirable, but the two concepts are nevertheless quite different. All policy-making, by its intrinsic nature, is discretionary, but only a part of it has to do with justice. Whether to aim at six years or twelve years for putting a man on the moon is a problem of policy but not a problem of justice. The major decisions reached in the White House are all discretionary but seldom involve discretionary justice—foreign policy, military policy, domestic policy in programs planned for congressional enactment. Such policies may contain ingredients of what we call social justice, but such policies seldom include determinations of rights of individual parties. Of course, the President does administer discretionary justice to individual parties in granting or denying pardons, in signing or vetoing private bills, and in other instances.

5 "Individual parties" include corporations, associations, and even governmental units (such as a school board under the Civil Rights Act), as well as individuals.
6 On this subject, see especially Karl Llewellyn, *The Common Law Tradition* (1960).
7 See Harry Kalven and Hans Zeisel, *The American Jury* (1967).

If policy-making means determining what is desirable, then discretionary justice always involves policy-making, unless one thinks of policy-making as limited to the making of policies that can be stated in the form of generalizations that go beyond particular cases, and unless the determination of policy is thought to be unique or nonrecurring, so that generalization is inappropriate.

One approach to the administrative process—much the most common one—is to regard it as an instrument for carrying out policies enacted by the legislative body and as an instrument for the proliferation of subordinate policies. This approach emphasizes the regulatory agencies; indeed, it often tends to ignore all agencies that do not regulate. The usual criterion of judgment is then the broad economic and social consequences of the policies developed. Such an approach may be largely valid when it is not pushed too far, for regulation is a vital function.

Yet quite a different emphasis may also be a valid one. The administrative process is of many kinds, and each kind may have many facets. One dominant function other than the formulation of general policy is the administration of justice for individual parties, that is, working out fair dispositions of problems that affect particular parties. Whether or not the agency's function is to regulate, a proper focus in examining the agency's performance is the substantive and procedural fairness of what it does. To a greater extent than is usually recognized in the relevant literature, many federal, state, and local administrators are concerned primarily with problems of justice for individual parties and only secondarily with the formulation of general policy. Perhaps more than three-quarters of the eighty thousand formal adjudications in federal agencies each year involve no greater degree of policy determination than the average degree of cases in the federal courts.

Some of our most important agencies are no more striving to achieve policy goals than are the courts; their prime focus and even their almost exclusive focus may be the administration of justice. Take, for instance, the Social Security Administration in its adjudication of claims. The answers are highly crystallized for old age and survivors claims, and computers do most of the work; the tiny proportion of disputed claims are disposed of with great efficiency; significant policy questions still arise and probably always will, but they are highly exceptional. The difficulties are in disability claims, which are often controversial. A great many of them even spill over into reviewing courts after the Appeals Council has acted on them at an administrative appellate level. Far from being a crusader for expanding social welfare, the Administration is trying to follow the intent of Congress as expressed in the statute and its legislative history, and the Administration is in general much less liberal to claimants than are the reviewing courts, which in a startlingly large proportion of the cases reverse the Administration's denial of benefits. The task of the Administration is basically one of administering justice, not one of formulating general policies in some legislatively-designated direction.

Among the most important administrators in America are the police—all 420,000 of them. They make some of our most crucial policies and a large portion of their function is the administration of justice to individual parties.[8] Protective and service functions consume more of their time than law enforcement, but the two overlap, and both may involve the administration of justice. The police are constantly confronted with problems of fairness to individuals, and such problems are often intertwined with problems of policy. When should they not make an arrest that can be properly made? When should they stop and frisk? When should they say "break it up"? When should they make deals with known criminals, as with the addict-informer? What minor disputes should they mediate or even adjudicate? The surprising fact is, as brought out by the President's Crime Commission,[9] that these mixed problems of justice and policy are seldom decided by heads of departments but are left largely to the discretion of individual policemen, who often act illegally without disapproval of their superiors.

A mere list of agencies in which problems of justice to individual parties are the dominant ones is an impressive reminder that the regulatory function is only a small part of the total administrative process. In the area of criminal justice are not only judges

---

8   See pages 80–96, below.
9   President's Commission on Law Enforcement and Administration of Justice, *The Challenge of Crime in a Free Society*, (1967), 91–123.

and police but also prosecutors, parole boards, probation officers, the Pardon Attorney and his state counterparts, the Bureau of Prisons and similar state agencies. Innumerable state agencies administer discretionary justice—workmen's compensation commissions, unemployment compensation commissions, welfare agencies, tax collectors. Some examples of federal agencies whose primary function is more in the nature of administration of justice than of regulation include the Immigration and Naturalization Service, the Board of Immigration Appeals, the Visa Office of the State Department, the Internal Revenue Service, the United States Tax Court, the Renegotiation Board, seventeen separate Boards of Contract Appeals, courts martial, the Indian Claims Commission, the Patent Office, the Wage Appeals Board, the Bureau of Employees' Compensation and the Employees' Compensation Appeals Board, the Veterans Administration, the United States Parole Board, one or more selective service boards in almost every county in the nation, selective service appeal boards in every judicial district.

Of course, even the agencies that are primarily regulatory are also concerned with problems of justice—and with mixtures and compounds that include problems of justice. In regulatory agencies, an ever present objective is to find the most satisfactory accommodation of the needs of effectiveness to the often conflicting needs of fairness, both substantive and procedural.

4. *The flavor and variety of discretionary justice.* Discretionary decisions number in the billions annually, even though the yearly number of all civil and criminal cases commenced in all federal courts is under one hundred thousand and the number going to trial is under twelve thousand. The amount of thought that goes into a discretionary decision varies from a fraction of a second to many man-years. The interests affected vary from trifles to lives or liberties or millions of dollars.

Some typical examples will suggest the flavor and variety of discretionary justice:

(1) Through plea bargaining a prosecutor agrees with one defendant to reduce a felony charge to a misdemeanor but refuses to do so with another defendant.

(2) The manager of a public housing project, following the cus-

tomary system, evicts a mother and four children on the ground
of "undesirability" without giving any more specific reason.

(3) To prevent a riot, city police round up ninety Negro youths
and keep them in jail for a month through impossibly high bail
and delayed proceedings. (A real case, protested and publicized
by the American Civil Liberties Union.)

(4) The Federal Communications Commission announces an investigation of the American Telephone and Telegraph Company
and the Associated Bell Companies, and the market price of the
stock declines three and a half billion dollars during the ensuing
three months. (A real case; the announcement was made October
27, 1965.)

(5) A traffic policeman warns a violator instead of writing a ticket because the violator is a lawyer and the police of the city (Chicago) have a long-standing custom of favoring lawyers. (A real
case.)

(6) A government procurement officer in negotiating for an item
whose cost of production is likely to drop drastically because of
rapid technological developments suggests to a corporate executive that he is more likely to win the contract if he reduces his own
salary to a specified figure for the duration of the contract. (This
is a recent development but it is becoming a commonplace.)

(7) A social worker, who is without training in social work and
has serious psychiatric problems of her own, refrains from reporting evidence that a mother who is receiving aid for her dependent
children has a man in the house; then the social worker, over the
mother's bitter opposition, prescribes policies for controlling the
children, using as an effective sanction the threat of discontinuing
aid payments because of the man in the house. (A real case, but
the real-life facts are less clear than this statement of them.)

(8) A judge who has power to sentence a convicted felon to five
years in the penitentiary imposes a sentence of one year and sus-
pends it, even though he knows that one of his colleagues would
impose a five-year sentence. (A commonplace event.)

(9) The Federal Trade Commission, responding to pressure of
two Senators who come to the office of the commission's chairman,
grants a merger clearance to two corporations, without public announcement, without a systematic statement of the facts, without

a reasoned opinion, without a comparison of the case to relevant precedents, without supervision or check by any other authority, without the knowledge or participation of the commission's staff, and without opening any of the related papers to public inspection. (A common occurrence in the FTC.) [10]

(10) The intake officer who is helping administer the program of aid to families of dependent children rejects a woman's application on the ground that the woman cannot find her absent husband. The applicable regulation provides that the applicant must "aid" in finding an absent spouse but it does not require that the applicant "find" the spouse. (An accurate statement of a frequent occurrence in Illinois.)

(11) The United States Parole Board, without stating reasons, denies parole to a prisoner who has waited five years for eligibility. The Administrative Procedure Act requires a statement of reasons, but the board, in a 1964 printed pamphlet entitled "Functions of the United States Parole Board," explains that "the Board does not sit as a group" to decide cases, that each member votes separately, and that "it is therefore impossible to state precisely why a particular prisoner was or was not granted parole." (An accurate statement of the system long followed.)

(12) Two students study together in the same department of the same university. The facts about each that are relevant to the draft are identical. One is drafted because his draft board follows one rule. The other is given a student deferment because his draft board, a different one, follows another rule. No administrative, judicial, or legislative authority requires the two boards to decide the same question the same way. (A hypothetical case but an accurate statement of the system.)

(13) The Assistant Attorney General in Charge of the Antitrust Division institutes a prosecution against a corporation. His successor, disagreeing with his prosecution policy, dismisses the prosecution, without stating facts, without stating reasons, without publicly relating the case to policies developed in other similar cases, and without any public statement of the basic policies involved. (A real case, widely publicized during 1966.)

10 See pages 113–16, below, for an elaboration of the FTC secret system of merger clearances.

(14) A student in India wins a scholarship in an American university, studies chemistry, leads his class, receives an offer of an excellent position in a large American corporation, but is ineligible to have his student visa changed to allow him to remain legally in the United States. Responding to the pressures of the corporation, the Immigration Service nevertheless agrees informally not to prosecute. The Indian excels and is rapidly promoted. Then he receives a message that his mother is dying in India. An executive of his corporation asks the Immigration Service to approve his visiting India for two weeks. A top officer of the Service says no. The Indian must choose between keeping his position and visiting his dying mother. (A real case, 1965, unreported.)

5. *Illegal discretionary action.* A startlingly high proportion of all official discretionary action pertaining to administration of justice is illegal or of doubtful legality. This is true in all units of American government—federal, state, and local. Yet the problem raised by the illegality of official action is an exceedingly complex one that clearly cannot be solved by some decision somewhere that all officers must obey the law. Of course, some officers are on occasion lawless in such a way that everyone would agree that the only proper course is to compel them to obey the law. The difficult problems have to do with choices by conscientious officers to exceed the strict limits of their authority in order to do justice or to protect the public interest or to produce the results that common sense requires; yet minds may differ as to what is justice or the public interest or common sense. Furthermore, the law-making authorities often acquiesce in or even encourage illegal official action. Sometimes the proper course may be to make legal the illegal official practices that have long been a part of our system; this is one way the law grows.

Of the illustrations of discretionary justice listed in the preceding section, more than half may involve illegality. Some degree of illegality may be involved in numbers 1, 3, 5, 6, 7, 9, 11, and 14. Almost all prosecutors engage in plea bargaining, but it is unauthorized in most jurisdictions, and it often rests upon misrepresentation. Thus, a recent study says that

. . . the parties typically act as if no prior negotiations had occurred.

Trial judges, although they are aware that negotiation for pleas is a common practice, routinely ask the defendant whether any promises have been made to him. Notwithstanding the fact that the plea has been the subject of negotiation, the defendant usually answers in the negative, and the prosecutor and defense counsel seldom indicate to the contrary.[11]

The President's Crime Commission reports: "Under existing practice the fact that negotiations have occurred is commonly denied on the record, and so is the explicit or tacit expectation that the judge will impose the agreed punishment." [12] The dominant thinking, however, is that plea bargaining is a necessary part of criminal justice.

Preventive detention is not only clearly illegal but clearly unconstitutional. But police, prosecutors, and judges nevertheless often find it necessary. That illegal preventive detention was a main factor in preventing race riots in Chicago during the summer of 1967 is widely believed. The American Civil Liberties Union made charges that two hundred persons were victims of "indiscriminate arrest and imprisonment prior to trial for long periods up to a month, due to the setting of excessive bail." Judge Louis J. Gilberto explained: "There is a legal theory that in these unusual circumstances people should be detained until the unrest is over."

Of course, the Chicago system of police favoritism to lawyers in traffic violations is unjust and pernicious and ought to be eradicated. But it continues.

The government procurement officer may lack authority to fix the salary of the corporate executive but what counts is power, not authority, and the officer may be conscientiously serving the public interest by informally controlling the salary. Even so, what happens when the officer is not conscientious? What are the realities about correction of abuses? The case is typical of a common phenomenon; an officer's practical power far exceeds the authority that has been conferred upon him.

Essentially the same phenomenon, with a different twist, is in-

11 "American Bar Association Project on Minimum Standards for Criminal Justice, Pleas of Guilty" (Tentative Draft, 1967), 61.
12 *The Challenge of Crime in a Free Society*, 135–36.

volved in the case of the social worker who abuses her power. The mother submits to the injustice and to the illegality because in one aspect she benefits from it and the only available alternative is worse.

Whether the Federal Trade Commission in secretly giving a merger clearance on the basis of political pressure is acting illegally is doubtful and depends on the case, but even if what it does is legal its action is atrocious from the standpoint of good government.[13]

The Parole Board's refusal to give reasons for a denial of parole is a clear-cut violation of the Administrative Procedure Act, and the violation has continued from the time that act was made law in 1946. The result is illegal and seems to me also unjust. At the same time the board is denying parole without telling the prisoner why, it makes public claims that it is "rehabilitating" prisoners.

The intake officer's denial of public assistance to the woman who cannot "find" her husband is in clear violation of the applicable regulation, and this particular illegality has been frequent in Illinois. The cure is interesting and significant: The Independent Union of Public Aid Employees has prepared a Welfare Handbook, manages to get it into the hands of many applicants, and helps applicants to assert their rights.[14]

The Immigration Service does not always prosecute deportable aliens. In this instance, yielding to the chemical corporation's pressure was easier. But when the Indian wanted to visit his dying mother for two weeks, leniency required more than mere inaction, and the Service was unwilling to take illegal affirmative action. That illegal inaction is much easier than illegal action seems to be a basic truth.

The problems of what to do about official illegality are one major focus of this essay. Some may have simple solutions but some are especially difficult.

13   See the full account of the practice, pages 113–16, below.
14   A management consulting firm in 1960 found that 32 percent of reasons for denial of applications for aid to families of dependent children in Cook County were "unlawful" or "questionable". Greenleigh Associates, Inc., *Facts, Fallacies and Future—A Study of the Aid to Dependent Children Program of Cook County, Illinois* (1960), 56.

6. *Why discretionary justice—why not rules?* In the administration of justice in court, few cases are decided without either applying rules or using rules as guides for discretionary decisions. Why is administrative discretionary justice so much dominated by discretion which is unguided by rules or even by standards?

This question has three answers: (1) Much discretionary justice not now governed by or guided by rules should be. (2) Much discretionary justice is without rules because no one knows how to formulate rules. (3) Much discretionary justice is without rules because discretion is preferred to any rules that might be formulated; individualized justice is often better, or thought to be better, than the results produced by precise rules. The second and third answers overlap. Each answer will now be explained.

(1) One major thesis of this essay is that the degree of discretion is often much greater than it should be. The problem is not merely to choose between rule and discretion but is to find the optimum point on the rule-to-discretion scale. A standard, principle, or rule can be so vague as to be meaningless, it can have a slight meaning or considerable meaning, it can have some degree of controlling effect, or it can be so clear and compelling as to leave little or no room for discretion. The degree of discretion depends not only on grants of authority to administrators but also on what the administrators do to confine and structure their own power, and on what they do to enlarge their power. In general, the thesis later developed is that the degree of administrative discretion should often be more restricted; some of the restricting can be done by legislators but most of this task must be performed by administrators. The need for "confining" discretion is the subject of Chapter 3.

(2) Sometimes no one knows how to write governing rules or even meaningful standards. Shortly after the United States entered the Second World War, Congress in early 1942 enacted a Renegotiation Act, authorizing administrative officers to recover for the government "excessive profits" made by those who supplied goods to the government. A few months later in 1942, Congress provided a definition: "The term 'excessive profits' means any amount of a contract or subcontract price which is found as a result of renegotiation to represent excessive profits." Did this definition

tell the administrators what profits were excessive? The administrators were at work trying to make that determination in concrete cases, and they were gradually building something less than meaningful standards—a mere list of the factors that would be taken into account in deciding what profits were excessive. When the statute was first written, Congress was unable even to furnish such a list. As experience in adjudication developed—and it included adjudication even though it was called renegotiation—the administrators gradually learned what they were doing on some types of problems. The Supreme Court upheld the delegation of discretionary power even though, at the time it did so, many problems still had to be governed by unguided administrative discretion.[15] Clearly, no one knew how to write rules that would answer all the questions, not even all the principal questions. The best way to get answers was by allowing the administrators to invent answers as they were confronted by each concrete case. This was responsible government, because the degree of discretionary power was commensurate with the need for discretionary power, because the administrators were developing guides for the exercise of discretion as fast as they reasonably could, because legislative committees carefully supervised the administrators to protect against abuses, and because review by the Tax Court was readily available to correct misuse of power.

The history of renegotiation since enactment of the Act of 1951 is an outstanding example of discretion which is needlessly broad. Senator Taft aptly said in 1951 that "this Board would have perfectly unlimited discretion." [16] The Renegotiation Board has not significantly confined its own discretion through regulations, policy statements, or adjudicatory opinions. The thousands of decided cases could have become important guides for discretion, but a regulation explicitly provides that opinions and orders are unavailable to the public "inasmuch as they are regarded as confidential for good cause shown, by reason of the confidential data furnished by contractors and relating to their business." The regulation also provides that "Opinions and orders are not cited as precedents in any renegotiation proceedings." [17] Although the

15   Lichter v. United States, 334 U.S. 742 (1948).
16   97 Congressional Record 1347.
17   32 CFR § 1480.8.

board properly protects confidential business information, its concealment of its grounds for decisions seems clearly unjustified. Whatever standards, principles, or rules it has developed should be out in the open. This kind of disclosure can easily be accomplished without revealing confidential information; even when facts need to be stated, the identification of particular parties can be withheld.

(3) Even when rules can be written, discretion is often better. Rules without discretion cannot fully take into account the need for tailoring results to unique facts and circumstances of particular cases. The justification for discretion is often the need for individualized justice. This is so in the judicial process as well as in the administrative process.

Every governmental and legal system in world history has involved both rules and discretion. No government has ever been a government of laws and not of men in the sense of eliminating all discretionary power. Every government has always been *a government of laws and of men*. A close look at the meaning of Aristotle, the first user of the phrase "government of laws and not of men," shows quite clearly that he did not mean that governments could exist without discretionary power.[18]

Even in the administration of justice (a small portion of all governmental processes) no government has ever come close to a government of laws and not of men. Every system of administration of justice has always had a large measure of discretionary power. Thus, Dean Pound tells us, very simply, that "in no legal system, however minute and detailed its body of rules, is justice administered wholly by rule and without any recourse to the will of the judge and his personal sense of what should be done to achieve a just result in the case before him. Both elements are to be found in all administration of justice." [19]

A leading English work on jurisprudence says: "The total exclusion of judicial discretion by legal principle is impossible in

18 For a full analysis of the position of Aristotle, see Jerome Frank, *If Men Were Angels* (1942), 190–211, abundantly supporting this conclusion at 203: "This much we can surely say: For Aristotle, from whom Harrington derived the notion of a government of laws and not of men, that notion was not expressive of hostility to what today we call administrative discretion. Nor did it have such a meaning for Harrington."
19 2 Pound, *Jurisprudence* (1959), 355.

any system. However great is the encroachment of the law, there must remain some residuum of justice which is not according to law—some activities in respect of which the administration of justice cannot be defined or regarded as the enforcement of the law." [20] Of course, many of the tasks assigned to administrative agencies obviously call for a much greater degree of discretion than the typical tasks of judges.

Even in something generally supposed to be so much controlled by law as the administration of criminal justice, administrative discretion is far more important than rules. All the rules that call for punishment can be nullified by any one of five sets of discretionary power—the discretion of the police not to arrest, the discretion of the prosecutor not to prosecute or to trade a lesser charge for a plea of guilty, the discretion of the judge in favor of suspended sentence or probation, the discretion of the parole officer to release, the discretion of the executive to pardon. We have not yet found a way to eliminate discretion with respect to arresting, prosecuting, sentencing, paroling, and pardoning without destroying crucial values we want to preserve.[21] Perhaps it is not too much to say that the essence of criminal justice lies in the exercise of discretionary power, despite the continuing importance of the jury trial.

On the civil side of the court, the need for discretion along with rules is manifest in the rise of equity, which is essentially a reaction against the tendency to govern too much through rigid rules and the main purpose of which is to replace rules with some measure of discretion. Both the Greeks and the Romans recognized the need for equity. For instance, Aristotle wrote: "An arbitrator decides in accordance with equity, a judge in accordance with

---

20 *Salmond on Jurisprudence* (11th ed. by Glanville Williams, 1957) , 44.
21 Judge Charles D. Breitel, of the New York Court of Appeals, said in "Controls in Criminal Law Enforcement," 27 Univ. of Chi. L. Rev. 427, 428 (1960) : "There is more recognizable discretion in the field of crime control, including that part of its broad sweep which lawyers call 'criminal law,' than in any other field in which law regulates conduct." With all regulatory agencies specifically in mind, I agree. And I also agree with Judge Breitel's concluding observation: "Recourse to rule of law in an effort to eliminate or reduce discretion is a natural reaction to the abuse of discretion; but it is, nevertheless, a naive reaction. For, in recognizing the place of discretion we perforce accept the limitations on verbalized law." We cannot eliminate discretion and we should not try to. But we can and should eliminate unnecessary discretion.

law; and it was for this purpose that arbitration was introduced, namely, that equity might prevail." [22] The Roman praetor, with his *jus praetorium,* was introduced for the purpose of relieving the rigidities of the older law, the *jus civile.* Of course, the story of the rise of equity in English law is familiar: The law courts became too much addicted to rigid and technical rules, and parties suffering from the resulting injustice went to the King for relief; the King appointed a Chancellor to help him, gradually the number of Chancellors was increased, and the significant power gradually went over into what became known as the Court of Chancery. In time, of course, the Chancery Court developed its own rules, but it kept a better balance between rule and discretion.

A formulation by Morris R. Cohen seems especially appealing:

[L]egal history shows, if not alternating periods of justice according to law and justice without law, at least periodic waves of reform during which the sense of justice, natural law, or equity introduces life and flexibility into the law and makes it adjustable to its work. In course of time, however, under the social demand for certainty, equity gets hardened and reduced to rigid rules, so that, after a while, a new reform wave is necessary.[23]

Note that in Cohen's statement, when equity is reduced to rules, reform is needed. Rules will not suffice. Rules must be supplemented with discretion. When discretion shrinks too much, affirmative action is needed to recreate it. For many circumstances the mechanical application of a rule means injustice; what is needed is individualized justice, that is, justice which to the appropriate extent is tailored to the needs of the individual case. Only through discretion can the goal of individualized justice be attained. Only through discretion can what Cohen calls "the life and flexibility" of equity be achieved.

Of course, the vast experience that proves the need for discretion in equity courts also proves the need for even greater discretion for the complex tasks assigned our modern administrative agencies. Some who have confused the existence of discretionary power with the abuse of discretionary power have cried out for

22 Rhet. I. 13. 19.
23 *Law and the Social Order* (1933) , 261.

eliminating or minimizing administrative discretion, and at times our system has responded to such voices, as it did, for instance, in developing the judicial doctrine that legislative power may not be delegated. But the legislative bodies, sensing the need for administrative discretion on one problem after another, have gone on delegating, as even the most conservative legislatures have felt compelled to do. The result is that perhaps the most significant twentieth-century change in the fundamentals of the legal system has been the tremendous growth of discretionary power. And the prospect is, for better or for worse, that discretionary power will continue to grow. The three main reasons for the continued increase of discretion are that (1) our governments—federal, state, and local—are likely to go on undertaking tasks for the execution of which no one is able to prepare advance rules, (2) even when we have capacity to formulate rules discretion is often desirable for individualized justice, and (3) in this country we have developed a habit of allowing discretionary power to grow which far exceeds what is necessary and which is much less controlled than it should be. What we need to do is to work on the third reason, not to minimize discretion or to maximize its control, but to eliminate unnecessary discretion and to find the optimum degree of control.

On a somewhat different level, creativity is impossible without discretion. No governmental authority—neither a legislative body nor an executive nor a court nor an agency—can make new policy or new law without exercising discretion. Everyone recognizes the necessity for creative action through legislation, but the most difficult creative thinking is usually introduced through executive or administrative solutions of specific problems. What happens over and over is that a legislative body sees a problem but does not know how to solve it; accordingly, it delegates the power to work on the problem, telling the delegate that what it wants is the true, the good, and the beautiful—or just and reasonable results, or furtherance of the public interest. Then the delegate, through case-to-case consideration, where the human mind is often at its best, nibbles at the problem and finds little solutions for each little bite of the big problem. Creativeness in the nibbling sometimes opens the way for perspective thinking about the whole big problem, and large solutions sometimes emerge.

Of course, what has just been described is the basic process of the creation of common law. Most of American law is the product of adjudication—of creativeness in the process of deciding particular cases. Case-to-case adjudication, when the system works satisfactorily, gradually develops rules, which are then used to guide adjudication of later cases. Without discretionary power to create in the process of deciding particular cases, the tribunal, whether judicial or administrative, might never be able to develop rules. The crucial point in the process is discretionary power to be creative in particular cases.

The conception of the common-law method that the judge must be free to create, and the conception of equity that discretion is needed as an escape from rigid rules are a far cry from the proposition that where law ends tyranny begins. The ideal toward which we should strive is this: Where law ends individualized justice begins.

7. *The lifeblood of the administrative process.* In the recent literature of administrative law, a false impression has become widespread that the most crucial administrative function is that of informal adjudication (that is, adjudication without trial-type hearings). No one can deny that informal adjudication is far more vital than formal adjudication (through trial-type hearings). For instance, to choose an extreme illustration, last year the Federal Communications Commission issued more than 800,000 licenses, each an "adjudication" as the term is defined in § 2 of the Administrative Procedure Act, but the FCC held only 115 formal hearings. The ratio here is about seven thousand to one. All over the government, the ratio of informal adjudication to formal may be fifty or a hundred to one.

Even so, informal adjudication is not the most vital portion of the administrative process. Discretionary action is, and *informal adjudication is only a small portion of discretionary action.*

Probably what has given rise to the misimpression is the much-quoted statement by the Attorney General's Committee on Administrative Procedure that "informal procedures constitute the vast bulk of administrative adjudication and are truly the lifeblood of the administrative process." [24] The statement never should have

24 Report (1941), 35.

put administrative adjudication at the center; the lifeblood is informal procedures, but informal procedures far transcend administrative adjudication.

Not many questions for discretionary justice ever reach the stage of adjudication, whether formal or informal. Discretionary justice includes initiating, investigating, prosecuting, negotiating, settling, contracting, dealing, advising, threatening, publicizing, concealing, planning, recommending, supervising. Often the most important discretionary decisions are the negative ones, such as not to initiate, not to investigate, not to prosecute, not to deal, and the negative decision usually means a final disposition without ever reaching the stage of either formal or informal adjudication.

Choices not to act as well as choices to act in any of these ways may involve not only the whether but also the who, the how, the when, and the how much. For instance, a decision to investigate calls for further discretionary determinations of what to investigate, what parties, by what methods, when, how broadly and how deeply. Each facet of each question necessarily involves a separate discretionary determination. Even a negative decision has to determine what and who will not be investigated when.

All along the line an enormous discretionary power is the power to do nothing. For instance, the power not to prosecute may be of greater magnitude than the power to prosecute, and it certainly is much more abused because it is so little checked. The power to do nothing, or almost nothing, or something less than might be done, seems to be the omnipresent power. Every regulatory agency has a statutory assignment to carry out a program enacted by the legislative body, and the agency always can be more active or less active, more effective or less effective. The agency is always considering whether to push out its frontier or to recede from it.

8. *The importance of interim decisions.* Interim decisions may be of greater consequence to discretionary justice than final decisions. The handling of a single case may require a hundred or more discretionary determinations, whether or not the case is developed all the way to formal or informal adjudication. An agency looks at available facts about the X Company and makes a discretionary determination whether or not to institute an investigation proceeding. Or whether to make it a prosecutory proceeding. Or

whether to make it ambiguous—somewhat investigatory and some-what prosecutory, allowing its nature to change as it progresses. Then a discretionary determination may be made whether to give the X Company a chance to escape by agreeing to comply, or whether statutory objectives can be better accomplished by making a public example of the X Company. Or the discretionary choice may be between a cease-and-desist order proceeding and a recommendation to the Department of Justice of a criminal prosecution.

At every step the agency administers more discretionary justice, and each step may make a tremendous difference to the X Company. Even if it is found guilty of nothing the investigation may cost it half a million. Or its license worth several millions may be jeopardized. The adverse publicity may cripple its business, and the agency's decision whether to promote or discourage such publicity may itself be a part of discretionary justice.

The agency's members are constantly confronted with discretionary choices. Shall we make the proceeding public or private? Shall we publicize the decision to make it private and then provide press releases calculated to get the results we want? Shall we barter nonpublication of facts adverse to X for a consent order? Shall we push for a consent order even after the publicity question is resolved? Shall we be lenient if X asks for clemency? Will a cease-and-desist order be enough? Shall we suspend the license or shall we revoke it? Shall we recommend a criminal prosecution not only of X but also of X's officers? Or to carry out our policy, shall we be less severe on X and more severe on Y? Or shall we wait for a more strategic case?

Problems of discretionary justice seep into administrative activities other than those preceding and accompanying adjudication. For instance, discretionary justice may be one facet of problems about rule-making—choosing between clarity and vagueness, choosing between legislative rules and interpretative rules, choosing between rules and policy statements, choosing between rules adopted through rule-making procedure and generalizations in adjudicatory opinions, choosing between a minimum procedural protection (issuing tentative rules and inviting written comments) and maximum procedural protection (trial-type hearings) or some intermediate procedural system. In most circumstances, the more the private party can know about the agency's law and policy the fairer the system; the less the private party can know the lower the quality of justice.

9. *Pressures, personalities, and politics.* Discretionary justice is often complicated—or sometimes simplified—by pressures, personalities, and politics. Agencies' formal rules limiting ex parte communications are limited to hearings with determinations on the record, and most discretionary justice involves no such hearings. The merits must often be weighed not only on scales of justice but also on political scales, which sometimes changes plusses to minuses. Is the alienation of the X Organization, with which we have a continuing relation, too high a price to pay? Some may think that in an ideal system of justice such considerations should be excluded; others may think that a democratic element is appropriate whenever policy questions, even those affecting only a single party, are decided; whatever the ideal may be, the reality is that such considerations do often affect discretionary justice. Senator Y is helping us to get a statutory amendment we much need; should we consult him about this important problem of discretionary justice even though he may take a position we will want to reject? Representative Z of the House Appropriations Committee has a special interest in this subject; will it be better, even so, to confront him with a fait accompli instead of consulting him in advance? Shall we sacrifice a part of the substance we want in order to pacify the chairman of our sister agency, which has a proper concern with this subject?

Even the simplest question of discretionary justice may have multiple dimensions. Whether to prosecute or to refrain from prosecuting X may involve questions of justice, law, facts, policy, politics, and ethics. One question of justice may be whether prosecuting X is unfair when the known offenses of other parties who are not prosecuted are greater. A question of law may be a new one or the subject of conflicting decisions. The factual picture may be incomplete and agency members may have to fill it in through intelligent guesswork. A policy question which may divide agency members is whether the agency's resources may better be devoted to another area. A problem of politics may be appraisal of the capacity of X's supporters to retaliate. And a problem of ethics may be whether pressures applied on X's behalf are beyond the pale.

Anyone who will ponder these samples of discretionary justice should quickly realize the impossibility of modern government without discretionary power. One may dream of a system in which X cannot be prosecuted if known offenses of others who are not prosecuted are greater, in which questions of law are always clearly answered by statute or by case law, in which decisions are never made when some essential facts are missing, in which legislative bodies have always laid down guides as to use of agencies' resources, in which political reprisals are always irrelevant to problems of justice, and in which ethical lines are always clearly drawn concerning the application of pressures. Whether we are moving toward such a dream system or away from it, clearly we have not achieved it and we are not about to achieve it. Until we do, questions of discretionary justice will often be decided on the basis of considerations other than justice.

10. *Some tentative conclusions about discretion.* Discretion is a tool, indispensable for individualization of justice. All governments in history have been governments of laws and of men. Rules alone, untempered by discretion, cannot cope with the complexities of modern government and of modern justice. Discretion is our principal source of creativeness in government and in law.

Yet every truth extolling discretion may be matched by a truth about its dangers: Discretion is a tool only when properly used; like an axe, it can be a weapon for mayhem or murder. In a government of men and of laws, the portion that is a government of men, like a malignant cancer, often tends to stifle the portion that is a government of laws. Perhaps nine-tenths of injustice in our legal system flows from discretion and perhaps only one-tenth from rules.

And every truth warning of dangers or harms from discretion may be matched by a truth about the need for and the benefits from discretion.

Let us not overemphasize either the need for discretion or its dangers; let us emphasize both the need for discretion and its dangers.

Let us not oppose discretionary power; let us oppose unnecessary discretionary power.

Let us not oppose individualization of justice through discretion; let us oppose individualization when rules should control.

Let us not oppose discretionary power commensurate with the tasks undertaken by government; let us oppose discretionary power that outruns those tasks.

Let us not oppose discretionary justice that is properly confined, structured, and checked; let us oppose discretionary justice that is improperly unconfined, unstructured, and unchecked.

II

The Rule of Law and the
Non-delegation Doctrine

1. *Failure to prevent growth of excessive discretionary power.*
As we have seen in the preceding chapter, discretionary power is a
necessary governmental tool but excessive discretionary power is
dangerous and harmful. What is obviously needed is balance—discretionary power which is neither excessive nor inadequate.

In the United States today, all levels of government—federal,
state, and local—lack that balance. Our governmental and legal systems are saturated with excessive discretionary power which needs
to be confined, structured, and checked.

What has caused this imbalance? The system we have evolved
is the product of thousands of instances of exercise of judgment
about concrete problems; how can such judgments have gone
wrong? Can some central deficiency be identified that has given
rise to the imbalance?

My opinion is that, paradoxically, today's excessive discretionary power is largely attributable to the zeal of those who a generation or two ago were especially striving to protect against excessive discretionary power. If they had been less zealous they would
have attempted less, and if they had attempted less they might
have succeeded. They attempted too much—so much that they
could not possibly succeed—and they were decisively defeated.
They tended to oppose all discretionary power; they should have
opposed only unnecessary discretionary power.

The two governmental or legal doctrines that are largely responsible for the damage are (1) an extravagant version of the

rule of law or supremacy of law and (2) the unconstitutionality of legislative delegation of power unless accompanied by meaningful standards. These two doctrines were developed by conscientious people, including legal philosophers and judges, whose worthy purpose was protection against governmental excesses. But both doctrines grossly overshot, and both have been decisively defeated. The worst of it is that milder and sounder opposition to excessive discretionary power became identified with the extravagant version of the rule of law and with the non-delegation doctrine and was largely pulled down in the defeat of those two doctrines. And our legal system has not yet recovered its balance.

This chapter will summarize the story of the defeat of the extravagant version of the rule of law and of the non-delegation doctrine.

2. *The extravagant version of the rule of law.* Jurisprudential thought has had its main impact on exercise of discretionary power through a vague idea known as the rule of law or supremacy of law.[1] The concept has many meanings, and in some of its meanings it is highly beneficial and widely accepted. For instance, in international relations the idea or the ideal of the rule of law means that law should in great measure replace use of force; one facet of this idea is that justiciable disputes should be decided by an international court. Similarly, in domestic affairs, one version of the rule of law is that a system of rule by law is to be preferred to a system of private use of force. Almost everyone agrees with Aristotle's statement that "The rule of law is preferable to that of any individual." Of course, the rule of law even in this sense has its occasional opponents; civil rights groups recently have often acted in defiance of the rule of law in this sense.

The historical subordination of the king to law—to what a parliament enacts or to the law declared by judges—can be regarded as a victory for the rule of law. This sense of the rule of law is about the same as the concept of government under law, or what Aristotle and others and finally the Massachusetts constitution

---

1 The literature of jurisprudence, down through the centuries, is astonishingly inadequate in the whole area of discretionary power. Most of the especially significant problems about exercise of discretion are hardly recognized in that body of literature.

called "a government of laws and not of men." The idea shades into such concepts as due process, natural law, higher law, democracy and fairness, absence of arbitrariness. Hardly anyone can oppose such vaguenesses in the abstract; opposition develops only when concrete meaning is put into such concepts.

We approach areas of trouble when we find the reference by the British Committee on Administrative Tribunals and Enquiries, the Franks Committee, to "the notion of what is according to the rule of law, its antithesis being what is arbitrary." [2] The committee continues:

The rule of law stands for the view that decisions should be made by the application of known principles or laws. In general such decisions will be predictable, and the citizen will know where he is. On the other hand there is what is arbitrary. A decision may be made without principle, without any rules. It is therefore unpredictable, the antithesis of a decision taken in accordance with the rule of law.

The word "arbitrary" in English dictionaries has two meanings; the one that dominates American usage is synonymous with unreasonable, capricious, despotic, and the other is synonymous with discretionary. If the committee had in mind the first sense, then I cannot agree, for a decision may be unguided by known principles or by law and still be reasonable and just, as when the Supreme Court overrules a batch of precedents, a judge imposes a sentence, a governor denies a pardon, or a policeman chooses not to arrest a known violator. If the committee meant to use the term in the second sense, its meaning is less objectionable, but even then I think the committee's statement is contrary to both the British and the American legal systems. My opinion is that neither country does have or should have a rule of law which requires decisions to be made by the application of known principles or laws; both countries allow many decisions to be discretionary, that is, to be made without "the application of known principles or laws."

Not only the Franks Committee but many other writers often interpret the rule of law to mean that discretionary power ("arbitrary" in the sense of discretionary) has no place in any system of

2 Report (1957), 6.

law or government. This proposition is at first seemingly innocuous, and men do respond to the fervent recitation of high ideals. Even so, I think the proposition that arbitrary power has no place in our system is pernicious to the extent that it falsifies, and it falsifies to the extent that all modern governments tolerate a good deal of arbitrary power. The principle which should guide practical action is that arbitrary power (in either sense) should be eliminated to whatever extent it can be eliminated without undue sacrifice of other values that may be deemed more important.

For instance, even though the lives of millions or hundreds of millions may have been at stake, the President of the United States unquestionably had the authority to make an arbitrary decision in 1962 when the United States was confronting the Soviet Union over missiles in Cuba. He could make his decision alone or with advisers. He could act contrary to the unanimous opinion of his advisers. When he ordered the Navy to intercept Soviet ships, his power was absolute. No one else could review the decision before it was carried out. Our view that such arbitrary power is necessary in order to protect our liberties overrides our fear of arbitrary power. And so it is in many other instances.

But what about the proposition that arbitrary power has no place in taking action that drastically affects the vital interests of named individuals? Will this more limited proposition withstand analysis? The answer seems to me quite clear that it will not. The enforcement officer has an arbitrary power to be lenient—or not to be lenient. The governor has arbitrary power to pardon—or not to pardon. The government contracting agent may have arbitrary power to buy from X when competitive bidding is not required— or to buy from Y. The parole board has arbitrary power to parole the prisoner—or not to parole him.[3]

Yet what I am calling the extravagant version of the rule of law, asserted by a good many writers, declares that legal rights may be finally determined only by regularly constituted courts or that legal rights may be finally determined only through application of previously established rules. What this version of the rule of law especially opposes is discretionary power exercised outside courts and not fully subject to judicial control.

3   See discussion of the United States Parole Board, pages 126–33, below.

Perhaps the outstanding American writer to take this position is Dickinson:

[N]othing has been held more fundamental to the supremacy of law than the right of every citizen to bring the action of government officials to trial in the ordinary courts of the common law. That government officials, on the contrary, should themselves assume to perform the functions of a law court and determine the rights of individuals, as is the case under a system of administrative justice, has been traditionally felt to be inconsistent with the supremacy of law. . . . In short, every citizen is entitled, first, to have his rights adjudicated in a regular common-law court, and, secondly, to call into question in such a court the legality of any act done by an administrative official.[4]

European writers often state what they call "the principle of legality" as meaning that discretion must be guided by rules previously announced. An example is a statement by Leon Duguit: "No organ of the State may render an individual decision which would not conform to a general rule previously stated." [5] Of course the fact is that much discretionary power is exercised in France without guiding rules and without review by the Conseil d'Etat. For instance, officers of the foreign ministry make deals with representatives of a foreign government, conclusively determining commercial issues between French and foreign citizens. Some such deals may be guided by rules, but many are not.

Dicey, the influential British writer, in 1885 assigned the rule of law three principal meanings, one of which was: "The absolute supremacy or predominance of regular law as opposed to the influence of arbitrary power [excluding] the existence of arbitrariness, of prerogative, or even of wide discretionary authority on the part of the Government." [6] The attacks upon Dicey's formulation of the rule of law were so completely devastating that the writer of the introduction to the ninth edition of Dicey's book declared: "Had he chosen to examine the existing scope of administrative law he would have been forced to enumerate, even in

4 John Dickinson, *Administrative Justice and the Supremacy of Law* (1927), 33, 35.

5 Leon Duguit, *Traite de Droit Constitutionnel* (2d ed., 1923), 681: "Il n'est pas un organe de l'État qui puisse prendre une décision individuelle qui ne sout conforme à une disposition par voie générale antérieurement édictée."

6 A. V. Dicey, *The Law of the Constitution* (8th ed., 1915), 198.

1885, a long list of statutes which permitted the exercise of discretionary powers which could not be called in question by the courts." [7] If Dicey had sought to protect against *excessive* discretionary power, his great influence might have been largely effective. By objecting to "wide discretionary authority," he squandered his influence, for his ideas were brushed aside. They had to be.

Perhaps the outstanding recent proponent of the extravagant version of the rule of law has been Friedrich A. Hayek, who in *The Road to Serfdom,* which became a best-seller in the United States, praises what he calls "the great principles known as the Rule of Law" and says: "Stripped of all technicalities, this means that government in all its action is bound by rules fixed and announced beforehand—rules which make it possible to foresee with fair certainty how the authority will use its coercive powers in given circumstances and to plan one's individual affairs on the basis of this knowledge." [8] Whether such an absurdity could have been intended by Hayek or whether the statement was an inadvertence does not appear; Congress in deciding how to legislate cannot be bound by rules fixed and announced beforehand, nor can the President in conducting foreign relations, nor can the Supreme Court in breaking new constitutional ground, nor can the planner of a network of highways.

Later Hayek took a less extreme position, although still extreme, in *The Constitution of Liberty*:

The rule of law means that government must never coerce an individual except in the enforcement of a known rule. . . . Under the rule of law, government can infringe a person's protected private sphere only as punishment for breaking an announced general rule. . . . The rule of law requires that the executive in its coercive action be bound by rules which prescribe not only when and where it may use coercion but also in what manner it may do so . . . . The decision must be deducible from the rules of law and from those circumstances to which the law refers and which can be known to the parties concerned. The decision must not be affected by any special knowledge possessed by the government or by its momentary purposes and the particular values it attaches to

7   E. C. S. Wade, page lxxviii.
8   *The Road to Serfdom* (1944) , 72.

different concrete aims, including the preferences it may have concerning the effects on different people.[9]

Hayek even goes so far as to say: "It is only when the administration interferes with the private sphere of the citizen that the problem of discretion becomes relevant to us; and the principle of the rule of law, in effect, means that *the administrative authorities should have no discretionary powers in this respect.*" [10] Hayek is forced to grant that "not all the acts of government can be bound by fixed rules" and therefore that "considerable discretion must be granted to the subordinate agencies," but he reconciles this inescapable concession by saying that such discretionary power "must be controlled by the possibility of a review of the substance of the decision by an independent court." "What is required under the rule of law is that a court should have the power to decide whether the law provided for a particular action that an authority has taken." [11]

The Franks Committee–Dickinson–Dicey–Hayek versions of the rule of law express an emotion, an aspiration, an ideal, but none is based upon a down-to-earth analysis of the practical problems with which modern governments are confronted. The men of action in all governments of the world have summarily rejected such philosophical yearnings. "If it is contrary to the rule of law that discretionary authority should be given to government departments or public officers, then the rule of law is inapplicable to any modern constitution." [12]

The reasons for the universal rejection of the extravagant version of the rule of law may be best understood by examining a single government. The next two sections will be devoted to a demonstration that American law has decisively rejected the extravagant version of the rule of law, and that the reasons for the rejection are overwhelming.

3. *American rejection of the extravagant version of the rule of*

9   *The Constitution of Liberty* (1960) , 205, 206, 211, 213–14.
10   Id. at 213. Italics added.
11   Id. at 213, 214.
12   Wade and Phillips, *Constitutional Law* (7th ed. by Wade and Bradley, 1965) , 67.

law. Here are a few samples of everyday violations of the extravagant version of the rule of law:

(1) The sentencing judge has no guidance except a statute authorizing one to five years and another statute authorizing suspension of sentence. The judge sentences one defendant to five years and another to one year, suspended. Rules fix boundaries for the judge's discretion, but no rule guides the judge in making choices within the boundaries.

(2) An equity judge writes a complex decree in an injunction proceeding. All the details and nearly all the major provisions are entirely discretionary, although precedents may be helpful on some of the major provisions. The state coerces the defendant to comply with every provision of the complex decree. A reviewing court keeps the judge within the bounds of reasonableness but refuses to substitute judgment.

(3) The Supreme Court of the United States overrules a batch of constitutional precedents. The only relevant "rules" are directly opposed to what the court decides.

(4) A common-law court decides a case of first impression. No statute governs, and no precedent is applicable. Broad principles that bear on the problem pull both ways.

(5) Two airlines apply to the Civil Aeronautics Board for certificates for an overseas air route. The board grants one application and denies the other. The statute provides that issuance or denial of a certificate for overseas transportation "shall be subject to the approval of the President" but says nothing about the basis on which the President may approve or disapprove. The President approves both the grant and the denial but states no reasons. The statute explicitly provides for judicial review. The Supreme Court nevertheless holds that the courts may not review because "the very nature of executive decisions as to foreign policy is political, not judicial" and because "the Judiciary has neither aptitude, facilities nor responsibility." [13]

(6) The Michigan Legislature during the nineteenth century authorized a board of registration to grant or deny certificates for the practice of medicine. Rejecting arguments that the statute was

13   Chicago & So. Airlines v. Waterman S. Corp., 333 U.S. 103, 111 (1946).

unconstitutional, the Supreme Court of the United States declared: "[W]e know of no provision in the Federal Constitution which forbids a State from granting to a tribunal, whether called a court or a board of registration, the final determination of a legal question. . . . Due process is not necessarily judicial process. . . . Neither is the right of appeal essential to due process of law." [14]

(7) By 1935 airlines in the United States were carrying 763,-000 passengers annually and more than a million ton-miles of freight and mail, and the Air Commerce Act of 1926 made no provision for economic regulation. The Federal Aviation Commission was appointed to make an intensive study of air transportation and brought in a report in 1935, recommending comprehensive regulation of air carriers, including subsidies. As to competition, the commission said: "To allow half a dozen airlines to eke out a hand-to-mouth existence where there is enough traffic to support one really first-class service and one alone would be a piece of folly. To try to maintain a multiplicity of services in such a case by giving direct governmental aid to all of them would be folly thrice compounded." [15] Congress in 1938 enacted the Civil Aeronautics Act but, failing to agree upon a precise policy about competition, it required the board to "consider," among other things, "competition to the extent necessary to assure the sound development of an air-transportation system properly adapted to the needs of the foreign and domestic commerce of the United States, of the Postal Service, and of the national defense." [16] In granting or denying applications for certificates for air routes, the board would have to decide when to allow monopoly and when to have two or more carriers on one route, with no meaningul guidance from Congress. The board held in 1940 that Congress "clearly intended to avoid the duplication of transportation facilities and services." [17] But a few years later it began certificating more than one carrier for some routes, finding "a strong, although not conclusive, presumption in favor of competition on any route which offered sufficient traffic to support competing services without unrea-

14 Reetz v. Michigan, 188 U.S. 505, 507–508 (1903).
15 Senate Documents, No. 15, 74th Cong., 1st Sess. (1935), 61.
16 72 Stat. 740 (1958), 49 U.S.C. § 1302 (d).
17 Northwest Airlines, Duluth-Twin Cities Operation, 1 C.A.A. 573, 577–78 (1940).

sonable increase of total operating cost." [18] By 1951 the board abandoned the presumption, holding instead that competition would be required only when it would contribute to high standards of public service.[19] Then in 1955 the board seemingly returned to the presumption doctrine,[20] and by 1956 competition had been authorized for 348 of the 400 most important routes.[21] The board's fluctuations show that it was clearly exercising a broad discretionary power to try to work out the extent to which competition should be permitted or required. Of course, a determination of what airlines are to be certificated is backed up by government coercion; operating without a certificate is a criminal offense. And courts had no authority to substitute their judgment for that of the board as to whether or not or to what extent competition should be allowed or required.

A hundred or even a thousand illustrations could easily be given of the use of coercive governmental power over individuals by authorities other than courts and without binding rules. Reviewing judges are customarily without power to substitute their judgment as to how the discretion should be exercised. All our governments—federal, state, and local—are violating, on a broad scale, the extravagant version of the rule of law. Indeed, every year almost every legislative body authorizes additional such violations.

4. *Reasons for rejecting the extravagant version of the rule of law.* Showing that American law *should* allow nonjudicial agencies to exercise final discretionary power over personal and property rights without guiding rules is less easy than demonstrating that it *does* allow this. Yet an appeal to authority as to what should be is easy: All legislative bodies at every level of government in the United States do in fact provide for such discretionary power. Indeed, all legislative bodies throughout the world provide for it, without exception. One sensible way to answer the question of what should be is to take a vote of the people's representatives,

18   Transcontinental & W. Air, North-South California Service, 4 C.A.B. 373, 375 (1943).
19   Southern Service to the West Coast, 12 C.A.B. 518, 533 (1951).
20   New York—Chicago Service Case, 22 C.A.B. 973 (1955).
21   Paul W. Cherington, *The Status and Economic Significance of the Airline Equipment Investment Program* (1958), 10; D. Philip Locklin, *Economics of Transportation* (6th ed., 1966), 801–806.

since the question is basically one of political philosophy. But some voices still assert that what all legislative bodies want is wrong. At the risk of expounding the obvious, let us inquire into the reasons that support the results in each of the seven illustrations in the preceding section.

(1) For centuries, broad discretionary power of sentencing judges has been traditional in the Anglo-American system, because the belief has been that the sentence should reflect the facts and circumstances about the individual human being. My opinion is that a good deal can be done that usually has not been done to confine and to structure the discretionary power, but the very idea of rules which will altogether replace discretion in sentencing seems almost preposterous.[22]

(2) When the interests of opposing parties are intricately intertwined, the best of judicial minds may have to strain to work out a suitable decree, even after all the facts of the particular problem have been fully spelled out. Beyond the intellectual power of any judges or legislators is the capacity to write rules that will be satisfactory for all future cases without knowing the facts of such cases. This is why the equity judge in the preparation of a complex decree is usually given a free rein. If a feasible alternative is possible, the developers of our system have not discovered it. Nor have the proponents of the extravagant version of the rule of law.

(3) All courts occasionally depart from judge-made rules; otherwise judge-made law could not keep pace with the developing times or with new understanding. For many decades the British House of Lords, although retaining the power to change the law by distinguishing precedents, was the only highest court of any nation in the world that formally pretended that it could not change the law, but at last in 1966 even that court acknowledged that it could overrule precedents.[23] The result is that the highest court of every nation in the world can depart from previously existing law, thus rejecting the extravagant version of the rule of law.

(4) When neither statutes nor precedents give meaningful guidance on a problem that comes before a court or an adjudicating officer, broad principles may conflict and may only aggravate the

22 For a full discussion of sentencing, see pages 133–41, below.
23 [1966] 1 Weekly L.R. 1234.

problem. The only sensible way out is a discretionary determination, for no practical alternative has been found.

(5) The President's approval of certificates for overseas air transportation may involve confidential information about international diplomacy that cannot be spread on a court record. Even when private rights are at stake, discretionary power of the President and the State Department is so clearly essential that the Supreme Court in the Chicago & Southern case cut off judicial review even in the face of a statute which clearly and unequivocally provided for judicial review.[24] Officers in all nations of the world necessarily have discretionary power to determine some private rights through international dealings.

(6) Even before 1900, such state agencies as the Michigan Medical Board were freely exercising discretionary power. The right to practice medicine is a precious right but the Michigan Legislature entrusted it to the board's discretion. The Supreme Court's holding that due process is not necessarily judicial process and does not require judicial review is a basic one in the American system, even though reviewability is normally desirable.

(7) In any area of economic regulation, discretionary power over valuable interests is probably inevitable. Theories that the legislative body must state all policies and that administrators must have no discretion except to apply the legislative policies always yield to the reality that legislative bodies cannot answer all policy questions. Indeed, much experience shows that American legislative bodies have been unable to anticipate and to answer even all *major* questions of policy in regulatory fields.

Four fundamentals are: (1) No matter how expert their helpers may be, legislators are less than omniscient and usually are wise, when they establish an agency, to attempt no more than to legislate broad frameworks for administrative policy-making. (2) Problems of policy are often beyond the highest expertness, so that meaningful answers have to come from focusing on facts and circumstances of concrete cases, limiting the decision to a single set of facts, and leaving the policy open for other circumstances. (3) A legislative body is ill-equipped to resolve controversies of

24   Chicago & So. Airlines v. Waterman S. Corp., 333 U.S. 103 (1944).

named parties; that function usually calls for court procedure or for the adjudicative procedure of an agency. (4) Even questions suitable for legislative determination are often delegated for some such reason as failure of legislators to agree, preference of legislators to compromise disagreements by tossing the problem to administrators, draftsmanship which is intentionally or unintentionally vague or contradictory, or some combination of such factors.

These fundamentals can be confirmed by examining any field of regulatory activity. The Civil Aeronautics Act of 1938, reenacted and modified by the Federal Aviation Act of 1958, is typical.[25] We have already seen that Congress left open the fundamental problem of the extent to which competition should be allowed or required and that the board's policy on that problem has fluctuated widely in deciding the rights of particular parties, who have no right to judicial substitution of judgment for the board's judgment. Congress also left open many other *major* questions of policy. A mere listing of samples of such questions will show how much discretionary power was necessarily conferred upon the board: Of the eleven domestic trunklines, the big four at first had about 70 percent of the business; should they be further strengthened or should the smaller trunklines be strengthened? Should new trunklines be allowed entry, or should all major routes be divided among the existing eleven? Should trunklines be allowed to provide local service? Should they be required to? Should the board compel service which a carrier does not voluntarily provide? Should local-service lines be allowed to compete with trunklines? Should the service of local-service lines and of trunklines be kept separate or should it be mixed? Should certificates for local-service lines be for limited periods only or should they be permanent? Should all-cargo carriers be certificated to compete with the trunklines which carry cargo? Should all-cargo carriers be eligible for subsidies? Should they be authorized to carry mail? Should the all-cargo carriers have the exclusive right to sell "blocked space" (reduced rates for specified space for designated periods)? Should nonscheduled carriers be exempt from regulation? Can an unregulated system of nonscheduled carriers be made compatible with a

25 72 Stat. 740 (1958), 49 U.S.C. § 1301.

regulated system of scheduled carriers? What activities should be classified as nonscheduled? What consolidations, mergers, and acquisitions of control are "consistent with the public interest"? What are the factors that should determine what transfers of certificates of convenience and necessity are in the public interest? In the statutory system of basing air mail pay on "need" of the carrier, does a carrier's profit from sale of a route reduce its "need"? Does profit from nontransportation service reduce a carrier's "need"? In finding "need," what rate of return on investment should be allowed? To what extent may mail pay rates be made retroactive? Should mail rates be of two kinds—a rate based on "need," and a rate based on cost of service when subsidy is inappropriate? When two or more carriers of mail between two cities have different rates, may the Post Office Department allocate mail to the carrier whose rates are lowest, or must the board make the mail rates the same for carriers whose "need" differs? May the board fix mail rates for classes of carriers or must the rates be fixed for each carrier separately? In what circumstances should the board fix minimum rates to check competition which causes operating losses? When may promotional or developmental rates below the cost of service be justified? Should the rate base be actual investment or cost of reproduction? Should the rate of return be the same for fixing mail pay as for fixing fares? Can fares be varied so as to stabilize annual earnings? If the fare level is fixed on the basis of earnings of the whole industry, should high-cost carriers receive mail subsidies or should they raise fares on noncompetitive lines above the industry level?

The foregoing questions do seem to involve *major* policy. Yet Congress in the statute gave no clear answer to any of these questions. Statutory provisions and legislative history have some bearing on many of the questions but in no instance enough to foreclose administrative discretion. The courts have answered some of the questions, and in some instances the courts' answers differ from those of the board. Several of the questions have been answered by later legislation and one by an executive reorganization. In our present context, the important observation is that such major questions of policy had to be answered through resort to officers' discretion.

The reason for committing *major* policy questions to the

board's discretion was that someone had to answer them, the courts were ill-equipped to do so, and Congress was neither equipped nor willing. A statute requiring judges to make regulatory policies would probably unconstitutionally violate the principle of separation of powers. Although Congress could not conceivably anticipate all the major policy questions, it could conceivably legislate on each question as it arose. But Congress has neither time nor inclination for that. As for time, Congress during 1938 enacted public laws filling 1,258 pages of the statutes at large, and the provisions on air carrier economic regulation fill only 18 pages; Congress or its committees considered ten or twenty times as much proposed legislation that was not enacted. As for inclination, should any authority other than the electorate try to require Congress to legislate in greater detail than it is inclined to? The attempt of the courts to develop a non-delegation doctrine ended in almost complete failure, as we shall shortly see. The degree of delegation should depend upon legislative appraisals of the need for delegation and of comparative qualifications of legislators and administrators. Even the Internal Revenue Code, said to be our most detailed federal legislation, contains more than a thousand express delegations, and through vague or inadequate language perhaps thousands more.

Staffs attached to committees of Congress could conceivably do all that the CAB and its staff now do, and everything that is done could be put through the legislative mill, so that all policies would be determined by statutory enactments. Even if such a system were feasible for one or a few fields of governmental activity, it could not be feasible for all. An individual congressman could not possibly follow even the general nature of more than a tiny portion of all the discretionary action now taken by 2,500,000 federal employees.

The extravagant version of the rule of law is incompatible with any regulatory program. Indeed, it is at variance with the fundamentals of any modern government. The very identifying badge of the American administrative agency is power, without previously existing rules, to determine the legal rights of individual parties. For instance, the Attorney General's Committee on Administrative Procedure said: "The Committee has regarded as the distinguishing feature of an 'administrative' agency the power to determine, either by rule or by decision, private rights and obligations." [26] The Congress of the United States did not respond to that statement by saying it violates the rule of law. Instead, it accepted the statement as a foundation for the Administrative Procedure Act.

One may confidently predict that every legislative body in the world will go on providing for discretionary determinations by administrators, even when legal rights are at stake, even when coercive governmental power is used, and even when courts are forbidden to substitute their judgment.

Inventing rules to answer all regulatory questions is far beyond the intellectual capacity of the ablest men. Rules are essential, but discretion is also essential—and the right mixtures of rules and discretion. Our objective should be to find for each case or each problem the right proportion of rule and discretion.

Speaking of "the need of and the place for discretion in the administration of justice," Dean Pound has written: "The problem is not to discover the fundamental principles or ultimate conceptions from which a complete and perfect body of rules may be deduced, but to define rightly the respective provinces of these two elements in the administration of justice and to give to each its proper development in its province." [27] That statement is based on thinking about courts, and not especially about administrative agencies. Because of the nature of the tasks assigned, the need for administrative discretion is often much greater than the need for judicial discretion. But in both the judicial process and the administrative process, the need is for giving to rule and to discretion its proper province.

Elimination of all discretionary power is both impossible and undesirable. The sensible goal is development of a proper balance between rule and discretion. Some circumstances call for rules, some for discretion, some for mixtures of one proportion, and some for mixtures of another proportion. In today's American legal system, the special need is to eliminate *unnecessary* discretionary power, and to discover more successful ways to confine, to structure, and to check necessary discretionary power.

5. *Can administrative rules eliminate discretion in individual cases?* The problem just discussed—whether the extravagant ver-

26 Report (1941), 7.
27 2 Pound, *Jurisprudence*, 374.

sion of the rule of law has been properly rejected—is a rather crude one, for only a superficial understanding suffices to answer it. A somewhat more sophisticated question, but still one that can be answered without delving very deeply, is whether something less than the objectives of the extravagant version of the rule of law can be accomplished through administrative rule-making which will eliminate discretion in individual cases. This would mean that justice in individual cases would always depend upon rules, not upon discretion, even though discretion would still be necessary for putting the content into the rules. Discretion to determine content of rules applicable to classes of private parties is of course less likely to involve injustice than discretion about individual cases.

The answer seems reasonably clear: Elimination of discretion through administrative rule-making is sometimes both possible and desirable, but sometimes it is impossible, and sometimes it is undesirable even when it is possible. To fix as the goal the elimination of all discretion on all subjects would be utter insanity.

A single illustration should suffice: The most precise and detailed set of administrative rules I know of is the Federal Tax Regulations, which fill more than four thousand double-column pages of rather fine print. These rules are the product of the effort of thousands of federal employees over many decades, and the whole set of regulations seems to me an especially admirable body of law, even though the process of correcting imperfections seems endless. Although nearly every rule is probably susceptible to revision to cover more detail, and although the long-term direction seems toward more detail, one may be sure that the time will never come when discretion about the substantive tax law will be completely eliminated. Expanding the four thousand pages to four million pages or to four hundred million pages would be *possible,* but it would be neither practicable nor desirable.[28] As it is,

28 An administrator who wants to reduce the discretionary power of his staff with respect to complex subject matter might gradually increase the detail of the rules that guide the staff, thus gradually diminishing their discretion. But the process of increasing the detail and reducing the discretion cannot be continued indefinitely. At some point, any reasonable human beings who are expected to apply the rules will inevitably rebel against excessive detail, and the result of increased detail will be increased discretion, as the Internal Revenue Service has on occasion discovered by experience. Probably administration of the federal tax laws through millions of pages of regulations would be *impossible* even if it were thought by the Hayeks of the land to be desirable.

millions of discretionary decisions must be made every year and many questions spill over into reviewing courts.

The sensible goal, in the federal tax field as in other fields, is not to try to replace discretion with rules but to locate the proper balance between rule and discretion. I think that in many areas our existing practice misses that proper balance by a wide margin; the usual need is for reduced discretion and more elaborate rules. But on many subjects we cannot eliminate all discretion, and on other subjects we should not even when we can.

6. *The non-delegation doctrine.* One way to enforce the extravagant version of the rule of law would be through judicial holdings that constitutional principles forbid legislative delegation of power unless "rules fixed and announced beforehand" will guide the exercise of the delegated power. I know of no single American judicial decision, federal or state, that has ever taken such an extreme position in a holding. The usual idea has been that "standards," not rules, are required. During the first three or four decades of the twentieth century, many courts were requiring meaningful standards, but the tendency of the last two or three decades has been to uphold delegations with vague and almost meaningless standards or even with no standards whatsoever.

The Supreme Court at one time paid lip service to a non-delegation doctrine embodying something like the extravagant version of the rule of law: "That Congress cannot delegate legislative power to the President is a principle universally recognized as vital to the integrity and maintenance of the system of government ordained by the Constitution." [29] If that were true, one would have to say that as of the 1960's we no longer have the system of government ordained by the Constitution. But of course it never was true. The court gradually changed its doctrine to a requirement of standards: "Congress cannot delegate any part of its legislative power except under the limitation of a prescribed standard." [30] But the court has upheld many delegations without meaningful standards and even many without any standards. When a district court took literally what the Supreme Court said about the requirement of standards, the Supreme Court reversed, upholding

29   Field v. Clark, 143 U.S. 649, 692 (1892).
30   United States v. Chicago, M., St. P. & P. R. Co., 282 U.S. 311, 324 (1931).

the delegation despite absence of standards.[31] The Supreme Court was yielding to realism when it acknowledged: "Delegation by Congress has long been recognized as necessary in order that the exertion of legislative power does not become a futility." [32]

Why has the court about given up in its one-time efforts to require that delegations be accompanied by meaningful standards? Perhaps the most important reason is that Congress has gone right on delegating, with vague standards or with no standards, and the Supreme Court has gradually bowed to the will of the people's representatives. The main reason that Congress resisted the non-delegation doctrine is stated above in our discussion of the major questions of policy decided by the Civil Aeronautics Board without significant guidance from the statute: Congress deemed itself both unequipped and unwilling to answer the major questions of policy; it decided that the job could better be done by the board, within the framework established by the statute. Anyone who will study the list of major questions the board has decided, as well as the kind of work that has gone into those decisions, is likely to begin to appreciate the wisdom in this arrangement. The most practical way to determine the major questions of policy within the statutory framework for regulating air transportation is through some such agency as the Civil Aeronautics Board, following some such procedure as the board follows. Indeed, no practical alternative has been invented.

7. *Statutory standards may sometimes be undesirable.* Even when a court will not use the delegation doctrine to strike down a delegation without standards, a legislative body still has to face the question of whether and when and to what extent a statement of standards is desirable.

A clear statement of legislative objectives in every delegation of

---

31 Fahey v. Mallonee, 332 U.S. 245 (1947).

32 Sunshine A. Co. v. Adkins, 310 U.S. 381, 397 (1940). In our entire history the Supreme Court has held only two congressional delegations to governmental authorities unconstitutional. Panama R. Co. v. Ryan, 293 U.S. 388 (1935); A.L.A. Schechter P. Corp. v. United States, 295 U.S. 495 (1935). The true judicial attitude about delegation often comes out more clearly in cases not directly involving delegation; for instance, in FCC v. RCA Communications, 346 U.S. 86 (1953), the commission, having no meaningful statutory guide, tried to create one, and the court struck it down, holding that the commission should rely on "its own evaluation of the needs of the industry rather than on what it deemed a national policy."

power is unquestionably desirable whenever the legislative body is itself clear about its objectives. Furthermore, legislative bodies should unquestionably strive for such clarity. But the lack of meaningful standards in statutes which delegate power seldom stems from a draftsman's failure to put into words the objectives that have taken shape in the minds of legislators, of committee members, or of committee staffs. The lack of meaningful standards almost always results from one or more of three facts and usually from a mixture of all three: (1) Each legislator and each assistant to a legislator concerned with a bill has limited confidence in his own capacity in the time available to dig very far into the specialized subject matter, and such a state of mind produces general and vague formulations of objectives, not specific and precise ones. (2) Developing policies with respect to difficult subject matter often can best be accomplished by considering one concrete problem at a time, as an agency may do; generalizing in advance is often beyond the capacity of the best of minds. (3) Subject matter calling for delegation is often highly controversial; the more specific the statement of legislative objectives the more difficult the achievement of a consensus that can be supported by a majority of each house and win the signature of the executive; the more vague and general the statement of legislative objectives the more likely is the achievement of such a consensus; if bills are to be enacted, the legislative process must be allowed to make its own determination of what degree of specificity or generality is attainable.

One can read a hundred or even a thousand judicial opinions on the subject of delegation and never encounter any mention of such realities as these. Indeed, I think the courts are usually at their worst in writing opinions about delegation,[33] even though

33   The court in Butler v. United Cerebral Palsy of Northern Kentucky, 352 S.W. 2d 203 (Ky. 1961), quoted with approval from my Administrative Law Treatise (§ 2.15) the severe criticism of state court opinions about delegation: "The typical opinion of a state court on a delegation problem is quite unfortunate both in what it says and what it fails to say. It says that (1) legislative power may not be delegated, (2) that 'filling up the details' is not an exercise of legislative power, (3) that legislative power is not delegated if the Legislature has laid down a standard to guide the exercise of the power, and (4) that presence or absence of vague verbalisms like 'public interest' or 'just and reasonable' make all the difference between valid legislation and unlawful delegation. The typical state court opinion on delegation fails to say anything about (1) the reasons for the legislative choice to make the particular delegation, (2) the practical consequences of allowing the Legislature

the *holdings* during the last decade or two are in general quite satisfactory. When a legislative body has done competent committee work, when the subject matter is of such a nature that case-to-case adjudication is likely to yield better results than generalization in a statute, and when the degree of specificity in the statutory statement of objectives is about as great as is readily attainable by the processes of persuasion and compromise, I think the legislative body deserves commendation. Disapproval when those conditions are met, whether by reviewing courts or by scholarly critics, seems to me based on misunderstanding.

Judge Henry Friendly, in an especially perceptive little book, *The Federal Administrative Agencies,* has written: "We still live under a Constitution which provides that 'all legislative Powers herein granted shall be vested in a Congress of the United States, which shall consist of a Senate and House of Representatives'; even if a statute telling an agency 'Here is the problem: deal with it' be deemed to comply with the letter of that command, it hardly does with the spirit." [34] Although I agree with the main thrust of Judge Friendly's excellent book, this particular thought seems to me unsound and harmful. The remark is opposed to dozens of Supreme Court decisions upholding such delegations, it wrongly assumes that the words "all legislative Powers" do not include the power to determine how much delegation is desirable, it does not mention the power "to make all Laws which shall be necessary and proper for carrying into Execution the foregoing Powers," and it ignores the realities that impel legislative bodies to delegate as they do.

The first Congress, made up largely of the same men who wrote

---

to do what it is trying to do, (3) the usual lack of practical advantage in compelling the Legislature to dress up the statute with vague verbiage that judges call standards, (4) the question whether in the circumstances good government calls for a headlong choice of policy by the legislative body or whether it requires the working out of policy by case-to-case adjudication conducted by those who have the advantage of knowing the facts of particular cases, (5) the need for protection against unfairness, arbitrariness, and favoritism, (6) the importance of procedural safeguards, or opportunity for a judicial check, and in some circumstances of a proper legislative or even administrative supervision or check, or (7) the need for providing help to the Legislature in its search for practical and efficient ways of accomplishing legislative objectives."

34 *The Federal Administrative Agencies* (1962), 21–22.

the Constitution, did not bother with standards when it delegated to the courts the power "to make and establish all necessary rules for the orderly conducting of business in the said courts, provided such rules are not repugnant to the laws of the United States";[35] when it delegated district courts power to impose "whipping, not exceeding thirty stripes";[36] when it provided for military pensions "under such regulations as the President of the United States may direct";[37] when it authorized the President to fix the pay, not more than prescribed maxima, for military personnel wounded or disabled in the line of duty;[38] when it conferred discretionary power upon the Secretary of the Treasury to mitigate or remit fines and forfeitures in designated circumstances, without requiring him to mitigate or remit.[39] Nor did the first Congress define the word "proper" in authorizing superintendents to license "any proper person" to engage in trade or intercourse with the Indian tribes; it provided no standard to guide the President in providing that such superintendents "shall be governed in all things touching the said trade and intercourse, by such rules and regulations as the President shall prescribe." [40] I think it fair to say that Judge Friendly finds a "spirit" in the Constitution that members of the first Congress did not find there, even though many of them had participated in drafting the Constitution.

In my treatise I have said of the vague standards that the courts usually approve: "Sometimes telling the agency to do what is in the public interest is the practical equivalent of instructing it: 'Here is the problem. Deal with it.' " The courts do and should sustain delegations that do even less than that. What Congress says in some such statutes is, in effect: "We the Congress don't know what the problems are: find them and deal with them." In many circumstances this is sound government. And the determination of whether or when it is sound government is primarily for Congress to decide.

Samples of major questions of policy that the Civil Aeronautics

35   1 Stat. 83.
36   1 Stat. 77.
37   1 Stat. 95.
38   1 Stat. 121.
39   1 Stat. 123.
40   1 Stat. 137.

Board has decided are listed in Section 4 of this chapter. One who examines those major questions can readily see that many could not have been dealt with by Congress when it enacted the Civil Aeronautics Act in 1938, because no one could anticipate the nature of the problems that would arise. Furthermore, even to the extent that the questions could have been anticipated, the congressional process for answering such questions seems clearly inferior to the board's process, despite various deficiencies in the board's process. And even if Congress had tried to answer the questions it could anticipate, must it be compelled to refrain from legislating at all if it cannot produce a consensus on questions so specific?

Legislative clarification of objectives may sometimes be undesirable, even though it is always desirable when the legislative body knows what it wants. When the society is sharply divided, when the problems are new and opinions have had insufficient time to crystallize, when biting off one concrete problem at a time is clearly preferable to trying to legislate in gross, or when sustained staff-work may contribute significantly to policy choices, a legislative body may wisely keep the policy objectives largely open. Vague or meaningless standards may then be preferable to precise and meaningful ones. This is so not merely from the standpoint of legislators' normal desires to escape the disadvantage of turning the losers into political opponents but also from the standpoint of facilitating the process of ultimately arriving at policies which are both sound and acceptable. When both the understanding of the merits and the weighing of political pressures are about in even balance, or when one of these factors points one way and the other the other way, or when these factors and a host of additional factors impel hesitation, a period of pulling and hauling, of vagueness, of inconsistencies, and of ad hoc decisions without standards may often be better than an early clarification, depending, of course, on an appraisal of the losses that may stem from the uncertainty.

Of course, some statutory delegations are clearly deficient in the extent to which they fail to clarify objectives. Some questions can be better answered by the legislative process than by the administrative process, such as broad questions on which major political parties oppose each other. Occasionally inadequate draftsmanship or haste in the closing days of a legislative session yields products that deserve to be struck down through use of the non-delegation doctrine. Perhaps the most frequent deficiency of legislative bodies has to do with failures to follow through in the development of policy after the delegation has been made. Even when vagueness or absence of standards has been necessary or desirable in the initial delegation, meaningful standards may become feasible after a few years of experience with a new program. The legislators then should either clarify the standards through amending the statute or they should prod the administrators to clarify through regulations or otherwise.

By and large, however, the emphasis should not be on legislative clarification of standards but on administrative clarification, *because that is where the hope lies.* Yet the objective is seldom complete clarification; the objective should be clarification to the extent that the subject matter and the available understanding permit, but not more than is consistent with needed individualizing. In succeeding chapters we shall consider further what administrators can and should do to clarify the law they administer.

8. *Some hindsight about the rule of law and non-delegation.* Early in the twentieth century some mistakes were made which were hard to see at the time but which can be more easily discerned during the second half of the century. One mistake was to allow the rule of law to take an extravagant form that could never prevail, to attract to it the opponents of excessive discretionary power, and thereby to crowd out more moderate versions of the rule of law that might have had more success. Another mistake was to overreach with a non-delegation doctrine; the idea that meaningful standards must always be stated by the legislative body was destined from the beginning to retreat from the battlefield and to disappear.

Both the rule of law and the non-delegation doctrine could have been turned into effective and useful instruments. The goal of the rule of law could have been to distinguish between necessary discretionary power and unnecessary discretionary power, the one welcomed and encouraged and the other forbidden or discouraged. *The courts could have been enlisted to help determine what discretionary power is necessary and what is unnecessary; if that had been their assignment, I think a good deal of today's excessive discretionary power could have been avoided.* Similarly, the non-delegation doctrine should never have aimed at always requiring meaningful standards; the courts could have succeeded if they had limited their objectives to designing legal devices for proper confinement and control of discretionary power.[41]

The last third of the twentieth century is not too late a time for turning the rule of law and the non-delegation doctrine into effective and useful legal tools for minimizing injustice from improper discretionary power. The chapters that follow will present some wondering about how to confine discretion, how to structure it, and how to check it. Half the problem is to cut back *unnecessary* discretionary power. The other half is to find effective ways to control *necessary* discretionary power.

41 For a specific proposal of such legal device, see pages 57–59, below.

III

Confining
Discretion

1. *The optimum breadth for discretionary power.* Discretionary power can be either too broad or too narrow. When it is too broad, justice may suffer from arbitrariness or inequality. When it is too narrow, justice may suffer from insufficient individualizing. Americans unquestionably err much more often by making discretion too broad than by making it too narrow, but we must nevertheless recognize that we do sometimes err by too much confinement of discretionary power.

Everyone has encountered the problem of rigid rules which are a misfit for the business at hand but which some clerk is enforcing without power to modify the rules or to make their application sensible. This is a common occurrence not only in government but also in private business. The cure, of course, is less inflexible rules, that is, more discretionary power; the cure may also be better organization, improved rules which anticipate the difficulties, and higher intelligence of the clerks. The remedy for the aggrieved party is usually to go to a superior of the clerk, who may have the requisite discretionary power to depart from the rules or to change them.

Discretion which is too narrow at higher levels is less common and is seldom a problem. Yet statutes are sometimes too rigid. In interviewing immigration officers, I have often inquired whether the result in a particular case does not seem unjust, and the answer has often been: "Yes, but we had no choice; the statute compels the answer we gave." My next question would usually be:

"Did you make a note of the case, with a view to recommending a statutory change?" The answer was invariably no. The attitude is that as long as the injustice is caused by the statute, the administrator has no reason for concern.

One major responsibility of every agency, too often neglected, is to watch for deficiencies in the legislation it administers, and to make systematic recommendations for changes, based upon understanding of the details of administration. Administrators must share the responsibility for producing legislation that is sound, workable, and just; legislators need the help of administrators in providing the legislation that is needed. An administrator may properly say that "the result was unjust, but I can't help it, because Congress required it" only if he has recommended a statutory change and only if his recommendation has been rejected. The attitude that an administrator never has responsibility for refining statutory provisions is rather common but seems inexcusable. Many agencies systematically report to legislative committees results which are deemed unjust or otherwise unsatisfactory.

Discretionary power which is too narrow at a high level can usually be felt by one trained in American law who observes English judges in action. English judges characteristically deny themselves the discretionary power to change the law as American judges customarily do. American judge-made law is constantly shifting in response to new needs and new understanding; English judge-made law is relatively static. English judges often answer twentieth-century questions with eighteenth-century or nineteenth-century thinking—or so it seems to one who is accustomed to the creative thinking that the best American judges dare to undertake.[1] Although the House of Lords announced during 1966 that it is abandoning its longstanding rule against overruling precedents, English law is still an outstanding example of unduly narrow discretion at high levels. Administrators in both England and America are more like American judges; they generally realize that the law and policy they create, whether or not it grows out of adjudication, must pro-

---

1 For a full development of this theme, see my article "The Future of Judge-Made Public Law in England: A Problem of Practical Jurisprudence," 61 Col. L. Rev. 201 (1961).

vide modern answers to modern problems, and that the answers must be tailored to the special needs of individual cases.

Top administrators in America seldom adopt rules for application to themselves which leave insufficient room for needed individualization. If a formal rule ever does this, it is immediately changed. But administrative rules which are too rigid do sometimes grow out of administrative adjudication. The Supreme Court has sometimes held that an agency has gone too far in limiting its own power to render individualized justice. An outstanding example is FCC v. RCA Communications.[2] The commission authorized a second company to compete with an established company in providing transatlantic radio-telegraph service, because of what the commission called "the national policy in favor of competition." The Supreme Court found no such "national policy" for a regulated industry, and it sent the case back for an individualized determination on the record of the one case as to whether or not competition was desirable in all the particular circumstances. Instead of a general principle—a "national policy" for all—the court required an ad hoc determination. The case, as well as many other such cases, is a reminder that for some circumstances a rule may be unsatisfactory as compared with an individualized decision.[3]

A rule is undesirable when discretion will serve better.

Although American administrators usually manage to produce individualized results when they are needed, and although this usually means satisfactory protection against discretionary power which is too narrow, I think that protection against discretionary power which is too broad is clearly inadequate. For that reason, undue breadth of discretion is the focus of all that follows in this chapter and in succeeding chapters.

2. *An approach to confining discretion.* If, as has just been said, the problem about discretion at all governmental levels in the United States is almost entirely that of excessive discretionary power and is seldom that of inadequate discretionary power, the

2   346 U.S. 86 (1953).

3   For an excellent discussion of the relevant judicial case law, see Ralph Fuchs, "Agency Development of Policy Through Rule-Making," 59 N.W. Univ. L. Rev. 781 (1965).

two principal needs are the elimination of unnecessary discretionary power and better control of necessary discretionary power. The principal ways of controlling are structuring and checking. Structuring includes plans, policy statements, and rules, as well as open findings, open rules, and open precedents, as we shall see in the next chapter. Checking includes both administrative and judicial supervision and review. Our present concern is with eliminating and limiting discretionary power, that is, confining discretion. By confining is meant fixing the boundaries and keeping discretion within them. The ideal, of course, is to put all necessary discretionary power within the boundaries, to put all unnecessary such power outside the boundaries, and to draw clean lines. The ideal is seldom realized, and many of the failures are rather miserable ones, for they frequently result in avoidable injustice.

Statutes which delegate discretionary power often fix some of the boundaries but leave others largely open. By and large, although some opinions differ, I think that legislative bodies usually do about as much as they reasonably can do in specifying the limits on delegated power, but they are often deficient in failing to provide further clarification after experience provides a foundation for it, and they are almost always flagrantly deficient in failing to correct the administrative assumption of discretionary power which is illegal or of doubtful legality. Perhaps the greatest single area of discretionary power which legislative bodies should cut back is the power of the police to nullify legislation through non-enforcement or partial enforcement; this problem is discussed in Sections 11–14 of the present chapter.

Altogether, the chief hope for confining discretionary power does not lie in statutory enactments but in much more extensive administrative rule-making, and legislative bodies need to do more than they have been doing to prod the administrators.

3. Administrative rule-making to confine discretion. When legislative bodies delegate discretionary power without meaningful standards, administrators should develop standards at the earliest feasible time, and then, as circumstances permit, should further confine their own discretion through principles and rules. The movement from vague standards to definite standards to broad principles to rules may be accomplished by policy statements in any form, by adjudicatory opinions, or by exercise of the rule-making power. When rule-making procedure is used, even a statement which changes a vague statutory standard into an administrative standard which is as vague or only slightly less vague is called, in our somewhat confusing language, a "rule." [4]

Earlier and more diligent use of agencies' rule-making power is a far more promising means of confining excessive discretionary power than urging legislative bodies to enact more meaningful standards. This is not because administrative clarification of law is preferable to legislative clarification; the opposite is often true. The reason administrative clarification is more promising is that legislative bodies may not be *expected* to provide the needed clarification. Legislators and their staffs know their own limitations, they know they are ill-equipped to plan detailed programs, and they know that administrators and their staffs are better equipped because they can work continuously for long periods in limited areas. On the basis of careful examination of what happens when legislative bodies undertake to determine detailed policies, as distinguished from broad outlines of policy accompanied by largely unguided delegation, one may conclude that legislators are usually wise in refraining from trying to legislate detailed policies. But anyone who doubts that conclusion is immediately confronted with the undeniable fact that legislators at all levels—federal, state, and local—make the choice with increasing frequency in favor of delegation of broad discretionary power without meaningful guides, and, even if opinions may differ about the wisdom of that choice, perhaps the people's representatives should be allowed to govern on the question of how far they should refrain from governing detail.

The hope lies in administrative clarification of vague statutory standards. *The typical failure in our system that is correctible is not legislative delegation of broad discretionary power with vague standards; it is the procrastination of administrators in resorting*

---

4 The accepted usage is somewhat unsatisfactory: A "rule" is a specific proposition of law, a "principle" is less specific and broader, and a "standard" is still less specific and often rather vague. Even so, the product of legislative action of administrators, called administrative "rules" or "regulations," may include rules, principles, and standards in the sense in which these terms are used in the preceding sentence. If we were reformulating the language, we could easily do better.

to the rule-making power to replace vagueness with clarity. All concerned should push administrators toward earlier and more diligent use of the rule-making power: Affected parties should push, legislators and legislative committees should push, appropriations committees should push, bar groups should push, and reviewing courts should push.

The typical tendency of agencies to hold back from resort to the rule-making power is understandable and often it is justifiable. Waiting for a case to arise, then clarifying only to the extent necessary to decide the case, and then waiting for the next case is one way to build cautiously. In some circumstances, the slow process of making law only through adjudication is a necessity, for administrators may be truly unable to do more than to decide one case at a time. And sometimes, even when they can do more, they properly refrain from early rule-making. Building law through adjudication is a sound and necessary process; the great bulk of American law is the product of that process.

Even so, I think that American administrators, by and large, have fallen into habits of unnecessarily delaying the use of their rule-making power. They too often hold back even when their understanding suffices for useful clarification through rule-making. This is the point at which significant reform is needed, and this is the point at which significant reform can be accomplished.

4. *Should courts require administrative rule-making?* The courts' traditional doctrine has been that legislative delegation is unconstitutional unless accompanied by meaningful standards. But the courts have been largely frustrated in trying to impose this doctrine. Legislative bodies have gone on delegating, often with vague standards or with no standards. Yet the main purpose of the courts, at least with respect to that portion of delegation which confers power to decide individual cases, has been entirely sound; the main purpose has been to try to protect against unguided discretionary power that can and should be guided. Can the courts in some way still accomplish that purpose or a part of it?

I think they can and I think they should. Only a slight shift in the doctrine is needed. The fundamental reason that the courts' doctrine has so largely failed is that legislative bodies have often been unable or unwilling to provide meaningful guidance for administrative discretion. Perhaps the courts should recognize the plain reality that legislative bodies often are not equipped—or often strongly believe that they are not equipped—to do more than to establish a legislative framework within which administrative discretion must be left largely free. But when legislators are incapable of supplying the desired standards, the courts can require the administrators to supply them.

The important part of the basic judicial purpose is to protect against unguided discretionary power to decide individual cases, whenever meaningful guides are feasible. From the standpoint of justice to the individual party, guides created by the administrators can be about as effective as guides imposed by a statute. Accordingly, *I propose that the courts should continue their requirement of meaningful standards, except that when the legislative body fails to prescribe the required standards the administrators should be allowed to satisfy the requirement by prescribing them within a reasonable time.*

The slight change I suggest in the non-delegation doctrine merely moves from a requirement of guides furnished by a legislative body, which has little or no hope of success, to a requirement of guides furnished by the administrators themselves, which has great hope of success. The change is necessary if the non-delegation doctrine is to be saved from virtual extinction.

The change I am recommending will also yield another rather important gain, for it will leave the doctrine more room for growth. The requirement of standards has always been a somewhat artificial one, for it has often been satisfied by adding some verbiage to a bill—verbiage that has sometimes had little or no practical effect, even though it has satisfied judicial requirements.[5] What is needed is something more than verbiage; what is

5 The New Jersey court held unconstitutional a delegation to a board of arbitration, which the legislature had authorized to decide disputes between public utilities and labor unions. The court held that "delegation of legislative power must always prescribe the standards that are to govern." State v. Traffic Tel. Workers' Federation, 2 N.J. 335, 353–54, 66 A.2d 616, 626 (1949). The legislature then amended the statute to state five factors for the board to consider. The court then upheld the statute. New Jersey Bell Tel. Co. v. Communications Workers of America, 5 N.J. 354, 75 A.2d 721 (1950). The two cases seem to me a fair example of the prevailing unrealism of the non-delegation doctrine, for any sensible board would necessarily consider the five factors, whether or not a statute so instructs it.

needed is as much clarification of purpose as is feasible in the circumstances. The requirement of standards, as soon as it can be met by administrators as well as by legislative bodies, ought to grow into a requirement that goes beyond standards. *The requirement should gradually grow into a requirement that administrators must strive to do as much as they reasonably can do to develop and to make known the needed confinements of discretionary power through standards, principles, and rules.*[6]

The non-delegation doctrine might also be gradually shifted from a constitutional base to a common-law base. Much more than is commonly realized, the courts have been fashioning a body of common law about administrative action. An outstanding example is the law requiring administrative findings, a remarkably uniform body of case law created by both federal and state courts. With a few exceptions now largely rejected, the findings requirement has no constitutional base. Like the law of findings, the modified non-delegation doctrine might gradually become common law.[7]

5. *An idea that can encourage earlier rule-making.* My conversations with many administrators lead me to believe that one main reason for undue delay in making rules is an administrator's lack of confidence in his own capacity and that of his staff to strike off a rule that will not cause unforeseen and unwanted consequences. Preparing an abstract generalization that will contain all the needed qualifications and limitations is often not only difficult but hazardous, and administrators typically believe that such an undertaking ought to be avoided until their understanding of the subject matter is fully rounded out. Although I think that delaying the use of rule-making authority is often justifiable on such grounds, still I believe that administrators often delay when they

6 The words "as much as they reasonably can do" can acquire meaning from case to case. Obviously, many questions can appropriately be left for law-making through adjudication. The sound holding in SEC v. Chenery Corp., 332 U.S. 194 (1947), has become more deeply established during the past two decades and should not be upset. But when an agency can easily clarify, when the substantive problems are of such a nature that parties especially need the clarification, and when no very good reason supports the agency's failure to clarify, judicial intervention seems to me desirable.

7 The great advantage of common law over constitutional law is that the legislative body is uninhibited about changing it. If an agency thinks a court has been too exacting, it probably should prevail over the court if it succeeds in persuading the legislative body.

ought not to. At this point a new but simple idea can be of great importance: Seeing all around a complex subject is not a prerequisite to making a sound rule, because *a rule need not be in the form of an abstract generalization; a rule can be limited to resolving one or more hypothetical cases, without generalizing.*

That the proposition just stated involves a departure from a deeply established custom is not a good argument against it. Our statutes have always taken the form of abstract generalizations, and so have administrative rules. But the custom of always couching statutes and rules in such a form is unsound and needs to be changed. The practical need, especially with respect to administrative rules, is for clarification of uncertain law—confinement of discretion—at as early a time as is feasible. An administrator who postpones making a rule until he is prepared to hazard an abstract generalization is falling far short of doing the clarifying he can safely do. The typical administrator, long before he gets around to preparing rules on a subject, has formulated in his own mind—and perhaps even in his files—some firm answers to significant hypothetical cases on each side of a line that must be eventually drawn.

As soon as an administrator knows his answers to such hypotheticals, he should issue a rule which is limited to stating the agency's position on the hypotheticals and which refrains from generalizing.

No agency, so far as I know, has ever issued any rule along this line. The closest approach may be illustrations in the Treasury Regulations, but they are always used to illuminate generalizations. My point is that *a rule need not contain any generalization.*

Moving away from the false assumption that a rule has to contain a generalization can narrow the gap between what an administrator and his staff understand about the law they administer and what outsiders to the agency have opportunity to understand. The goal in any good system should be to narrow that gap as much as feasible. The false assumption that a rule must always generalize is an unnecessary barrier to earlier clarification of the law the agency administers and hence to earlier confinement of the agency's discretion.

When clarification of law can be of great benefit to affected parties, an agency should strive to do all it can reasonably do to help the affected parties, and, in my opinion, an agency does less than it can reasonably do if it refrains from rule-making merely because it quite properly feels unprepared to locate the lines that will have to be located if a generalization in a rule is to have any significance, or because it deems itself unable to draft all the qualifications and exceptions that may be needed if a generalization is to be attempted. In such circumstances—circumstances that very frequently exist—the agency can enlarge its capacity to serve the interests of affected parties if, instead of attempting to generalize in a rule, it will think in terms of a rule in the form of (1) a hypothetical set of facts, (2) a statement of the problem raised by the facts, (3) an indication of the agency's answer to the problem, and, when appropriate, (4) a statement of the agency's reasons for its position.

In proposing such rule-making through hypotheticals, I do not assert that an agency should refrain from law-making through adjudication; such law-making seems to me obviously essential. Nor do I assert that rule-making procedure can do all that adjudication procedure can do; obviously it cannot. Nor do I assert that an agency can always make useful rules on any subject matter, either through generalizations or hypotheticals; agencies often wisely refrain from rule-making in many circumstances. My point is the simple one that an agency can often—quite often—make rules through hypotheticals when it is unable to make rules through generalizations. *An agency which uses three tools for making law— adjudication, rules in the form of generalizations, and rules in the form of hypotheticals—is much better equipped to serve the public interest than an agency which limits itself to the first two of the three tools.*

A ready example of an ideal set of circumstances for rule-making through hypotheticals is the Securities and Exchange Commission's famous Rule 10b-5. Neither this rule nor the anti-fraud statutes it reflects says anything explicit about corporate insiders' dealing in the corporation's stock, but in 1961 the SEC made some crucial law on that subject through adjudication in the Cady Roberts case.[8] That case left many vital questions open,[9] and businessmen everywhere need to know the legal restrictions on insider dealing, but the SEC in the years since 1961 has refrained from use of its rule-making power to clarify the law it declared in Cady Roberts. And the case law of the commission and of the courts seems to develop at a glacial pace.

My opinion is that the commission is unjustified in refraining from amending its Rule 10b-5 to answer most of the usual questions that businessmen ask (and yet I intend this remark as a part of an effort to push out the frontier of understanding of the uses of rule-making, and not as an adverse criticism of the commission). My opinion is that the commission can and should increase the degree of clarity of its rule even though I fully agree with its apparent belief that the subject can be better developed through case-to-case consideration than through attempted generalizations. Awaiting the exceedingly slow process of case-to-case adjudication seems to me undesirable even though generalizing may be premature. What is needed is case-to-case rule-making, that is, rule-making through hypotheticals, which can develop the law much faster than it is likely to be developed through adjudication

8 Cady, Roberts & Co., 40 S.E.C. 907 (1961). Rule 10b–5, 17 CFR § 240.10b–5, provides: "It shall be unlawful for any person, directly or indirectly, by use of any means or instrumentality of interstate commerce, or of the mails or of any facility of any national securities exchange,

" (a) To employ any device, scheme, or artifice to defraud,

" (b) To make any untrue statement of a material fact or to omit to state a material fact necessary in order to make the statements made, in the light of the circumstances under which they were made, not misleading, or

" (c) To engage in any act, practice, or course of business which operates or would operate as a fraud or deceit upon any person, in connection with the purchase or sale of any security."

9 See William L. Cary, *Politics and the Regulatory Agencies* (1967), 84: "Yet the decision itself leaves open many questions. Does it apply to persons other than broker-dealers? What is material information? Who are insiders? How long should an insider refrain from trading? How far do the sanctions extend, and to what extent is there liability to private persons? All these can be gradually developed through succeeding opinions."

I agree with Chairman (now Professor) Cary that these questions can be developed through adjudication, and I also agree with his view that rule-making for enunciating policy should not be "relied upon exclusively." I think adjudications are necessary and even inevitable. But the commission should answer many questions long before they are raised in adjudications. Rules in the form of hypotheticals should be especially useful for earlier clarification than is likely to be brought about through the slower process of law-making through adjudication.

but which at the same time can avoid attempting more than the commission feels prepared to attempt.

Rule-making through hypotheticals can do a great deal that cannot be done by rule-making through generalizations, just as rule-making through generalizations can do a great deal that cannot be done by rule-making through hypotheticals. Each tool has its proper use. A generalization tries to answer a question in the abstract, without a concrete set of facts, and the draftsman can be surprised by the application of his generalization to facts he failed to imagine; such a surprise is much less likely in rule-making through hypotheticals. A generalization inevitably has some limits and therefore to some extent tends to draw lines; a precise generalization fixes the lines, and a vague generalization indicates something about the general location of the lines. If an agency wants to deal only with the central portion of a main question, without either locating the lines or throwing light on their location, it is likely to be baffled if it attempts to generalize in a rule; its purpose can be easily accomplished if it limits its rule to one or more hypotheticals. A rule in the form of a hypothetical case can deal only with ordinary, usual, typical business circumstances and with factual patterns that most frequently recur, and it can say nothing whatsoever about either unusual circumstances or circumstances that push the problem toward the borderland. A series of hypothetical cases can be designed to answer only the questions the agency is ready to answer and to avoid the questions it prefers not to answer.[10]

10 In adjudicatory opinions, administrators may speak rather freely, because what they say is largely dictum, and readers of dictum properly discount it. If hypothetical cases are discussed in rules, what will be the authoritative effect of dictum included in the explanation? I think the answer is rather easy: It will have the same effect as it would have if it were a part of an adjudicatory opinion. After all, the Administrative Procedure Act, 5 U.S.C. § 553 (c), provides that "the agency shall incorporate in the rules adopted a concise general statement of their basis and purpose."

Another parenthetical thought: Rules in the form of hypotheticals will seldom be entirely unsupported by generalizations somewhere in their backgrounds. For instance, a hypothetical under Rule 10b–5 will be dependent on the generalizations in that rule. A hypothetical may give meaning to generalizations about "the public interest" in the statute, or "due process of law" in the Constitution. The extremely broad generalizations need not be given meaning by narrower generalizations; they may also be given meaning, or partial meaning, by rules in the form of hypothetical cases.

The chairman of the SEC and his legal assistant have published an unusually perceptive and helpful discussion of administrative rule-making.[11] With the thesis that law-making through adjudication is essential for such an agency as the SEC I am in full agreement.. My only significant doubt has to do with the implication in the statement concerning a formal rule that "there is a tendency to evaluate it in terms of the maximum possible scope of its language," but that "a statement in an adjudicatory opinion is evaluated against the specific factual content." The implication is that a rule cannot be formulated which, like an adjudicatory opinion, will be evaluated against a specific set of facts. I think it can be. A rule can be written in the form of a set of facts and an answer, and the rule can specifically provide that all words used in the rule are to be evaluated against the single set of facts. A rule can do anything an adjudicatory opinion can do. It can have any degree of precision or vagueness, with or without one or more generalizations, with or without one or more illustrations, with or without one or more sets of real facts, with or without one or more sets of hypothetical facts. Whatever an agency is able to say in an adjudicatory opinion it can likewise say in a rule. *An adjudicatory opinion can never say anything that cannot be said as well or better in a rule.*[12]

11 Manuel F. Cohen and Joel J. Rabin, "Broker-Dealer Selling Practice Standards: The Importance of Administrative Adjudication in Their Development," 29 L. & Contemp. Prob. 691 (1964).

12 My main point—that a rule need not generalize—seems to be unusually hard to get across to those who are accustomed to the usual assumption that a statute or a rule has to be in the nature of a generalization. I made the point in § 6.13 of the 1965 Supplement to my Administrative Law Treatise—somewhat unsuccessfully. For instance, such an astute reader as Judge Henry Friendly, in his illuminating essays called *Benchmarks* (1967) says at page 145: "I would not go so far as to give the affirmative answer evidently sought by Professor Davis' rhetorical question, 'Can anything be accomplished in an adjudicatory opinion that cannot be accomplished as well or better in a rule?' I hope this is not merely vocational bias. As to the very instance discussed by him, the SEC's decision in Cady, Roberts & Co., with respect to the use of inside information, I agree with Chairman Cohen that initial formulation through adjudication was preferable. The Commission was entering into what was largely terra incognita; it simply did not know enough to draft a rule, even when one takes account of the variety of drafting techniques which Professor Davis helpfully develops." In addition to the incidental fact that Judge Friendly must mean "negative" when he says "affirmative," I think I have failed in two respects to make my meaning clear to Judge Friendly: (1) My discussion was not about adjudication versus rule-making; if it had been, I would have favored adjudication for many circumstances, such as for controversies about facts pertaining to particular parties, as well as for circumstances that an agency is

6. *Rule-making procedure is one of the greatest inventions of modern government.* When more than a handful of parties are affected, creation of new law through either statutory enactment or administrative rule-making is much more desirable than creation of new law through either judicial decision or administrative adjudication. True, the Supreme Court of the United States decides great policy issues affecting millions of people, but its procedure is geared to a few parties, not to many, even though occasionally it may receive a dozen or even two dozen briefs from amici curiae. By contrast, the legislative committee system at its best is a superb procedure for the development of understanding and for the reflection of democratic desires.

The procedure of administrative rule-making is in my opinion one of the greatest inventions of modern government. It can be, when the agency so desires, a virtual duplicate of legislative committee procedure. More often it is quicker and less expensive. The usual procedure is that prescribed by the Administrative Procedure Act,[13] the central feature of which is publishing proposed rules and inviting interested parties to make written comments. Anyone and everyone is allowed to express himself and to call attention to the impact of various possible policies on his business, activity, or interest. The agency's staff sifts and summarizes the presentations and prepares its own studies. The procedure is both fair and efficient. Much experience proves that it usually works beautifully.[14]

For making policy affecting large numbers, rule-making proce-

---

not likely to foresee. My discussion was limited to adjudicatory opinions versus rules as a means of declaring an agency's law, and my point is that nothing can ever be better said in an adjudicatory opinion than in a rule. (2) When Judge Friendly says that "the Commission simply did not know enough to draft a useful rule, even when one takes account of the variety of drafting techniques which Professor Davis helpfully develops," I think he has ignored the drafting technique I have suggested. Using that technique, the commission could state the Cady Roberts facts in a rule and then could say precisely what it did say in its opinion in that case.

13 5 U.S.C. § 553. The prescribed procedure does not apply to interpretative or procedural rules, and various other exceptions and qualifications are made.

14 Many states have discovered the advantages of such procedure. See, for instance, Calif. Gov't Code §§ 11420-27, providing for notice, including "Either the express terms or an informative summary of the proposed action" and "opportunity to present statements, arguments, or contentions in writing, with or without opportunity to present the same orally."

dure is superior to adjudicative procedure in many ways, including the following six: (1) All who may be interested are systematically notified; for instance, the Administrative Procedure Act requires that notice of rule-making be published in the Federal Register. Notice to non-parties of contemplated policy-making through adjudication is unusual. (2) Tentative rules are usually published and written comments received before final rules are adopted. In an adjudication a tribunal may adopt a policy without knowing and without having means of discovering what its impact may be on unrepresented parties. (3) Rule-making procedure which allows all interested parties to participate is democratic procedure. Adjudication procedure is undemocratic to the extent that it allows creation of policy affecting many unrepresented parties. (4) An administrator who is formulating a set of rules is free to consult informally anyone in a position to help, such as the business executive, the trade association representative, the labor leader. An administrator who determines policy in an adjudication is usually inhibited from going outside the record for informal consultation with people who have interests that may be affected. In policy-making through adjudication, either the quest for understanding is likely to be impaired or the tribunal's judicial image is likely to be damaged. (5) Even when retroactive law-making through adjudication is not so unfair as to be a denial of due process, the retroactive feature may still be sufficiently unfair that good administrators ought to try to avoid it. Much law-making that is now retroactive can and should be avoided. For this reason alone, prospective rules often should be preferred to retroactive law-making through adjudication. (6) Congressional committees often provide useful supervision of administration, even though it is usually unsystematic and spotty. Such supervision can be quite effective in reaching contemplated rule-making, but is almost always ineffective in influencing administrative law-making and policy-making through adjudication.

The last item raises an interesting philosophical question which is of general application but which can best be stated through a concrete illustration. In its decision in the Cady Roberts case,[15] the

15   40 S.E.C. 907 (1961).

SEC held that one who had inside information violated the anti-fraud provisions of the statutes and of the regulations merely by dealing in the corporation's securities on an exchange, without making representations of any kind to anyone. The case broke new ground, for the anti-fraud provisions had not previously been extended that far. The policy was created through an adjudication. Neither the industry nor the congressional committees had a chance to exert their influence before the commission's adoption of the policy had become fait accompli. Yet on the basis of conversations with commissioners and some staff members, I think the commission probably would not have adopted the policy if it had first announced it in the form of a proposed rule; pressures from the industry and from the committees would have been too strong. The philosophical problem is this: Even if one assumes that the new policy is in the public interest, as the unanimous commission strongly believed it to be, should the policy have been adopted through an adjudication if pressures from regulated parties and from their representatives in the congressional committees could have blocked it in the form of a proposed rule? [16] The problem, of course, is one facet of the age-old issue of government by experts versus the will of the people, or what the Greeks thought of as the benevolent philosopher-king versus demos.

Recognition of the superiority of rule-making procedure over adjudicative procedure for making law or policy affecting more than a few parties means that agencies should strive to use rule-making procedure to the greatest extent they find feasible, but it does not mean that agencies should avoid making law or policy through adjudication. For complex subject matter, rules can never provide all the answers in advance. When facts about parties are in dispute, the methods of adjudication are indispensable, and whole problems must be disposed of, including whatever law-making or policy-making may be necessary. The vastly increased rule-making that I think desirable can never be carried so far as to eliminate all development of law and policy through case-to-case adjudication.

By and large, federal agencies should resort to rule-making

16   See Cary, *Politics and the Regulatory Agencies,* 83–84.

much more often than they do.[17] And so should state and local
agencies, whether or not their governing statutes so require.

7. *Power to make rules always accompanies discretionary power
and need not be separately conferred.* Any officer who has discretionary power necessarily also has the power to state publicly the
manner in which he will exercise it, and any such public statement can be adopted through a rule-making procedure, whether
or not the legislative body has separately conferred a rule-making
power on the officer.

The preceding sentence is (a) especially important to successful control of discretionary power, and it is (b) exceedingly
simple and clearly incontrovertible, even though (c) the legal
effect of such a public statement by an officer depends upon extremely complex law that often baffles the best judges and the
best lawyers.

(a) That an officer having discretionary power can make a public announcement of what his response will be to specified problems is especially important because such announcements are often the most practical and the most effective means of confining
discretionary power. If legislators must—or at all events do—limit
themselves to main outlines, the task of filling in the outlines necessarily falls to administrators, and if the power of the adminis-

17 Unfortunately, even when rule-making procedure is clearly required by statute, some agencies refuse to follow the prescribed procedure. The outstanding such
federal agency is the National Labor Relations Board, which has illegally and in-
excusably used the procedure of adjudication for rule-making in such cases as De-
luxe Metal Furniture Co. and Sheet Metal Workers International Assoc., 121
N.L.R.B. 995 (1958), and General Cable Corp., 139 N.L.R.B. 1123 (1962). Both
cases were adjudications but both involved rule-making for thousands of nonparties.
In the second case the board said that it received letters, telegrams, and memoran-
dums from "the overwhelming majority of labor and management representatives."
It violated the Administrative Procedure Act by failing to publish notice in the
Federal Register, by publishing no proposed rules for parties to comment on, and
by failing to publish final rules in the Federal Register. Even worse is the board's
rule-making by press release. See, for instance, the 1963 annual report, page 34, concerning jurisdictional limitations: "These self-imposed standards are primarily expressed in terms of the gross dollar volume of the business in question. Those prevailing on Aug. 1, 1959, were those announced on Oct. 2, 1958. Press Release (R-
576) Oct. 2, 1958. . . ." The Administrative Procedure Act, 5 U.S.C. § 552, requires publication of substantive rules in the Federal Register. For an expression
of "regret" over failure of the NLRB to use its rule-making power, see NLRB v.
Majestic Weaving Co., 355 F.2d 854, 860 (2d Cir. 1966). And see Peck, "The At-
rophied Rule-Making Powers of the National Labor Relations Board," 70 Yale L. J.
729 (1961).

trators is to be confined, the most eligible authorities to do the confining are the administrators themselves, who are clearly in the best position to act because they have the most direct knowledge of practical needs with respect to the power. A main hope— probably *the* main hope—for needed confinement of discretionary power lies in administrative self-confinement. Furthermore, administrators in some circumstances have incentives to make rules which will confine their discretionary power, because regularization through rules can mean getting more accomplished with less effort; application of a rule may be easier than thinking out each individual problem. Yet in other circumstances inertia or lethargy are strong forces for inaction, and sometimes the incentives must be supplied from the outside, as from affected parties, superior officers, legislative committees, or reviewing courts. Whatever the source of the incentives, announcements by officers having discretionary power of what they will do in various circumstances are an especially important means of confining discretionary power.

(b) The proposition that an officer with discretionary power may state how he will exercise his power has the merit of being both simple and obvious. The Attorney General may announce, as one once did, that the Department of Justice never prosecutes for criminal libel.[18] A police chief may announce: "We don't arrest for five miles in excess of the speed limit." What is simple and obvious is that these announcements may be made and that they may have the desirable effect of confining discretionary power; what is simple and obvious nevertheless does not include the drawing of a line between legal and illegal announcements or finding the exact legal effect of such announcements.

(c) When an officer with discretionary power states how he

18   The announcement was made by Attorney General Robert H. Jackson, who refused to prosecute Drew Pearson and Robert S. Allen for allegedly libeling Senator Millard Tydings. For a full account of the incident, see Hearings before Subcommittee of the Senate Judiciary Committee, 77th Cong., 1st Sess., on Nomination of Robert H. Jackson to be an Associate Justice of the Supreme Court (1941), 47–69. The statute provided: "Whoever publishes a libel shall be punished by a fine not exceeding $1,000, or imprisonment for a term not exceeding 5 years, or both." The Attorney General told the Senator "that he did not intend to prosecute under it until hell froze over." The Attorney General said to the subcommittee: "I know that as Attorney General I must have made hundreds of mistakes, hundreds of bad mistakes, but this is not one of them." He was confirmed.

will exercise his power in given circumstances, he may be in some degree making law, but the degree to which the statement is legally binding on him or on someone else who is affected is far from simple and far from obvious. More than a hundred pages of my Administrative Law Treatise and its Supplement[19] are devoted to this subject, and this is not the place to elaborate that discussion. The fundamental problem is to distinguish legislative rules, which have the force of law if valid, from interpretative rules, which sometimes have the force of law, sometimes have some degree of authoritative effect less than force of law, and sometimes have little or no authoritative effect. Legislative rules are always the product of a grant of legislative power, whether or not explicit or specific, by the legislative body. Equally clear is the proposition that interpretative rules may have some degree of authoritative effect, sometimes even force of law, in absence of any separate grant of legislative power to make rules having such authoritative effect.

8. *The Federal Trade Commission as an example.* The laws administered by the Federal Trade Commission revolve around characteristically vague terms—restraint of trade, monopolize, lessen competition, unfair methods of competition, unfair or deceptive acts or practices. A major purpose of the commission, in my opinion, should be to give meaning to those vague terms, and the most important tool should be rule-making procedure. But the commission has done remarkably little in that direction, even though in recent years it has been enthusing about its new methods of industry guidance, consisting mainly of advisory opinions and trade regulation rules. The commission's adjudications and cease and desist orders have declined drastically, and the commission proclaims: "Statistics simply don't tell the true story. The Commission's purpose is not to bring an even greater number of adversary actions; *its function is essentially one of guidance.* And whatever can be done to persuade American business to heed that guidance is infinitely more important than to exhibit proudly the futile scalps of the too few." [20]

Although the commission's view that its function should be one

19 Chap. 5.
20 1966 Annual Report 9. Commission's italics.

of guiding businessmen is highly commendable, the commission is doing far less than it reasonably can do to provide such guidance. Adjudicatory opinions currently provide less guidance than ever before; the total number of cases disposed of after hearings before examiners has fallen in one recent year to twenty-nine.[21] Beginning with its 1962 annual report, the commission has been emphasizing guidance given through advisory opinions and through trade regulation rules, but the supporting figures seem quite unimpressive. The commission during 1966 issued only forty-six formal advisory opinions.[22] Furthermore, during the years 1962 to 1966, the commission was so eager to give guidance to businessmen that it carefully kept all its advisory opinions secret! It still does, except that in 1966, "in response to urgent requests from businessmen, the trade press and members of the bar," it began publishing digests of them in that year.[23] The digests are so skimpy that one can seldom extract significant law or policy from them, and each digest recites: "The advisory opinion itself and all background papers are confidential and are not available to the public."

The indiscriminate withholding from public inspection of all advisory opinions and all background papers reveals an underlying attitude that is totally inconsistent with giving businessmen guidance. All advisory opinions and all background papers clearly should be open to public inspection except to the extent that some special reason requires confidentiality for particular information; businessmen are entitled to know what the commission does in advising parties having problems similar to theirs. Furthermore, the Information Act[24] requires disclosure of "all opinions" and of "identifiable records" except what is covered by the act's nine exemptions, and much that is contained in advisory opinions and background papers is not within the nine exemptions.

The commission has never given an advisory opinion except upon request of a private party. Yet in many instances the commission could skip its lengthy and expensive fact-finding process

21   Id. at 69.
22   Id. at 15.
23   Id. at 16.
24   5 U.S.C. § 552.

and say, after allowing the private party to assert its position about the question of law or policy, in effect: "If the facts are thus and so, our opinion is that the applicable law is such and such, for the following reasons." The effect on a private party who knows that the assumed facts can probably be proved could often be about as strong as the effect of a cease and desist order; the legal effect of an unsolicited advisory opinion would be the same as that of a requested one.

Since 1962 the commission has carried on a sustained campaign to give the impression that trade regulation rules are a major new means of giving guidance to businessmen. A trade regulation rule is unquestionably a good device; a single rule can sometimes have more effect on business practices than a hundred cease and desist orders. The fundamental is that nearly all businessmen will normally comply with law they understand. Spending a few hundred thousand of taxpayers' dollars for an order against a single company that says "buy one and get a second one free" might not pass any test concerning cost-effectiveness, as the commission should know, but a trade regulation rule can declare such a practice unlawful, can apply to all and not just to a single respondent, and costs far less than a cease and desist order. The trade regulation program of the commission is splendid as far as it goes, but the whole program hardly reaches the edges of the job that can and should be done. The total number of trade regulation rules issued by January, 1967, was nine, applying to sleeping bags, electric sewing machines, prismatic binoculars, dry cell batteries, tablecloths, leather content of waist belts, previously used lubricating oil, cigarettes, and size of television pictures. Whether all nine of the trade regulation rules in the aggregate reach one per cent of products sold seems doubtful.

What the program of trade regulation rules needs is multiplication by about one hundred. The commission's inflated boasts about its great accomplishments through trade regulation rules raises the question whether the commission itself is committing unfair or deceptive acts or practices, under the standards it uses for measuring the representations of others.[25]

Although the commission's trade practice rules are more nu-

25 The extent of the loafing seems to me greater in the Federal Trade Commission building than in any other government building I have entered. I keep won-

merous and more extensive, the degree of their emptiness is appalling. Open at random the 770 pages of trade practice rules, as printed in 16 CFR, and here is a sample of what one finds:

§ 214.4 "It is an unfair trade practice for any industry member to make or publish, or cause to be made or published, any advertisement, offer, statement, or other form of representation, which directly or by implication is false, misleading or deceptive: (a) Concerning . . . (b) Concerning . . . "
§ 214.5 "It is an unfair trade practice for any industry member falsely to represent . . . in his advertising or otherwise: (a) That . . . (b) That . . . (c) That . . . ; or to misrepresent in any other material respect the . . . "
§ 214.6 "In connection with the sale or offering for sale of industry products, it is an unfair trade practice for any industry member to represent, directly or by implication, that . . . when such is not the fact."
§ 214.7 "It is an unfair trade practice for any industry member: (a) To represent, directly or by implication, through the use of such words or expressions as . . . that . . . unless such is the fact."

Does specification of the items that may be misrepresented, or of the ways that misrepresentations may be made, have any value? If it does, the printing of the 770 pages of trade practice rules may not be a complete waste of taxpayers' money. Perhaps the value lies in educating businessmen, or their representatives, in the proposition that misrepresentation is unlawful concerning this, concerning that, and concerning something else.

The commission's affirmative accomplishments seem singularly small, and whether or not they are offset by the harm it does is unascertainable because the commission keeps secret some of its major activities. For instance, the commission apparently considers that its major function of providing pre-merger clearances cannot stand the light of day. For all that an outsider can learn, the commission may be freely giving pre-merger clearances that are contrary to the public interest and contrary to the intent behind the laws it administers.[26]

Altogether, what the Trade Commission most needs is a much

---

dering whether a single able administrator, with a selected staff and one-tenth the budget, could do the commission's job more effectively than it is being done. I do no such wondering about any of the other independent regulatory agencies.
26 See the full presentation of the commission's violation of the Information Act with respect to pre-merger clearances, pages 113–16, below.

stronger push toward trade regulation rules.[27] The beginning in that direction is splendid, except that it is too tiny. The commission should no longer boast about issuing forty-six formal advisory opinions in one year and nine trade regulation rules in five years. It should be ashamed of that record.

9. *Rule-making power not separately granted—the Cigarette Rule.* One trade regulation rule issued by the Federal Trade Commission—the Cigarette Rule—deserves special mention because it was accompanied by an opinion which I regard as one of the outstanding administrative opinions of the twentieth century.[28] Even though a statute has superseded the Cigarette Rule, the opinion has enduring value as an especially astute analysis of the administrative power to make rules even when such power has not been separately granted. The analysis is of general applicability—far beyond the Trade Commission—and it merits a prominent role in future thinking.

The commission at the outset explicitly stated that the rule was not "legislative in the sense of adding new substantive rights or obligations." Congress had not delegated to it a separate power to make substantive rules. Section 6 (g) of the Federal Trade Commission Act authorizes the commission "to make rules and regulations for the purpose of carrying out the provisions of this Act," but the commission acknowledged in a footnote, as I believe it was obliged to do, that: "At most, the legislative history suggests that the Commission was not intended to promulgate 'legislative' rules." Support for the Cigarette Rule did not rest on § 6 (g), for the commission asserted: "Even if 6 (g) were not in the Act, it could not be persuasively maintained that the trade regulation rule procedure is ultra vires." The commission's support for this view was § 5 (a) (6), providing that the commission is "hereby empowered and directed to prevent persons . . . from using unfair methods of competition in commerce and unfair or deceptive acts or practices in commerce." The commission argued that deciding cases necessarily involves substantive rule-

27 See Philip Elman, "Rulemaking Procedures in the FTC's Enforcement of the Merger Law," 78 Harv. L. Rev. 385 (1964).

28 The rule is printed in 29 F.R. 8324–75, and the part we are concerned with is Chap. 6, pp. 8364–73.

making, that both the courts and the commission evolve rules
through adjudication of cases, and that making rules through
rule-making procedure has ten advantages over making rules
through adjudication. The commission specified each of the ten.
In concluding that use of rule-making procedure was appropriate,
it nevertheless asserted that it would continue to make rules
through adjudication.

The commission's opinion developed the idea that discretionary power to give meaning to such terms as "unfair or deceptive
acts or practices" in individual cases carries with it the power to
announce the commission's views about the meaning of such terms
apart from individual cases. Making such an advance announcement does not involve a claim of additional power but has the effect of confining discretionary power, and it helps affected parties
to know the commission's position at an earlier time. The commission persuasively said that

. . . when an agency's consideration of a problem has progressed to the
point at which a specific legal standard has crystallized, it is plainly to
the advantage of the persons who might be affected thereby that the
agency announce its determination in a formal, public, explicit, and
prospective manner. Otherwise such persons may violate the law and
incur heavy sanctions because of uncertainty as to the law's requirements.

The reasoning is important because it means, for instance, that
every enforcement officer has the power to announce in advance
how he interprets and applies the law he is authorized to enforce.
And the reasoning is important because the law—somewhat ob-
scure law—is in accord with the commission's position. The best
single authority may be Skidmore v. Swift & Co.[29] Even though
Congress in enacting the Fair Labor Standards Act considered the
question whether or not to confer upon the Wage-Hour Administrator a general rule-making power *and decided not to,* the Supreme Court nevertheless gave weight to an interpretative bulle-
tin in which the administrator announced his position on various
questions of interpretation. The court declared that the adminis-

29   323 U.S. 134, 139–40 (1944).

trator's interpretations "determine the policy which will guide applications for enforcement by injunction on behalf of the Government," and that "this Court has long given considerable and in some cases decisive weight to Treasury Decisions and to interpretative regulations of the Treasury and of other bodies that were not of adversary origin."

Enforcement officers and agencies thus have an intrinsic authority to issue interpretative rules. And under Section 4 of the Administrative Procedure Act, interpretative rules are explicitly exempt from the prescribed rule-making procedure. But the exemption obviously does not mean that the rule-making procedure may not be used; the Treasury Department has long been winning general approval by using the prescribed rule-making procedure for its interpretative regulations even though it is not required to do so. The position of the tobacco companies in the case of the Cigarette Rule that "the commission lacks authority to conduct such a proceeding" was utterly without merit. Even so, the companies were clearly entitled to refuse to participate in the proceeding.

Of course, the hard question is what degree of authoritative effect interpretative rules may have. A safe statement is that of the Supreme Court in the Skidmore case: Such rules have "considerable and in some cases decisive weight," but that statement hides many intricacies.[30] The theory is that interpretative rules clarify existing law but do not add to it; they cannot create new rights or new obligations. The commission claimed very little for its Cigarette Rule: "The Commission could, in a subsequent adjudicative proceeding, rely not only on the propositions of law contained in the rule, but also on the underlying factual matters determined." The commission in deciding policy positions may obviously "rely on" not only law and facts developed in rule-making proceedings but also on facts and ideas its members find in newspapers, in conversations with businessmen, and in any other written or unwritten sources.

The commission may "rely on" the Cigarette Rule and all that comes to light in the proceeding, and it may also reject or modify

30   See §§ 5.03–5.05 of my Administrative Law Treatise.

its views and any basis for its views in a later adjudicative proceeding. But that does not mean that the rule is without legal effect. Anyone, whether or not in the legal profession, who has studied a question thoroughly and announced a position, is likely to take the same position again unless new considerations come to his attention. And this is true of the Trade Commissioners. The commission claims no more.

If the commission in a later adjudicative proceeding takes official notice of facts or law developed in a rule-making proceeding, any party is entitled under § 556 (e) of the Administrative Procedure Act to full procedural opportunity to meet what is considered.

That enforcement officers have intrinsic authority to announce their positions and their policies and to use rule-making procedure as an aid to developing those positions and policies is a proposition of great consequence in the control of discretionary power. If the cure for some ills that grow out of discretion is rules, then the cure for some ills that grow out of excessive discretionary power of enforcement officers may sometimes be interpretative rules, even when no rule-making power has been separately conferred.

10. *Admission to and eviction from public housing.* The discretionary power of administrators of public housing seems grossly excessive. The best means of confining it may be through use of the rule-making power.

The congressional purpose of the program as stated in the basic legislation of 1937 is "to remedy the unsafe and insanitary housing conditions and the acute shortage of decent, safe, and sanitary dwellings for families of low income, in urban and rural nonfarm areas, that are injurious to the health, safety, and morals of the citizens of the Nation." [31] Congress in 1949 declared the objective of "the realization as soon as feasible of the goal of a decent home and a suitable living environment for every American family," [32] and in 1959 Congress declared "the policy of the United States to vest in the local public housing agencies the maximum amount of responsibility in the administration of the low-rent

31 50 Stat. 888 (1937) , 42 U.S.C. § 1401.
32 63 Stat. 429 (1949) , 42 U.S.C. § 1401.

housing program," [33] but 1961 legislation required that "the public housing agency shall adopt and promulgate regulations establishing admission policies." [34]

The unsatisfactory element is the extreme generality of the regulations. For instance, the New York regulation provides:

It shall be a ground for eligibility for admission to or continued occupancy in any Authority project that the tenant or applicant is or will be a desirable tenant. The standard to be used in approving eligibility for admission or continued occupancy of a family shall be that the family will not or does not constitute (1) a detriment to the health, safety or morals of its neighbors or of the community, (2) an adverse influence upon sound family and community life, (3) a source of danger to the peaceful occupation of the other tenants, (4) a source of a danger or a cause of damage to the premises or property of the Authority, or (5) a nuisance.[35]

The Chicago regulation likewise uses "undesirable" as the key concept: "An undesirable tenant is defined as one who imperils the health, safety or morals of his neighbors, or is a source of danger to the property or to the peaceful occupation of the tenants, or is remiss in his normal obligations as a tenant." [36]

The concept of "undesirable," so largely undefined, confers enormous discretionary power to control many aspects of the lives of tenants who are typically unable to fight against official arbitrariness. For many families, the difference between continuing in low-rent public housing and returning to high-rent slums is a crucial one; they may often be willing to sacrifice other vital interests in order to protect continuity of their housing. The power in an individual officer to put whatever meaning he chooses into the term "undesirable" and to enforce his determination against individual families by ousting them from their established homes is an arbitrary power that is inconsistent with sound government.

Congress and the state legislatures have quite properly delegated to administrators the power to determine through regulations who is eligible for admission to public housing or to continued oc-

33   73 Stat. 679 (1959) , 42 U.S.C. § 1401.
34   75 Stat. 163 (1961) , 42 U.S.C. § 1410 (g) (2) .
35   N.Y.C. Housing Auth. Res. 62–9–683, § 2.
36   Chicago Housing Auth. Res. 55–CHA–275, F.

cupancy. But administrative use of the largely undefined term "undesirable" is an inadequate discharge of the administrative responsibility to issue regulations. Discretionary power to make determinations in individual cases should not be so largely unconfined; it should be confined by regulations that are reasonably specific. Of course, discretion in the application of reasonably specific regulations is probably inevitable.

The regulations, for instance, should specify whether or not a family becomes "undesirable" because of such reasons as separation of husband and wife, divorce, imprisonment for a misdemeanor, imprisonment for a felony, suspended sentence for a felony, disclosure of a previous criminal record, an illegitimate birth, adultery, prostitution, membership in a teen-age gang, juvenile delinquency, irregular school attendance, dropping out from school, use of heroin, use of marijuana, alcoholism, quiet intoxication, membership in a subversive organization, membership in a radical organization, contraction of a contagious disease, mental illness, a mentally retarded child, gambling on the premises. The answers with respect to each such item need not be a simple yes or no and need not aim at cutting out all discretion, but the main policies with respect to each item should be fixed by the regulation and should not be left to the discretion of administrators in individual cases.

The regulations, of course, should be published and readily available to all who are affected. Every denial of admission or eviction should be explained, as is now at last required by a 1967 directive of the Department of Housing and Urban Development, and every such explanation should refer to the applicable provision of the regulations.[37] To assure against unfair or discriminatory practices in admitting, some such system should be required as classifying every applicant as eligible or ineligible and admitting eligible applicants in the order in which their applications are received.

---

37 The directive, dated Feb. 7, 1967, provides in part: "Since this is a federally assisted program, we believe it is essential that no tenant be given notice to vacate without being told by the Local Authority, in a private conference or other appropriate manner, the reasons for the eviction, and given an opportunity to make such reply or explanation as he may wish." The directive is quoted in full in Thorpe v. Housing Authority, 386 U.S. 670, 672 (1967).

The objective should be neither to eliminate legislative delegation without standards nor to eliminate all discretionary power. The objective should be to eliminate unnecessary discretionary power and to require that the main administrative policies be developed through rule-making.

The propositions that the government is not obligated to provide housing and that the typical tenancy in public housing is from month to month do not at all detract from the conclusions here stated, even though the courts have generally held that a Housing Authority may evict for whatever reason it chooses.[38] Good government requires the control of discretion in administration of public housing, and if the law does not require it, the law should be changed so that it will require it. Furthermore, the law is, at least to some extent, and ought to be that a public authority is subject to constitutional limitations even in administering a gratuity. Sound law was expressed by the Court of Appeals for the District of Columbia when it said: "The government as a landlord is still the government. It must not act arbitrarily, for, unlike private landlords, it is subject to the requirements of due process of law. Arbitrary action is not due process." [39]

11. *The police should make policy through rule-making procedure.* The thesis of this and the three succeeding sections is that the police should do a large portion of their policy-making through rule-making procedure along the line of what is required of federal agencies by the Administrative Procedure Act.[40] Some may be startled by the idea that police should make policy, and even more startled by the idea that they should use rule-making procedure, but the reasons in support of this thesis are powerful.

The President's Crime Commission has reported that 420,000 policemen work for about 40,000 separate agencies.[41] Each of the agencies is in every sense of the term an administrative agency, each makes important policy, and each plays a vital role in ad-

---

38 A leading case is Brand v. Chicago Housing Authority, 120 F.2d 786 (7th Cir., 1941).

39 Rudder v. United States, 226 F.2d 51, 53 (D.C. Cir., 1955). For an excellent article, see Michael B. Rosen, "Tenants' Rights in Public Housing," in Norman Dorsen and Stanley Zimmerman, *Housing for the Poor: Rights and Remedies* (1967).

40 5 U.S.C. § 553.

41 *The Challenge of Crime in a Free Society,* 91.

ministering justice to individuals. Comparing the relative importance of the police with regulatory agencies is difficult, but a clear
fact about the magnitude of the tasks performed is that we have
420,000 policemen (excluding assisting personnel) but that all
seven major federal independent regulatory agencies have an aggregate number of only about 10,000 employees (including all
personnel). Measured in manpower, the job of the police is more
than forty times as large as that of all seven major federal independent regulatory agencies combined.

The police are among the most important policy-making agencies, despite the widespread assumption that they are not. The
Crime Commission makes the basic observation that peacekeep-
ing and service activities consume most of the time of policemen,
and law enforcement takes only a minority of their time. Policy
has to be made about what private disputes to mediate and how
to do it, breaking up sidewalk gatherings, stopping undue noisi-
ness during sleeping hours, legally or illegally tapping wires and
using listening devices, helping drunks, deciding what to do with
runaway boys who refuse to go home, breaking up fights and mat-
rimonial disputes, deliberately destroying valuable property such
as gambling devices even when admissible evidence that it has
been used illegally is lacking, engaging in preventive detention in
violation of the Constitution, stopping citizens on the street, entering and searching premises, and deciding which crimes not to
investigate for lack of manpower. Policy has to be made for the
enormous field of police control of juveniles.[42] Policy has to be
made on such huge and troublesome subjects as the relations between the police and various minority groups. The Riot Commission listed in order of importance twelve deeply held grievances of
residents of the ghettos; in *first* place were "police practices." [43] The
Crime Commission said that police relations with minority groups
are "as serious as any problem the police have today." [44]

With respect to law enforcement, the problems of policy as to

---

42 For an outstanding piece of scholarship by students, see "Juvenile Delin-
quents: The Police, State Courts, and Individualized Justice," 79 Harv. L. Rev. 775
(1966), a study of seventeen cities based on about seventy-five interviews with police officers, probation personnel, and juvenile court judges.
43 *Report of the National Advisory Commission on Civil Disorders* (1968), 7.
44 *The Challenge of Crime in a Free Society,* 99.

whether and when to refrain in some degree from full enforcement are enormous, sometimes involving broad social problems,
and often raising difficult problems about justice to the individual. Some of the policy problems the police must somehow resolve are whether to refrain from arresting a violator because—
   the police believe the legislative body does not desire enforcement,
   the police believe the community wants nonenforcement or
   lax enforcement,
   a policeman believes another immediate duty is more urgent,
   a policeman interprets a broad term (such as "vagrancy") in
   his own unique fashion,
   a policeman is lenient with one who did not intend the violation,
   the offender promises not to commit the act again,
   the statute has long been without enforcement but is unre-
   pealed,
   lack of adequate police manpower is believed to require nonenforcement,
   the policeman believes a warning or a lecture preferable to an
   arrest,
   the policeman is inclined to be lenient to those he likes,
   the policeman sympathizes with the violator,
   the crime is common within the subcultural group,
   the victim does not request the arrest or requests that it not be
   made,
   the victim is more likely to get restitution without the arrest,
   the only witness says he will refuse to testify,
   the victim is at fault in inciting the crime,
   the victim and the offender are relatives, perhaps husband and
   wife,
   making the arrest is undesirable from the policeman's personal
   standpoint because of such reasons as the extra effort required, he goes off duty in ten minutes, the record keeping necessary when an arrest is made is onerous, or he wants to avoid
   the expenditure of time for testifying in court,
   the police trade nonenforcement for information or for other
   favors,

the police make other kinds of deals with offenders,
the police believe the probable penalty to be too severe,
the arrest would harm a psychiatric condition,
the arrest would unduly harm the offender's status.[45]

Some of the problems committed to personnel with average education of 12.4 years call for the best talents and specializations that the society can muster. Take, for instance, this question: "To what extent, if at all, is it ever justifiable to take into account the customs, practices, and prevailing standard of conduct of an identifiable subcultural group in determining whether the [criminal] process should be invoked against a member of that group?" [46]

Despite the extensive policy-making by the police, the continuing assumption by the community and by the police themselves has been that the police do not make policy. For instance, the Crime Commission says: "Probably the most pervasive reason that the police do not articulate policy formally is that they usually do not realize that they make policy informally every day." [47] An independent scholar says that "most departments attempt to maintain the existing stereotype of the police as ministerial officers who enforce all the laws, while they actually engage in a broad range of discretionary enforcement." [48]

The first step toward confining and structuring the discretionary power of the police is to bring to the consciousness of the community and of the police the significance of the policy-making role played by the police. The first step seems to be in process. For instance, the Crime Commission says: "The need for legislative and administrative policies to guide police through the changing world of permissible activity is pressing. . . . Clear police policies about ways of handling various juvenile situations would be of great help to policemen on the street. . . . It is incumbent on police departments to define as precisely as possible when arrest is a proper action and when it is not." [49] And the Riot Commission notes: "Contacts between citizens and the police in the ghet-

45 For a discussion of all such items and more, see Wayne R. LaFave, *Arrest* (1965).
46 Id. at 113.
47 *The Challenge of Crime in a Free Society,* 104.
48 LaFave, *Arrest,* 493.
49 *The Challenge of Crime in a Free Society,* 104, 106.

to require discretion which should be based upon carefully-drawn, written departmental policy. *The Commission Recommends* the establishment of guidelines . . . ." [50]

12. *Illegality and semi-legality of police policies.* A most astounding fact about police policy-making is that much of it is unauthorized by statute or by ordinance, that some of it is directly contrary to statutes or ordinances, and that the strongest argument for legality rests upon legislative inaction in the face of long-continued police practices. Nearly all of the policy-making power the police have assumed is beyond the reach of judicial review. Extremely incongruous is the juxtaposition in the same legal system of enormous undelegated power long exercised by the police without legislative guides of any kind and often directly contrary to policies embodied in legislative enactments, and a judicially created doctrine that legislative delegations are unconstitutional without meaningful standards. By and large, the uncontrolled discretionary powers that have been assumed by the police without delegation are more dangerous than any uncontrolled discretionary powers that have been delegated to the police.

To begin with, the flagrance of the illegality is often astonishing. For example, the law of Illinois seems entirely clear that gambling is a crime, and that gambling includes playing "a game of chance or skill for money or other thing of value." [51] The penalty is up to a year in jail, or up to three years in the penitentiary for a second offense. The law was first enacted in 1825 and has been reenacted fourteen times, the last three being 1953, 1963, and 1965. The statute makes no distinction between commercial gambling and social gambling. But when Chicago police arrested a group of prominent citizens who were playing a friendly game of poker, the superintendent of police announced on the front pages that he was sorry; his policy, he said, was not to arrest for gambling in absence of a commercial element. What the Illinois

50 *Report of the National Advisory Commission on Civil Disorders,* 313. The commission at pages 308–309 says of ghetto inhabitants: "They come to believe that an assault on a white victim produces one reaction and an assault on a Negro quite another."

For an excellent discussion of legal implications of less police protection in the ghetto, see 76 Yale L. J. 822 (1967).

51 Ill. Stat. 38 § 28-1.

legislature had enacted was partly nullified by the police chief. The law for Chicago is not what the legislature enacts; it is what the police chief says to the newspapers.

But where does the police chief get his power? An 1874 Illinois statute, reenacted in 1965 with a slight amendment, provides: "It shall be the duty of every . . . policeman . . . of any incorporated city . . . when any criminal offense . . . is committed . . . in his presence, forthwith to apprehend the offender. . . ." [52] A Chicago ordinance places "duties" on the police including the duty to "enforce the laws and ordinances throughout the city." [53] Another ordinance provides for a fine or discharge for neglect to perform a duty which "shall tend to . . . impair in any way the prompt and strict enforcement of any law. . . ." [54] The authority, if any, of the police chief to nullify the statute comes only from acquiescence by the community and by the legislative body.

A 1958 ordinance of the City of Chicago provides: "No pedestrian shall cross a roadway other than in a crosswalk in any business district." [55] A Chicago newspaper reported February 16, 1966:

Chicago Police Supt. Orlando W. Wilson said Tuesday that city policemen will continue to ignore jaywalking. On the basis of a two-month study of cities that enforce jaywalking laws, he explained, his men will leave well enough alone. He said that Chicago's pedestrian death rate is substantially lower than in cities that have had enforcement programs for years.

Yet a Chicago ordinance provides: "It shall be the duty of the traffic bureau [within the police department] to make arrests for traffic violations." [56]

The Chicago police seem to be typical of city police all over the country. Here is an item from the New York *Times* for October 18, 1963:

The police in Port Chester clamp down on professional card gambling when unwritten rules of procedure are violated, not on the basis of laws,

52   Ill. Stat. 125 § 82.
53   Chicago Munic. Code, Chaps. 11–24.
54   Id., 11–32.
55   Id., 27–282.
56   Id., 27–388.

testimony before the State Investigation Commission showed yester-
day. . . . Fred C. Ponty, chief of police, gave the commission his view in
these words: "We don't feel if local men are playing cards and there's
no money around—we know they probably divide up later—as long as
there are no strangers around, we feel we know what's going on and
who's there." . . . But when "outsiders" appeared, he said, "we don't
tolerate it."

The New York legislature writes the statutes but the Port Chester police modify them.

Probably every state has criminal statutes which express ideals
of the community but which are unreal in terms of accustomed
behavior. A well-known example is statutes making sex practices
of various kinds crimes; the police systematically nullify many
such statutes, or—what is worse from the standpoint of justice—
they enforce them only occasionally. For instance, in New York
adultery has been proved with evidence in thousands of divorce
cases; the statute makes adultery a crime, but the police usually
make it not a crime, even when already proved on official records.

State legislation is quite uniform over the country in imposing
a duty on the police to enforce criminal statutes.[57] Police manuals
are generally quite clear in imposing a duty of full enforcement.

Of course, police illegality is not limited to non-enforcement or
to selective enforcement. It includes destruction of property such
as slot machines or pornography, making deals with criminals,
as by trading non-enforcement for information, using the arresting power as a sanction when evidence is lacking to support a
charge. The discretionary power of the police, even when flagrantly lawless, is usually supreme.

Views differ as to what, if anything, should be done about the
extent of police illegality. One attitude is that expressed by the
President's Crime Commission:

Finally, the police should openly acknowledge that, quite properly, they
do not arrest all, or even most, offenders they know of. Among the factors accounting for this exercise of discretion are the volume of offenses

57 A systematic collection of statutes appears in Joseph Goldstein, "Police Discretion Not to Invoke the Criminal Process: Low-Visibility Decisions in the Administration of Justice," 96 Yale L. J. 543, 557–58 (1960). New Mexico seems to stand
alone in conferring a discretionary power of selective enforcement.

and the limited resources of the police, the ambiguity of and the public desire for nonenforcement of many statutes and ordinances, the reluctance of many victims to complain and, most important, an entirely proper conviction by policemen that the invocation of criminal sanctions is too drastic a response to many offenses.[58]

The Crime Commission's statement seems to be an approval of police illegality. To say that the police "properly" refrain from arresting known offenders is directly in opposition to statutory provisions that the police "shall" arrest known offenders. Similarly, saying that the police have "an entirely proper conviction" that criminal sanctions are too drastic is an explicit approval of direct police violation of clear statutes.

I recognize that the Crime Commission's attitude is dominant in the American society today. I also recognize the arguments in favor of that attitude: Legislative bodies have long acquiesced in the assumption of power by the police, legislation has long been written in reliance on the expectation that law enforcement officers will correct its excesses through administration, the legislation often reflects unrealistically high aspirations of the community and hence compels the law enforcers to temper the ideals with realism, and the system we have is the product of natural evolution through responses to the multiplicity of community needs.

Even so, despite the full or partial validity of some of these arguments, I wonder whether the degree of rejection of a sound version of the rule of law is too great. When a legislative body enacts that an act is a crime, and when it delegates no power to the police to substitute their judgment as to what should be a crime, police nonenforcement on the ground that the enactment is unwise seems clearly an unlawful assumption of power. When administrators flagrantly violate clear statutory provisions, they reject the central idea of the rule of law. The extremism that allows the police to set aside legislation on the ground that it is unwise may be as objectionable as the extremism in the opposite direction (labeled the extravagant version of the rule of law in Chapter 2) that forbids even such discretionary power as is necessary for in-

58 *The Challenge of Crime in a Free Society*, 106.

dividualized justice. The middle view between the extremes is the one that Americans have generally chosen in other contexts, and perhaps it is the one that should be chosen with respect to the police.

The harms from police violations of clear statutes are multiplied when the policy-making power is exercised by individual policemen. *The system is atrociously unsound under which an individual policeman has unguided discretionary power to weigh social values in an individual case and make a final decision as to governmental policy for that case, despite a statute to the contrary, without review by any other authority, without recording the facts he finds, without stating reasons, and without relating one case to another.* Yet that is precisely what happens when the legislation makes the act a crime, when the police department leaves the degree of enforcement to the judgment of the individual policeman, and when the policeman refrains in some cases from full enforcement, on the basis of his own ideas about social values.

13. *Subdelegation by the police and denial of equal justice.* Not only do the police make vital policy, and not only is much of the policy they make illegal or of doubtful legality, but police policy is made primarily by subordinates, not by the heads of departments.

No other federal, state, or local agency, so far as I know, delegates so much power to subordinates. No other agency, so far as I know, does so little supervising of vital policy determinations which directly involve justice or injustice to individuals. And no other agency, so far as I know, makes policy which in such a large degree is illegal or of doubtful legality.

The Crime Commission packed a tremendous amount of meaning into its simple statment that "law enforcement policy is made by the policeman." [59] The extreme decentralization of power has been planned by no one; it has simply grown out of the gigantic false assumption, deliberately fostered by some policemen who have full understanding but widely believed by many conscientious officers at all levels, that of course the police do not make policy. The surprise here is that not only does the Crime Commission seem to approve police illegality but it goes far in the di-

59 Id. at 10.

rection of approving important policy determination by individual officers: "Policemen cannot and do not arrest all the offenders they encounter. It is doubtful that they arrest most of them. . . . Crime does not look the same on the street as it does in a legislative chamber." [60]

A leading commentator says that effective control of police discretion within the department "is generally absent in the current criminal justice system." He emphasizes lack of reporting, lack of review by supervisory officers, and lack of guidance through stated criteria: "Either because of fear that any such criteria would be challenged, or for other reasons, nonenforcement decisions continue to be made on an ad hoc basis. . . . A decision not to arrest seldom comes to the attention of superior officers, and, if it does, there is no prescribed criterion for deciding whether it conforms to departmental policy." [61]

Can unconfined, unstructured, and unchecked discretionary power of an individual officer to make vital governmental policy in individual cases be good government? Can such power of an individual officer to make policy that is directly contrary to what a legislative body has enacted be good government?

What has happened is essentially that all the forms, all the machinery, all the organizational arrangements, and all the procedures are built on the false assumption, constantly furthered by many officers, that policy-making power is not being exercised. In general, top officers refuse to acknowledge that their departments are making important policy determinations and that they must accordingly plan a system for making such determinations. The legislative bodies have never knowingly delegated policy-making power to the police, and the heads of the departments have never explicitly subdelegated such power to their subordinates. Yet the policy-making power has grown tremendously. And the principal place of growth is in the lower levels of police organizations.

When "law enforcement policy is made by the policeman," one consequence is that social values are weighed and determined by

---

60 Ibid. The commission's seeming approval of the police illegality may be something less than a genuine approval; it may be a part of the commission's strategy for motivating the police toward favorable response to some of the commission's recommendations.

61 LaFave, *Arrest*, 158.

single individuals whose median education is 12.4 years; the average policeman has had less than half a year of college.[62] But what is worse is the unevenness of results; policies differ from one patrolman to another, and policies of one patrolman differ from one case to another, in whatever way his idiosyncracies move him. For instance, a policeman catches one boy in the act, gives him friendly advice, and perhaps drives him home; on another occasion he catches another boy in the same act but his mood is different and the boy is arrested, prosecuted, tried, convicted, and sentenced. A policeman makes a deal with a small narcotics peddler, bartering nonenforcement for information, but on another occasion in the same circumstances he arrests a smaller peddler. One policeman arrests for social gambling or for a particular sex offense, another arrests for one and not the other, a third arrests for the other and not for the one, and a fourth for neither, but none of the four administers evenhanded justice or has any special incentive to do so. The result of such uneven enforcement is often unequal justice, for whenever the evidence of an offense is clear, the decisive point in the entire criminal process is usually whether or not an arrest is made; if it is, prosecution and conviction may automatically follow, and if it is not, the offense forever goes unpunished. The crucial decision in the entire criminal process thus often depends upon the unguided discretion of an individual policeman, who exercises his great power of selective enforcement, without guidance from headquarters, partly on the basis of his emotions or even his whims of the moment, reacting to his own predilections and his own convenience, without regard to what his fellow officers do in similar cases or to what he himself has done in other such cases.

Equal justice can and should be better protected.

14. *What rule-making procedure can accomplish for police policy.* The objectives of a good program for reform of police practices should be (1) to educate the public in the reality that the police make vital policy, (2) to induce legislative bodies to redefine crimes so that the statutory law will be practically enforceable, (3) to rewrite statutes to make clear what powers are granted to the police and what powers are withheld, and then to keep the police within the granted powers, (4) to close the gap between

62 *Crime Commission Task Force Report: The Police* (1967), 10.

the pretenses of the police manuals and the actualities of police behavior, (5) to transfer most of the policy-making power from patrolmen to the better qualified heads of departments, acting on the advice of appropriate specialists, (6) to bring policy-making out into the open for all to see, except when special need exists for confidentiality, (7) to improve the quality of police policies by inviting suggestions and criticisms from interested parties, (8) to bring the procedure for policy determination into harmony with the democratic principle, instead of running counter to that principle, (9) to replace the present police policies based on guesswork with policies based on appropriate investigations and studies made by qualified personnel, and (10) to promote equal justice by moving from a system of ad hoc determination of policy by individual officers in particular cases to a system of central policy determination and a limitation of the subjective judgment of individual officers to the application of the centrally determined policy.

All ten objectives can be furthered and some can be fully accomplished through rule-making procedure, except that the second and third call for legislation.

In the total system of police discretion, one fundamental failure is the continued enactment of statutes which go far beyond the limits of effective law enforcement. *Criminal statutes which overshoot are a prime cause of avoidable injustice,* because such statutes inevitably result in selective enforcement, and cases are often selected for enforcement on irrational grounds. A major means of reducing injustice is by tailoring criminal statutes to what can be rather fully enforced.

Of course, even when legislative bodies have failed to tailor the substantive criminal statutes to bring them within the limits of effective enforcement, the police through rule-making can to a considerable extent eliminate unnecessary discretionary power to make decisions in individual cases. Both the President's Crime Commission and the American Law Institute have provided the beginning of thinking about the need for police rule-making, but it is only a beginning. The Crime Commission has recommended:

Police departments should develop and enunciate policies that give police personnel specific guidance for the common situations requiring exercise of police discretion. Policies should cover such matters, among others, as the issuance of orders to citizens regarding their movements or activities, the handling of minor disputes, the safeguarding of the rights of free speech and free assembly, the selection and use of investigative methods, and the decision whether or not to arrest in specific situations involving specific crimes.[63]

The American Law Institute's Model Code of Pre-Arraignment Procedure provides for issuance of regulations by the chief law officer of the state (usually attorney general), and for regulations by local authorities, subject to review by the state's chief law officer.[64] A note on the provision says that "there should be participation by both police and prosecutors in the drafting of the regulations, so as to encourage compliance with the procedures established by the Code." The proposals of the Crime Commission and of the institute are sound as far as they go, for they do recognize the need for rules. But neither the commission nor the institute has recognized the great gains that can be made not merely from having rules but from the use of public rule-making procedure.[65]

Having rules to guide police discretion will further several of the ten objectives, but for some types of subject matter *the process of making the rules* will be a much greater contribution to achieving the ten objectives. I repeat my view that rule-making machinery, such as that prescribed by the federal Administrative Procedure Act, is one of the greatest inventions of modern government.

Such procedure as applied to large portions of police policy-making will tend to educate the public in the facts of life that police departments are great policy-making agencies, will call to legislators' attention the nature of police policies—including the

---

63   *The Challenge of Crime in a Free Society*, 104.

64   Tentative Draft No. 1, not yet adopted, § 1.03 (1966).

65   The Crime Commission was nevertheless aware of need for community participation in working out policies of the police. For instance, it said at page 101: "In each police precinct in a minority-group neighborhood there should be a citizens' advisory committee that meets regularly with police officials to work out solutions to problems of conflict between the police and the community. It is crucial that the committees be broadly representative of the community as a whole, including those elements who are critical or aggrieved." I agree but I would emphasize more than the commission did that majority-group neighborhoods should have a voice in police policies, too. The commission never mentions rule-making procedure.

sometimes strong practical reasons for departing from statutes as now written, will make legislators aware of the need for granting policy-making powers to the police and for placing appropriate limits on those powers, will help provide the basis for writing police manuals that are built on natural police responses to practical problems instead of on unreal pretenses, will assume that the policy-making power is primarily in the heads of departments and not in subordinates, will bring policy-making out into the open, will gain the benefits of ideas contributed by the public, will make the machinery for determining policies more democratic, will pull qualified personnel into the process, and will greatly reduce the need for lowly patrolmen to make decisions on the basis of their weighing of social values.

For example, the typical state has a statute making gambling a crime, and by its terms the statute applies equally to the church bingo game, the poker game among friends, small bets on athletic contests, and commercial gambling that becomes a cornerstone of organized crime. What typically happens is that the police enforce selectively, whether the gambling is social or commercial, but without any clearly determined policies. Some commercial gambling, because of favoritism from particular officers, may be condoned, but some social gambling, because of attitudes of other officers, may be effectively stopped. The best solution would be for the legislative body to answer all the major questions with clarity and precision; failing that, the next best solution is for the police through rule-making procedure to give systematic and clear answers to all the major questions, thus reducing the power of selective enforcement in individual cases, and thereby reducing the injustice that results from uneven enforcement.

But can enforcement policies be determined through rule-making if substantial reformulation of enacted law results? For instance, if a statute flatly provides that gambling is a crime, can the police formally through rules provide that church bingo games and social poker games are not a crime? Surprisingly, the answer may have to be yes. Of course, if a choice can be freely made between full fidelity to enacted law and police illegality through a rule specifying what will and will not be enforced, the enacted law clearly should prevail. But realistically, that choice is not open to the police if the community refuses to tolerate full enforcement, as many communities do, and if the legislative body refuses to amend the statute, as many do. If the only realistic choice for the police is between (1) secret policies through ad hoc decisions of individual officers often resulting in flagrant denials of equal justice and (2) open policies adopted through rule-making proceedings with something approaching even application in all like cases, then the second choice is clearly better than the first.

A common kind of confused thinking is to prefer the secret ad hoc policies to the open uniform policies on the ground that the enacted law should be respected!

But can the police be expected to disclose to the public their own illegal behavior in refusing to enforce enacted law? The answer, I think, is sometimes yes and sometimes no. The extent to which the police do announce policies directly contrary to statutes or ordinances is astonishing;[66] to determine the announced policies through rule-making involves only a change in procedure. Yet the police may be expected to continue to strive for secrecy of some of their worst patterns of illegality, such as destruction of gambling devices when admissible evidence of crime is lacking, their use of arrest as a sanction when they have no intention of filing charges, their illegal corporal punishment of boys, their illegal deals with known criminals against whom they have evidence sufficient for conviction, and many other such practices.

Can the police be expected to act voluntarily in cutting down their own discretionary power through rule-making? The answer may be sometimes yes but usually no. One-third of all reported arrests are for drunkenness, involving much police time and much discretion; the police might willingly open up some of the difficult problems for public understanding and participation. Whether to shoot to maim looters during a riot is the kind of question the police may be willing to have someone else answer; recent public discussion of that issue has been surely helpful. On many less dramatic issues, the police may willingly allow opportunity for public expression. Of course, the police will usually prefer to retain their broad discretionary power to make ad hoc decisions about arrests

66 See pages 84–88, above.

in individual cases; even though clarification through rule-making of such concepts as "vagrancy," "disorderly conduct," and "loitering" may be clearly desirable, the police seem unlikely to take voluntary action in that direction.

The troublesome problem is not whether use of rule-making procedure for formulation of many police policies is desirable; clearly it is. The troublesome problem is how to bring it about. The police can be persuaded in some instances; they are more likely to resist than to initiate or to support such action in many other instances. Can legislative bodies be induced to require the police to resort to rule-making procedure? In the present climate of opinion, the answer may often be no. But many desirable programs of social change require long periods for accomplishment. A long-term strategy extending over a period of decades may be necessary, the first stage devoted to intellectual interchange, the second to gradual education of portions of the public who are interested, and the action stage coming only after sufficient educational foundation has been laid.

The unfortunate truth is that a large portion of accustomed police practices could never stand the light of day, and therefore much can be accomplished merely through public education. Indeed, even the police themselves need to be educated in the realities of what they are doing; many of them would refuse to participate if they were more sharply aware of the realities. The Crime Commission's Task Force on the Police made an astute observation that deserves applause:

Direct confrontation of policy issues would inevitably require the police administrator to face the fact that some police practices, although considered effective, do not conform to constitutional, legislative, or judicial standards. By adopting a "let sleeping dogs lie" approach, the administrator avoids a direct confrontation and thus is able to support "effective" practices without having to decide whether they meet the requirements of law.[67]

To give more meaning to the value of what the Task Force calls "direct confrontation of policy issues," let us choose at random an

67 *Crime Commission Task Force Report: The Police,* 17.

area of police illegality, and dress it up in the form of a formal rule. Here is a sample of an imaginary rule based on *real facts*:

Whereas, various statutes make distribution of narcotics a crime; whereas, the federal and state constitutions guarantee equal protection of the laws; and whereas, the Police Department of the City of X finds that law enforcement with resources at its disposal is inadequate when the statutes and constitutions are complied with; now therefore, the Police Department of the City of X, pursuant to power which it necessarily assumes but which no statute or ordinance has granted to it, does hereby promulgate the following rules, which shall supersede all constitutional provisions, statutes, and ordinances to the contrary:

1. The arresting officer may release a violator of a narcotics statute, no matter how clear the evidence against him, upon making a finding that he may become an informer.

2. Upon releasing such a violator, no officer shall interfere with his further purchase or sale of narcotics, so long as a finding is made that he is supplying information to the police or may be about to do so.

3. All transactions by which an officer trades nonenforcement for information shall be kept secret, so that the absolute discretion of the officer will be immune to check or review by any other governmental authority and immune to criticism by the public.

4. When two violators of the narcotics laws have committed the same offense in the same circumstances, no principle concerning equal justice under law or equal protection of the laws shall control when an officer chooses to trade nonenforcement for information; all provisions of constitutions, statutes, and ordinances to the contrary are hereby superseded.

5. Whenever an informer becomes recognized as such by the underworld, the officer who has made promises of immunity from arrest shall request another officer to arrest and prosecute the informer, and the second officer shall falsely pretend to have no knowledge of such promises of immunity; as soon as an informer's effectiveness has been spent, considerations of decency and fairness about keeping promises shall be given no weight.

The advantages of police resort to rule-making procedure can be enormous and can often mean a great gain for justice. Yet the problems of specifically what to do, how to do it, and how to provide incentives to get it done are challenging. These problems are very much in need of thorough and detailed study.

IV

Structuring
Discretion

1. *The meaning of structuring.* The principal question in this chapter is: How can administrators structure the exercise of their discretionary power, that is, how can they regularize it, organize it, produce order in it, so that their decisions affecting individual parties will achieve a higher quality of justice? One who thinks about this question is likely to discover that the answer has to grow out of particular subject matter, and I agree. But the question I am raising is more difficult: What can we do about structuring administrative discretion in general, irrespective of subject matter? The question leads into pioneer territory where the literature of jurisprudence, of public administration, and of administrative law is of little or no assistance.

Structuring discretionary power is different from confining it, although the two may overlap. The purpose of confining is to keep discretionary power within designated boundaries, and this can be accomplished through statutory enactments, through administrative rules, or by avoiding the development of discretionary power beyond the boundaries. The purpose of structuring is to control the manner of the exercise of discretionary power within the boundaries, and this, too, can be accomplished through statutory enactments, through administrative rules, and by other means. Administrative rule-making is an especially important tool both for confining discretionary power and for structuring it; rules which establish limits on discretionary power confine it, and rules which specify what the administrator is to do within the limits structure the discretionary power.

The seven instruments that are most useful in the structuring of discretionary power are open plans, open policy statements, open rules, open findings, open reasons, open precedents, and fair informal procedure. The reason for repeating the word "open" is a powerful one: Openness is the natural enemy of arbitrariness and a natural ally in the fight against injustice. We should enlist it much more than we do. When plans and policies and rules are kept secret, as through confidential instructions to staffs, private parties are prevented from checking arbitrary or unintended departures from them. Findings are a better protection against arbitrariness if affected parties can point to needed corrections. Reasoned opinions pull toward evenhanded justice but the pull is stronger if the opinions are out in the open. The difference between a system of precedents and a system of open precedents is enormous; for instance, because the Visa Office of the State Department uses a system of precedents but keeps them secret, parties often cannot ascertain whether discretion has been abused.

Plans, policy statements, and rules are three facets of essentially the same thing; all are designed to clarify and to regularize the purpose of the governmental activity. Similarly, findings and reasons are two facets of somewhat the same thing; findings summarize the facts, and reasons explain why the discretionary choices are made as they are. We have long realized the value of findings and reasons when cases go to hearing; we need to learn their value when discretionary determinations are made without hearings. The use of precedents—striving for consistency—has to be a central feature of any system which adequately structures discretionary power. Reasoned opinions and the use of precedents work together as a strong team, constantly structuring discretion as well as changing the exercise of discretion into the making of law. In addition to the procedural requirement of findings, reasons, and precedents, fair informal procedure includes opportunity for the affected party to know what is considered and to respond to it before a decision is made; requirements of fair procedure are not limited to hearing procedure.

Some discretionary power is beyond the reach of all seven methods of structuring, some can be reached by some of the seven, and some is subject to all seven. New discretionary functions may for long periods defy application of any of the seven methods of structuring and then may gradually yield to some or all of them. An exceedingly important fact is that when many or most apply, they help each other, producing an aggregate effect that may be profound, changing a disorderly system of ad hoc decisions that frequently result in avoidable injustice into an orderly system that may do reasonably well in minimizing injustice. Of course, even when the seven methods are possible, they are not always desirable for particular governmental tasks; *the purpose is not to maximize the use of the seven methods of structuring but to locate the optimum degree of structuring in each respect for each discretionary power.*

The main theme of this chapter is that many administrators are doing much less to structure their discretionary power than they should.

2. *Open plans.* The structuring of a particular discretionary power begins when the administrator first has some thoughts about his long-term objectives in the exercise of the power. Structuring occurs as the objectives take shape and as discretionary choices are made in the light of the objectives. In some circumstances executives are forced at an early time to do significant overall planning in order to instruct their staffs, who are immediately confronted with day-to-day choices. But regulatory agencies characteristically sit back and wait for questions to arise in particular cases, and the members of the agencies typically do little policy thinking except in the process of adjudicating single cases. Because the resulting case law is often spotty and even self-contradictory, the regulatory law remains uncertain over long periods. Indeed, regulatory agencies are notoriously deficient not only in doing the needed overall planning but also in announcing the results of such little planning as is done.

The seeming inability of regulatory agencies to take care of perspective problems, instead of merely treating the symptoms of those problems in the form of hundreds of cases annually, is one of the major weaknesses of the administrative process in its present stage of development. A new commissioner typically takes office with a determination to dig into the underlying problems of his agency but typically becomes absorbed in trying to keep his desk clear of the piles of routine work. Taking care of the inescapable day-to-day tasks consumes all his time; the wish for cutting through to the underlying considerations remains, but he has no energy for it now, and it has to wait until next week—or next month—or next year. In time even the wish seems to wear away.

The common administrative malady of debilitation about planning has many harmful consequences. It increases costs to the taxpayer. It increases legal expenses to regulated parties. It often defeats the democratic will embodied in the basic legislation which the agency is supposed to administer. It causes both inefficiency and ineffectiveness, and through prolonged uncertainties it significantly contributes to injustice.

Agencies are usually aware of their planning debilitation and sometimes make feeble gestures toward doing something about it. The most noteworthy planning office within a federal regulatory agency may be that of the Civil Aeronautics Board, which prepared an elaborate document entitled "Goals of the CAB," served it on airlines and other interested parties, and invited written comments. The planning office then made a systematic digest of all the comments and made revisions accordingly. But despite the excellence of the work done, the effort failed. The planning office was superseded. The CAB's 1966 annual report says: "The primary objective of the CAB's new planning, programming, and research activity is to analyze, interpret, and evaluate economic data relating to air transportation and to develop economic plans and programs related to the Board's mission of promoting and developing a sound transportation system." [1] The new emphasis seems to be on research that is ancillary to other activities, not on basic planning of a regulatory system.

One should not conclude from the CAB experience that a planning office must be manned by agency heads, for the Interstate Commerce Commission's planning committee of three commissioners is virtually a dead letter. A member of the committee could recall no significant accomplishment. The committee is not mentioned in recent annual reports or on the commission's organization chart.

The Federal Trade Commission has a Program Review Officer,

1   Page 59.

unmentioned in its annual reports, who tries to classify all business, establish units in the commission over each class of business, and allocate budget to each unit, so that the commission's work will no longer be hit or miss but will be planned and properly distributed. He finds that the great bulk of commission cases relate to small business, not big business, and he thinks this is wrong, but his ideas seem to have no effect on commission action. Apparently no one in the commission knows the cost to the government of typical cases of various classes, and no one has tried to appraise the value to the public of any such cases. No one knows whether the commission could sometimes render an unrequested advisory opinion which would be about as effective as a cease and desist order that costs taxpayers many thousands of dollars. The commission never gives unrequested advisory opinions.

The Communications Commission may be the federal regulatory agency that most urgently needs to do basic planning, but it has nothing in the nature of an overall planning office or committee. Advancing technology is revolutionizing some of the fundamentals of communication, but the commission does little by way of anticipating new needs. The government pays salaries of more than fifteen hundred employees who are supposed to think about communications problems, but what many believe to be the best communications idea in recent times came from the Ford Foundation. The President in a message of August 14, 1967, on Communications Policy seemed to slap at the commission's planning failures by establishing a Task Force on Communications Policy of sixteen members, only one of whom represents the FCC. The organizational arrangement seems highly questionable, for the cooperation of the FCC should be encouraged, not discouraged.

Surprisingly, the machinery by which planning for the regulatory agencies can be done has been fully thought out, tried, and found successful, although the general applicability of the machinery has been almost universally overlooked. The machinery that has succeeded is that of the Securities and Exchange Commission's Special Study, which was undertaken in 1961 and culminated in a three-thousand-page report in 1963, including 175 specific recommendations for correction of shortcomings in investor protection. The special study was directed by outsiders to the commission, who nevertheless used many members of the commission's staff and at all points had its close cooperation. The formula is an excellent one, and it should be used in other fields. We need a special study of antitrust enforcement, of natural gas regulation, of transportation regulation, and perhaps most of all we need a study of the systems of our city police departments, to carry further the good beginning made by the President's Crime Commission. The format of the Special Study might have been better for the communications field than the President's Task Force on Communications Policy established during 1967.

3. *Policy statements and rules.* When an agency knows what it is doing, it should say in some form what it is. The goal should be to close the gap between what the agency and its staff know about the agency's law and policy and what an outsider can know. The gap can probably never be completely closed, but the effort should always continue.

The means by which an agency can make known its law and policy range from the least formal to the most formal—an informal remark of a staff member, a whispered statement by an agency member, a public speech by a representative of the agency, a press release by the agency, a policy statement issued as such, a formal statement in an adjudicatory opinion, an interpretative rule, a legislative rule. All these means of communication are useful and all are used. Often the legal effect of what is said is difficult to ascertain. Sometimes a policy statement or rule is judicially reviewable and a less formal statement is not, but the lines are not clearly drawn.

Policy statements are usually looser than rules and are not necessarily binding on the agency, as legislative rules may be. Policy statements may still be very helpful. Such a statement may be appropriate when the agency feels that it is not quite prepared to issue rules; the agency may say, in effect: We are feeling our way in this direction, and this is where we want to go if we can get there. A policy statement may be essentially an announcement of a plan for an area of the agency's activities and therefore may be very helpful in structuring discretion. In general, policy statements should be used much more freely. Whatever understanding an agency may have about any subject that affects private parties should usually be made known to them, except when the agency has a sufficient reason for not doing so.

At some point policy statements shade into interpretative rules which in turn shade into legislative rules. Interpretative rules are considered slightly more formal than policy statements, and they usually have a slightly greater degree of binding effect on the agency—a degree that is seldom clear. Legislative rules are the product of grants of power to make law and when valid have substantially the same legal effect as a statute.

Most of the discussion of rules in Chapter 3 is relevant here and may be incorporated by reference, with a reminder of the difference between a rule which confines discretion and one which structures discretion: A rule may provide that over here at the right end the answer is always yes, and that over here at the left end the answer is always no; when it does that it confines discretion to the middle territory. But the rule may go on and structure the discretion in that middle territory. For instance, it may provide that in exercising discretion the agency will consider three factors. That much is a partial structuring of discretion. Then the rule may state the result when the three factors pull together but provide that the result will be worked out from case to case when the three pull against each other. Such a rule structures discretion, leaving many questions open. A rule which does not generalize but which gives illustrations may help structure discretion. Too many bureaucrats are slow to realize that rules may do much to structure discretion even when they leave many gaps that they do not purport to fill.

Of course, how fast discretion may be structured through rules is itself necessarily a matter for discretion. Almost all administrators do less structuring through rules than they can and should do. They should realize—as few do—that rules may be exceedingly useful even though they do not round out the coverage of a subject and even though they contain no abstract generalizations. The idea presented in section 5 of Chapter 3, that a useful rule may contain nothing more than an answer to a single hypothetical case, should be understood by more administrators.

4. *Findings and reasons.* Agencies systematically state findings of fact and write reasoned opinions whenever they hold trial-

type hearings, and they are required to do so whenever section 557 of the federal Administrative Procedure Act applies.[2] The reasons for findings and opinions are often just as strong, if not stronger, when discretion is exercised without hearings, for findings and opinions tend to protect against careless or hasty action, help assure that the main facts and ideas have been considered, make easier the supervision of the officer by a higher officer, and help parties to decide whether or not to seek administrative or judicial review.

Although findings and reasoned opinions obviously cannot be written in support of all discretionary determinations, they probably should be used much more than they are; the assumption is too general they are suitable only for cases that have gone to hearing.

Indeed, the Administrative Procedure Act in a provision that is seldom heeded specifically provides that "the denial in whole or in part of a written application, petition, or other request of any interested person made in connection with any agency proceeding . . . shall be accompanied by a simple statement of the grounds for denial." [3] And the act provides that the adoption of rules, with some exceptions, be accompanied by "a concise general statement of their basis and purpose." [4]

An example of the reason for reasons may be instructive. The Immigration Service disposes of about 700,000 applications per year, of which some 35,000 are denied. Almost all applications are handled without hearings. Some of the questions involved are of great moment to the particular aliens. When I discovered in 1964 that reasons were stated in support of denials in only a few classes of cases and not in about nine-tenths of them, I proposed to the commissioner and other top officers of the Immigration Service that an alien should always be entitled to have a written reason for the denial of any application. The initial response to this proposal was that it might require a doubling of the staff of some seven thousand and that the proposal was totally impractical. But on further study the service found the idea feasible. For

2 5 U.S.C. § 557 (c) .
3 5 U.S.C. § 555 (e) .
4 5 U.S.C. § 553 (c) .

each of thirty-six types of applications it prepared printed cards, listing all the usual reasons for denials. The officer was required to check the applicable reason and to give the card to the alien. I think this was a great gain. The alien now knows whether he should take some action to change his circumstances and file another application, whether the denial is based on a mistaken impression of the facts, and whether he should fight the case further by going to a superior officer. Furthermore, if the facts are in the file, a superior officer has the means of checking the officer's judgment. The new system has caused no increase in the size of the staff.

The prevailing assumption that decisions to prosecute or not to prosecute never call for reasoned opinions may well be reexamined. In some circumstances, I think the failure to write a reasoned opinion in support of a decision not to prosecute may be unfortunate. For instance, a Communications Commissioner told me one day that the seven commissioners had spent all the previous afternoon on a four-to-three division about a nice question of policy he told me about. When I asked for the name of the case, he said no opinion would ever be written and not even an announcement would be made, because the four had voted to permit a renewal to become effective without challenge. Even the broadcaster whose license was involved would not be notified that the problem was considered or that the commission had divided. In this instance, I think opinions should have been prepared and published.[5]

Although a system of reasoned opinions to justify discretionary determinations provides protection against arbitrariness when the true motivating reasons are spelled out, such a system has an intrinsic weakness which is hard to overcome. When administrators realize that the motivating reasons are unlikely to win approval, they naturally do what they can to set forth reasons that will look better. Of course, we commonly discern this sort of thing—or think we do—in opinions of both judges and administrators. Even the judges of the highest integrity sometimes pretend that a crooked line of decisions is straight or that a precedent on all fours is

5 The problem of stating reasons in support of decisions to prosecute or not to prosecute is discussed on pages 188–207, especially 188–90 and 203–205.

distinguishable. In any agency, the opinion-writing staff may be unaware of the motivating reasons but they know how to dress up a decision in verbiage that will make it look better than it is underneath. Some administrative opinions make me wonder whether the opinion-writing staff has ready-made boiler plate that will come close to fitting decisions of every size and shape, and sometimes the tailors even seem to forget to make the slight alterations that are needed.

Even though crafty administrators know how to avoid a requirement of reasoned opinions, and even though some opinions have little or no utility, nearly all administrators most of the time take the requirement seriously and conscientiously write reasoned opinions that include most of the motivating reasons. The many administrative opinions of excellent quality are encouraging. Opinions should more often be written in support of discretionary decisions that are made without hearings.

5. *Open precedents.* The main difference between what we call case law and what we call discretion lies in the presence or absence of an expectation that the tribunal will strive for consistency. As soon as a tribunal shows that it is in a sufficient degree striving for consistency, it is making law and not merely exercising discretion. Striving for consistency normally pulls along with it the writing of reasoned opinions, and opinion-writing tends to yield principles and then rules. The key element is the degree of attention given to consistency.

Law and discretion are not separated by a sharp line but by a zone, much as night and day are separated by dawn. Instead of the two categories of law and discretion, we could recognize five or fifty, as may be convenient. For present purposes, five seem convenient—those in which the tribunal's prevailing attitude is that precedents are (1) almost always binding, (2) always considered and usually binding, (3) usually considered but seldom binding, (4) occasionally considered but never binding, and (5) almost never considered. The first two categories fit what we usually call case law, the last two fit what we usually call discretion, and the third is the zone between law and discretion.

One's first impulse is to prefer law to discretion and therefore to suppose that the greater the role of precedents the better. After all, consistency is clearly desirable for two main reasons: Equality is a major ingredient of justice, and striving for consistency reduces arbitrariness. But other factors also must be considered. Turning all discretion into law would destroy the individualizing element of equity and of discretion. Binding precedents may make for undue rigidity. For instance, we do not want precedents to be as strongly binding on some of the looser problems of public law as they are and ought to be in some areas of real property law. Precedents have greater force in English courts than in American courts, and my opinion is that we would lose much if our courts were to imitate the English courts; we benefit by the flexibility which helps keep our law abreast of changing conditions and new understanding. Near the other end of the scale, we do not want the President and the State Department to be bound by precedents in making foreign policy, and the same is true of any agency's broad policy positions. We must remember that although the inequality caused by inconsistency can mean injustice, excessive rigidity can mean not only injustice but also a failure to make use of better understanding.

Our sound objective, therefore, is not to maximize law and to minimize discretion, and it is not to maximize consistency and to minimize inconsistency. Our sound objective is to locate the optimum degree of binding effect of precedents for each particular subject matter, so that the role of precedents will be in each instance neither too strong nor too weak.

But once we have rejected the goal of maximizing the role of precedents, our next step is to recognize that the optimum degree of binding effect of precedents for any particular subject matter usually is not a constant but a variable. For many types of administrative subject matter the normal and desirable progression is to start in category 5—wide-open discretion—and gradually move up the scale to categories 4 and 3 and 2 and sometimes even to 1.

Of course, some subjects properly stay permanently in category 5, where precedents are almost never considered. An example is the President's discretion in the selection of officers for his administration, or any other executive's selection of personnel. Another example is an agency's recommendations to Congress of

amendments to the legislation the agency administers or its recommendations of new legislation.

Most new administrative subject matter, however, must at first
be committed to discretion because no one is able to write rules or
even meaningful standards. But as administrators exercise discretion, they solve some of the recurring problems. Then they naturally follow precedents, for they find it inefficient to rethink a
question they have once resolved to their own satisfaction, in absence of special reason to do so. The precedents accordingly
grow, the opinions are soon stating some standards or other guides,
and the movement may go on toward principles and, for some
subjects, rules.

This normal progression from unguided discretion to some use
of precedents to clarification of standards to greater use of precedents to discovery of principles and finally to formulation of rules
is a phenomenon of major importance. Whenever the subject matter is right for it, as it very frequently is, we should encourage this
normal progression. This is not the same as saying that we should
maximize the binding effect of precedents; we should not do that.
We should find the optimum degree of binding effect of precedents, and that degree should be no more and no less than the
optimum. As experience with a subject develops, the optimum is
likely to shift upward, and when it does, the movement should be
upward. For new problems, the optimum is often wide discretion. For old problems, the optimum may be principles or even
detailed rules.

Perhaps I should point out parenthetically that the degree of
binding effect of precedents is not the only factor that determines
the extent of discretion. Discretion may be broad even when precedents are fully binding. An officer may have discretion to change
the framework of law, and he may also have discretion to make
choices within that framework.

Another parenthetical observation may be useful. The literature of jurisprudence abounds with discussions of our categories
1 and 2—whether precedents should be always binding or usually
binding—but it throws hardly any light on our categories 3, 4,
and 5. Perhaps this is because it focuses on judges and not on
administrators. One great challenge of the age in which we live is

the development of a useful jurisprudence of administrative law.

That we should encourage the normal progression from un-structured discretion to structured discretion and beyond often seems entirely clear when private interests are at stake and when the same issues often recur. We should not fail to clarify standards when we have the requisite understanding to clarify standards, we should not fail to develop principles when experience leads toward principles, and we should not fail to formulate rules when rules have become feasible.

What happens in fact, however, is that the normal progression from unguided discretion toward rules is often one or two stages behind the stage that the administrators' understanding makes feasible, with the result that the optimum may be category 1 or 2 but the agency goes on using category 3 or 4. I shall describe what happens by choosing an example that seems typical of the principle involved.

A statute provides for forfeiture of automobiles used in the narcotics trade and provides that if the Secretary of the Treasury finds specified facts he "may remit or mitigate. . . ." [6] Through executive reorganization the discretionary power to remit or miti-gate is now in the Attorney General, and although the top officers of the Department of Justice may supervise, a single attorney in day-to-day operations administers the power. He decides all ques-tions—law, fact, and discretion. The problems are largely recur-ring ones and the subject matter is obviously the kind that will readily yield rules. The officer is required neither by law nor by his superiors to follow precedents, but getting his work done re-quires him to, for he would waste time to do the same thinking over and over. To save time he not only follows precedents but he develops rules. He has a prefabricated answer to almost any question that may arise. For instance, he never mitigates a penal-ty; he either remits altogether or not at all. At one time he con-sidered mitigation, which is explicitly provided for by the statute, but he found it unsatisfactory and has never given serious thought to it since. On the main question of when he will remit or refuse

---

6   19 U.S.C. § 1618, explained and applied in United States v. One 1961 Cadil-lac, 337 F.2d (6th Cir., 1964), holding a refusal to remit a forfeiture judicially unreviewable for abuse of discretion.

to remit, his rules are highly crystallized. Discretion in a most natural fashion has properly given way to rules.

Now, the picture I have painted may seem beautiful, but if we look a little longer we see some blemishes. The precedents are there, but where are the open precedents? The decisions are there, but where are the reasoned opinions? The rules are there, but where are the published rules? Can the picture be beautiful if the affected parties have no access to precedents, if they never see a reasoned opinion, and if the rules which in fact control administrative discretion are neither published nor open to public inspection?

These missing elements are indispensable to a satisfactory system of justice. As soon as the administrator develops a system of following precedents, the precedents must be open to inspection. As soon as discretion gives way to rules, the rules should be available to affected parties. Precedents and rules provide a beneficial structuring of discretion, but not if they are kept secret, for the administrator then can ignore a precedent or violate a rule, engaging in discrimination and favoritism without detection. Discretionary power to depart from precedents and to change the rules should continue, but discretionary power to violate without changing should be cut off. Secret law, whether in the form of precedents or in the form of rules, has no place in any decent system of justice.

Why are the precedents and the rules not open to public inspection? The answers this officer gives seem to me especially significant because they seem to be natural responses and because other administrators seem to give somewhat the same answers. His first answer was: "Why should they be open? I am the only one that uses them." His next answer was: "The law does not require me to follow precedents or to formulate rules. The law confers a discretionary power. The precedents and the rules are only for my own guidance." His third answer disclosed a more important motivation and one that is very common: "Publishing the rules I use will only invite trouble. The lawyers for the finance companies are very able, and they can make it appear that almost any document has flaws in it. Everything is going smoothly now, and I am not going to go out of my way to ask for trouble."

He has not opened his rules or his precedents to public inspection, even though the Information Act clearly requires him to do so.[7]

6. *Openness as a protection against arbitrariness.* One valuable weapon in the fight against arbitrary exercise of discretion is openness. In absence of special reasons for closed proceedings or closed records, both courts and agencies usually hold open hearings and usually keep the records of the hearings open to public inspection, but both courts and agencies often bar the public from informal processes and from inspecting the records of informal processes. What is needed, I think, is increased openness of informal processes and the resulting records. The Information Act[8] is designed to open records to public inspection, but it falls far short of substantial accomplishment of its purpose, as we shall see.

Court trials, both criminal and civil, are based on a tradition of openness. Courtroom doors are open to the public, and so are trial records. The Sixth Amendment, which is read into the Fourteenth, guarantees a "public" trial in all criminal prosecutions. "Today almost without exception every state by constitution, statute, or judicial decision, requires that all criminal trials be open to the public." [9] Trials in civil cases are customarily open; Wigmore speaks of "the traditional common-law practice of holding trial with open doors." [10]

Records of trials, with all relevant papers, are customarily open to public inspection. For example, a federal statute provides for verbatim recording of all proceedings in open court "unless the parties with the approval of the judge shall agree specifically to the contrary" and further provides with no exception: "The original notes or other original records and the copy of the transcript in the office of the clerk shall be open during office hours to inspection by any person without charge." [11] The provision for open court records is closely limited; it fails to reach the large portion of non-trial proceedings that are not recorded.

7   5 U.S.C. § 552.
8   *Ibid.*
9   In Re Oliver, 333 U.S. 257, 267–68 (1948).
10   6 Wigmore, Evidence § 1834 (3d ed., 1940).
11   28 U.S.C. § 753.

The common-law tradition of openness of trials goes back into the centuries. Blackstone, for instance, spoke of "open examination of witnesses . . . in the presence of all mankind." [12] The tradition was bolstered by the strong and even perhaps excessive views of Jeremy Bentham, who insisted not only that "Publicity is necessary to good judicature" but also wrote:

> . . . suppose the proceedings to be completely secret, and the court, on the occasion, to consist of no more than a single judge,—that judge will be at once indolent and arbitrary: how corrupt soever his inclination may be, it will find no check, at any rate no tolerably efficient check, to oppose it. Without publicity, all other checks are insufficient: in comparison of publicity, all other checks are of small account.[13]

One need not go as far as Bentham to appreciate the advantage of openness as a check. Mr. Justice Brandeis, in an article first published in 1914, captured the fundamental in a few words: "Sunlight is said to be the best of disinfectants; electric light the most efficient policeman." [14]

In the administrative process, as in the judicial process, hearings are customarily open. The Attorney General's Committee on Administrative Procedure said: "Hearings should be, and almost invariably are, public. The few exceptions where hearings are private are for the benefit of the individual involved. [Open hearings are] an effective guarantee against arbitrary methods in the conduct of hearings. Star chamber methods cannot thrive where hearings are open to the scrutiny of all." [15] Yet no federal statute prescribes open administrative proceedings. The Administrative Procedure Act says not a single word about openness of hearings or of other proceedings, and it recognizes "nonpublic investigatory proceedings." [16]

The British Committee on Administrative Tribunals and Enquiries, the Franks Committee, gave rather extreme emphasis to

12   Max Radin, "The Right to a Public Trial," 6 Temp. L. Q. 381 (1932).
13   1 Bentham, *Judicial Evidence* 524 (1827).
14   Louis D. Brandeis, *Other People's Money* (1933), 62.
15   Report (1941), 68.
Of course, interests in confidentiality are sometimes respected even when hearings are open. But often they are overridden. See FCC v. Schreiber, 381 U.S. 279 (1965).
16   5 U.S.C. § 555 (c).

"openness," since from the beginning to the end of its report it insisted upon the three characteristics of "openness, fairness and impartiality." [17] Putting "openness" consistently ahead of "fairness" may be a desirable emphasis, which Americans may well heed.

Although administrative hearings are generally open, *more than 90 percent of the American administrative process is behind closed doors,* even though the need for openness as a check upon arbitrariness is especially strong when discretionary action is taken without hearings. Furthermore, the Information Act,[18] designed to open administrative records, is largely ineffective as a check upon arbitrariness.

The meaning of the important observation that administrative processes are closed except when hearings are held can be better understood through an illustration, the Federal Trade Commission's enforcement of antitrust law concerning mergers. The Commission has two procedures for deciding whether a merger is legal, the hearing procedure and the nonhearing procedure. *All papers and all law that may be created are open when the hearing procedure is used. All papers and all law that may be created are secret when the nonhearing procedure is used.*

When the nonhearing procedure is used, everything is secret (except some vague digests later discussed). The proceeding is secret, including discussions with the corporations' representatives and with Senators and Congressmen who may be helping the corporations. Some pre-merger clearance letters are so secret that they are even kept from the commission's own staff, according to what some staff members have told me. The applications are secret; briefs and letters in support of applications are secret; the facts bearing upon the merger are secret, including not only facts that businessmen normally keep confidential, but also facts readily available to the public through other sources; the law that emerges from the commission's decision is secret; the policy the commission declares is secret; the commission's legal analysis, if any, is secret; the political rewards to the commission's chair-

17   Report (1957), 5, 10, 89, 90.
18   5 U.S.C. § 552.

man, if any, are secret; and the commission's reasons, if any, for
conducting the public's business in secret are secret.[19]

All this secrecy is in clear violation of the Information Act, the
1966 legislation amending the Administrative Procedure Act.[20]
The act requires disclosure of "orders," "interpretations," and
"identifiable records," with nine exceptions. Disposition of an
application for clearance is obviously an "order," which is defined
as "the final disposition . . . of any agency in any matter other
than rule making." So is it an "interpretation." And obviously
it is a "record." Eight of the nine exemptions are here irrelevant,
as they pertain to defense or foreign policy, personnel rules, specific statutory exemptions, intra-agency or inter-agency communications, personnel and medical files and similar files, investigatory
files, financial institutions, and wells. The only one of the exemptions that is relevant to pre-merger files is "commercial or financial information obtained from any person and privileged
or confidential." Such information presented by a corporation to
the commission with an understanding that it will be kept confidential is clearly exempt from the disclosure requirements. Yet
even commercial or financial information often is not confidential;
the same information may have been sent to a hundred thousand stockholders, and it may appear in open records of the Securities and Exchange Commission.

As of late 1967, the commission had never publicly acknowledged its pre-merger clearance program, so far as I can find. Its
annual reports to Congress had never mentioned the subject. An
outsider could not learn whether the commission was granting
clearances, how many it granted, how many it denied, whether it
wrote reasoned opinions, whether it applied legal principles or
was actuated exclusively by political influence, or any of the other
significant facts about clearances. In response to my pressure for

19 The commission has asserted this policy of secrecy in two letters to me. In
the first letter, Nov. 27, 1967, it failed even to mention the Information Act, and I
urged reconsideration in the light of that act. In the second letter, April 30, 1968,
the commission mentioned the act but quoted no single provision from it. The
first letter was supported by a three-to-two vote. In both letters, Commissioner Elman wrote dissenting statements; in the second letter he stressed the Information
Act and concluded: "I regret that the Commission seems still to be dealing with
these matters in a pre-Act fashion."
20   5 U.S.C. § 552.

opening up the clearance program except to the extent that confidential information was involved, the commission in late 1967 issued some statistics about the clearance program, and then in a News Release of February 13, 1968, issued twenty-six digests of clearances. The digests are in such vague terms as to be virtually meaningless,[21] but the commission announced that "these news releases are the only material of public record. The advisory opinions themselves and all background papers are confidential and are not available to the public." This published statement is a flagrant violation of the Information Act, which requires the opinions and papers to be open to public inspection except to the extent that any specific information is within one of the act's nine exemptions.

The digests do show that information the commission keeps secret is not within any exemption to the Information Act. For instance, no such exemption permits the commission to refuse to disclose such facts as the following: (1) In No. 167, the facts showing the meaning of the statement that "The companies partially competed," (2) in No. 171, the facts showing the meaning of the statement of "probable adverse competitive effects somewhat less than were present in the Brown Shoe case," and (3) in No. 173, what competitive information was available which the commission characterized as "the paucity of competitive information."

Even worse than the secrecy about the facts is the secrecy about the commission's law and policy. For instance, in No. 179, according to the digest, "the Commission advised that an acquisition

21   Here is a sample of one digest, No. 165, in full:

"The Commission issued an advisory opinion on July 30, 1964, in which a request for pre-merger clearance from liability under Section 7, amended Clayton Act, was approved permitting acquisition of a deteriorating competitor.

"A national manufacturer and distributor of consumer goods sought clearance of its proposed acquisition of a smaller manufacturer and distributor of the same products. Most of the business of the smaller firm was in a limited geographical area. The industry involved could be entered with a relatively modest sum of money. The firm to be acquired had experienced declining sales, a deteriorating, nonviable financial situation, personnel problems and had made reasonable but unsuccessful efforts to sell to others.

"The Commission advised that basing its belief on the information currently available to it that the proposed transaction, if consummated, probably would not violate any of the laws which the Commission administers."

by another producer in the same field would not be in violation
of Section 7, amended Clayton Act, and in the event a sale is
made to a company which is under Commission order requiring
approval of such acquisition, said approval would be granted."
Because of the secrecy, an outsider cannot know what happened
in No. 179. Apparently the commission had openly issued orders
forbidding named companies from making further acquisitions
without commission approval, and then the commission may have
secretly pursued an opposite policy from the one openly declared.
The secrecy is a bar to determining (1) what open orders embodied the commission's openly-declared policies, (2) what legal
analysis, if any, supported the secret clearance, (3) whether the
secret clearance contradicts the open orders, (4) whether the
commission's true policy, reflected in the secret clearance, is the
opposite of what appears in the open orders and supporting opinions, if any.

My conclusion is that in the Federal Trade Commission's pre-
merger clearance system, openness is not a protection against arbitrariness, or against favoritism, or against decisions contrary to
law, or against political deals which ignore open law and open
policy, or against any other kind of administrative abuse.

Sunlight is a good disinfectant, as Brandeis said. A disinfectant
is surely needed for the Trade Commission's pre-merger system.

But my main point goes beyond the Trade Commission to all
governmental action. The tendency of our prevailing practice is
(1) to open proceedings and records of formal hearings, overriding interests in privacy and in confidentiality, and (2) to close informal proceedings and records, irrespective of the advantage of
openness as a check on arbitrariness or other abuse. We need to
reexamine both facets of this tendency. The question we should
explore is how far we can, irrespective of formality or informality,
protect legitimate interests in privacy and confidentiality and
open everything else.

7. *Fairness of informal procedure.* The American legal profession is too much focused on fairness of hearings and too little
concerned with fairness of administrative procedure when hearings are not held. Bar groups and other study groups should, over

a period of decades, try to develop procedural principles to guide informal action of administrators.

For instance, procedure used by the Small Business Administration in lending government money to businessmen needs attention, even though one's first impression might be that government bankers should simply use the methods of any other bankers. When government agents dispense government money, procedural protection is needed which goes beyond what is needed when private bankers are dispensing private money.

The outstanding example of unfairness of the procedure of the Small Business Administration is its use of information from the Federal Bureau of Investigation and from the House Un-American Affairs Committee as a basis for denying loans, without disclosing to the applicant that the information is used and without giving the applicant an opportunity to rebut or explain. Officers of the SBA have elaborate explanations of the need for the information and of the impracticability of disclosing it, but after listening to their arguments I believe that the advantages of the system they follow are insufficient to offset the unfairness of making a decision on the basis of information about the applicant which he has no chance to rebut or explain.

The Immigration Service handles 700,000 applications a year, only a handful of which go to hearing. A formal regulation of 1964 provided that "confidentially furnished evidence shall not be made available" to the alien.[22] That meant that applications could be denied on the basis of gossip or on the basis of facts fabricated by a personal enemy of an alien or on the basis of some other factual impressions that the alien might readily explain away. In early 1965 I recommended to the Immigration Service that it should change the regulation to allow rebuttal or explanation. In May, 1965, I debated the question with the Deputy Commissioner before the Association of Immigration and Nationality Lawyers. He insisted that the provision I objected to was essential for efficient administration. I am happy to say that shortly thereafter, the objectionable provision was removed.[23] I am

22   29 F.R. 11956 (1964).
23   30 F.R. 7516 (1965).

unhappy to say, however, that examples of this type of unfair informal procedure can be found throughout the government.

The same basic principle is involved when an agency regulating banking denies an application for a charter or for approval of a branch. Yet many practitioners and a few courts have failed to recognize the vital distinction between requiring a trial-type hearing and requiring a chance to know and to respond to adverse evidence. My position has been one of opposing trial-type hearings on problems involving economic imponderables: "Probably the outstanding example in the federal government of regulation of an entire industry through methods of supervision, and almost entirely without formal adjudication, is the regulation of national banks. . . . The system may be one of the most successful [systems of economic regulation], if not the most successful." [24] This position has been adopted by the courts.[25] The result has been case law that denial of a charter or of a branch approval need not be on the basis of trial-type hearing.[26] Although I believe that a trial-type hearing is inappropriate, that is not the same as saying that any information can be considered without making it known to the party adversely affected. The choice is not between requiring every element involved in a trial-type hearing and dispensing with every such element; a sensible choice may be to dispense with the hearing but to allow a party to know and to respond to the information considered. For instance, when an application is made for a bank charter, I think competitor banks should not be entitled to a trial-type hearing in absence of issues about specific facts, but I also believe that they should be entitled to see the application and the other materials submitted in support of the application, and they should have a chance to state their response to such materials, either orally or in writing.

The tendency of courts, aided and abetted by practitioners, has been to refuse to recognize any middle position between requiring a trial-type hearing and not requiring it. Often a trial-type hearing is either too cumbersome or too expensive or both, and yet some procedural protection is desirable. *Often a good*

24 1 Davis, *Administrative Law Treatise* § 4.04 (1958).
25 E.g., United States v. Philadelphia Nat. Bank, 374 U.S. 321, 330 (1963).
26 E.g., Webster Groves Trust Co. v. Saxon, 370 F.2d 381 (8th Cir., 1966); Citizens Bank of Hattiesburg v. Camp, 387 F.2d 375 (5th Cir., 1967), certiorari denied——U.S.—— (1968).

procedure is to let a party know the nature of the evidence against him and to listen to what he has to say, even though, in general, no such procedure is recognized either in statutory law or in case law. An example is revocation of parole. The key case, in an unsatisfactory opinion, held that the parolee is not entitled to a trial-type hearing.[27] Even if, as the courts seem to believe, the practical reasons against giving the parolee a trial-type hearing are strong, the practical reasons in favor of listening to what he has to say after summarizing for him the nature of the evidence against him may be stronger. The inconvenience of giving him that much procedural protection is slight; yet the protection against a serious miscarriage of justice is considerable, even though the parolee has no chance for either confrontation or cross-examination. Facts which, without the parolee's explanation, seem to add up to guilt may seem to add up to something quite different when the parolee explains them.[28]

Once the basic idea has been discovered that *procedural protection short of trial-type procedure may be valuable,* possible applications for the idea blossom in many areas. The idea can be useful not merely for informal adjudication as a substitute for formal adjudication, but it can be useful for totally different functions, such as prosecuting, for example. Suppose the SEC thinks it has sufficient evidence that a broker-dealer has violated the law and is considering whether to institute a revocation proceeding or to recommend to the Department of Justice a criminal prosecution. Giving the broker-dealer a hearing on the question whether to take a step leading to a hearing would be nonsense. But procedural fairness may require something short of hearing: Before the commission acts, should it allow the representative of the broker-dealer a chance to know what it is contemplating and why, and listen to what he has to say? Or, in the alternative, can circumstances be identified in which this should or should not be done? [29]

---

27 Hyser v. Reed, 318 F.2d 225 (D.C. Cir.), certiorari denied 375 U.S. 957 (1963).

28 For a full discussion of procedure for parole revocation and some musing about procedural safeguards less than trials, see 1 Davis, *Administrative Law Treatise* § 7.16 (1965 Supp.)

29 Milton V. Freeman, "Administrative Procedures," 22 The Business Lawyer 891, 892 (1967): "To the person who is the subject of a [Securities and Exchange] Commission investigation, perhaps the most important thing that will

Should cases in which prosecution itself will cause significant damage that cannot be corrected by a finding of innocence be recognized as a special category, and for this category should special principles be developed to guide the prosecutor?

Similarly, should an investigator be guided by special principles whenever the investigation itself may cause irreparable injury?

In coming decades, I think justice will gain if less attention is given to the overworked subjects of judicial review and formal hearings and if more time and energy are devoted to cutting paths into the wilderness of nonhearing procedures.

8. *Banking regulation as an example of needed structuring.* What has been said in the preceding seven sections about structuring discretion can be better understood through application to a specific subject matter. The opportunity to observe structured and unstructured discretionary power is extraordinary in the federal banking agencies because of the recent changes made in one of them. To describe the facts, I am compelled to discuss my own role, and I shall frankly do so, as objectively as I can.

The purpose of what follows is not to inquire into banking regulation; it is to understand in one practical context how discretionary power which has been unstructured for more than a century can be successfully structured. *What can be learned from the structuring of discretionary power over banks is largely transferable to a considerable portion of discretionary power whereever it is found.*

The four principal banking agencies are the Comptroller of the Currency, the Federal Reserve Board, the Federal Deposit Insurance Corporation, and the Federal Home Loan Bank Board. As of 1965, the chartering and branching functions of all four of these agencies were almost wholly without structuring: The agencies

---

ever happen to him in his life, perhaps the most disturbing thing, is that the Commission will bring or contemplate bringing a civil proceeding against him or will bring a proceeding to take away his license to do business as a broker or dealer, or will recommend to the Department of Justice that he be prosecuted.

"Now these are the most important areas, and in these areas, the Commission has no fixed and definite procedures. . . . Of course, counsel wants to talk to the Commission about the matter. . . . Does he get that chance? Well, sometimes he does and sometimes he doesn't. To a certain extent, this depends on his skill. To a certain extent, it depends on pure luck."

had done no open planning of substantive policies, followed a practice of keeping secret the materials submitted in support of applications, had issued no significant substantive rules or policy statements or other guides for making determinations in individual cases, made decisions without systematically stating findings of fact, decided many cases without reasoned opinions and failed to serve such opinions on the parties even when they were written for internal use, and kept secret all proceedings and all related papers. My study of the banking agencies began in 1965, with a principal focus on the Comptroller of the Currency. During 1966 a draft of my criticisms and affirmative ideas was presented to the Comptroller's Chief Counsel, and then in 1967 a revised draft was published as an article, the first two sentences of which asserted: "The banking agencies of the federal government have long maintained systems of secret evidence, secret law, and secret policy. The result has been a degree of unchecked and unstructured discretionary power that is far greater than it should be." [30] The Comptroller's Chief Counsel accurately stated in a responding article that "most of the criticisms that form the basis of Professor Davis's article appear to have been met," [31] and my published response to that concluded: "I applaud the Office of the Comptroller for its recent procedural progress, and I hope the other banking agencies will make their own studies and follow in the same general direction." [32] As of the present writing, the Federal Home Loan Bank Board appears about to make changes like those made by the comptroller, the Federal Reserve Board during 1967 delegated its whole power over charters and branches to the twelve regional banks whose practices are still in the formative stage, and the FDIC has made no change and seems disinclined to do so. The discussion that follows is devoted to the system of the Comptroller of the Currency, past and present.

One way that structuring of the comptroller's discretionary power might have been brought about would have been through allowing trial-type hearings on every contested application; for-

---

30 "Administrative Procedure in the Regulation of Banking," 31 L. & Contemp. Prob. 713 (published 1967, dated 1966).
31 Robert Bloom, "Hearing Procedures of the Office of the Comptroller of the Currency," 31 L. & Contemp. Prob. 723.
32 31 L. & Contemp. Prob. 731.

mal proceedings would pull toward opening facts to public inspection, openly making findings, openly stating reasons, and
developing a system of open precedents. My opinion is and has
long been that trial-type hearings are a clumsy way to determine
how many banks and which banks ought to serve a community.[33]
Some of the worst processes of the federal government are those
of the Federal Communications Commission and the Civil Aeronautics Board, whose proceedings in comparative application
cases often cost individual parties several hundred thousand dollars and yet seem to have little utility. I think hearings in the
banking cases should be held if, but only if, the prospects are
that in particular circumstances such hearings will be the most
efficient way to do what needs to be done; clearly trials are the
best way to resolve disputes about specific facts.[34]

What has happened during the 1960's is that the federal courts
have at last gone along with the idea that trial-type hearings on
contested applications for charters or branches are not required.
Three circuits have so held during 1966, 1967, and 1968, and the
Supreme Court has denied certiorari.[35] In a 1965 case,[36] however, another circuit held that when the comptroller does not

33 1 Davis, *Administrative Law Treatise* § 4.04 (1958) .
34 For a statement in support of avoiding trial-type proceedings in the banking
cases and at the same time emphasizing fair informal procedure, see Sec. 7 immediately above.
35 Webster Groves Trust Co. v. Saxon, 370 F.2d 381 (8th Cir. 1966) , held that
the comptroller in issuing a national bank charter was not required to "hold a
formal adversary hearing upon the request of a competitor bank." Citizens Bank
of Hattiesburg v. Camp, 387 F.2d 375 (5th Cir., 1967) , certiorari denied——U.S.——
(1968) , held that the comptroller need not "hold a formal adversary hearing in
determining whether to approve the chartering of a new national bank," that the
decision is not subject to "review by trial de novo," that the court could not substitute its judgment for that of the comptroller, and that the comptroller had not
"acted arbitrarily or otherwise illegally." Warren Bank v. Camp,——F.2d—— (6th
Cir., 1968) , held that a hearing is not required, and that the review is not de novo.
36 First Nat. Bank of Smithfield v. Saxon, 362 F.2d 267 (4th Cir., 1965) . The
authoritative effect of the case today, if any, is weak, for three reasons: (1) The
later decisions of the 5th, 6th, and 8th circuits are unanimous and clear in holding that de novo review is not required. (2) The dissenting opinion of Judge So-
beloff in the Smithfield case was especially powerful; the decision was two to one.
(3) The comptroller's failure to disclose to the competing bank the application
and supporting data may have influenced the decision; I think it should have.
The comptroller now discloses such materials, except when confidentiality is essential.

conduct a hearing, the review must be de novo; that holding caused the comptroller to hold hearings in a good many cases, and such hearings have had substantial effect upon the structuring.

As for secret evidence, the comptroller's traditional system has been to keep secret even from opposing parties the application, the supporting papers, and the results of the investigation, including such subjects as composition of the population, economic growth, banking needs, adequacy of the applicant's capital structure, and degree of public support. The comptroller in 1964 published a regulation that the examiner should "summarize his findings" but that his report was "confidential." [37] Although I agree that some information about an application may properly be confidential, I think that none should be in absence of special reason. In a letter of May 29, 1968, the Comptroller's Chief Counsel has stated: "In both our branch and charter hearings all written material submitted by either the applicants or protestants is made available for inspection by all interested parties with the exception of personal financial and biographical data submitted in confidence to the Comptroller's Office." This change seems to me exactly right, except that it should be embodied in a formal procedural rule and published in the Federal Register.

Findings of fact should be systematically made in every case and should be openly stated. Such findings are an important safeguard against careless or arbitrary action. Since the law requires such findings, the surprise is that the comptroller's traditional system has been to announce decisions without stating findings. The comptroller had three reasons for his practice: (1) A belief that protecting the public required rejection of an application on the basis of unconfirmed suspicion, when significant evidence either way was lacking, (2) a belief that appraisal of particular personalities, at the heart of many decisions, cannot be publicly disclosed, and (3) a disinclination to give ammunition to those who might want to fight further in a reviewing court. Each reason seems to me insufficient. Although admitting to the banking business some dubious characters who may have engaged in shady

---

37 Comptroller of the Currency, *Guidelines for National Bank Directors* (1964), 43–44. No formal regulation properly published in the Federal Register has ever taken the place of this *Guidelines* statement.

deals that cannot be proved seems undesirable, the alternative may be worse—uncontrolled discretion to decide without evidence and on the basis of nothing more than bare suspicion who may or may not enter the banking business, without findings, reasons, or checks. The answer to the second reason is that unfavorable findings about particular personalities need not be precise and detailed; what the case law calls "the basic facts"—not what it calls "the evidentiary facts"—can be satisfactorily stated without creating runs on banks or distrust for their managers. The third reason that findings will supply ammunition to those who seek judicial review is founded on the truth. It will, and some useless litigation will result. But so will some correction of—or prevention of—injustice.

The comptroller is now generally stating findings in nearly all contested cases. I think this is a great gain, even though findings are not stated in all cases or even in all contested cases.

The comptroller and the other banking agencies have been clearly violating the Administrative Procedure Act by denying applications without stating reasons. The act provides: "Prompt notice shall be given of the denial in whole or in part of a written application . . . made in connection with any agency proceeding. Except in affirming a prior denial or when the denial is self-explanatory, the notice shall be accompanied by a brief statement of the grounds for denial." [38] I think opinions should be written on all significant issues of law and policy, whether applications are granted or denied. The strange fact is that the files of chartering and branching cases in the comptroller's office usually contain staff memoranda in the nature of reasoned opinions, which, with a little editing, could have been opened to the parties and to the public.

Beginning in late 1966, the comptroller has systematically stated written reasons in nearly all contested cases. And he has adopted a formal regulation providing for availability for public inspection of "Final opinions when made in the adjudication of cases." [39]

The principal deficiency that remains in the structuring of the comptroller's discretionary power is the almost complete failure

38   5 U.S.C. § 555 (e).
39   32 F.R. 9513, 9515, § 4.15 (a) (2) (1967).

of open planning. The comptroller has done about as little as possible to clarify his policies. Until recently the closest approach to open planning has been vague statements in speeches and in testimony to congressional committees. In formal rules published in the Code of Federal Regulations, no amplification is provided for the statement that "The Comptroller of the Currency determines whether or not the national banking association is entitled to commence the business of banking," except that five "matters investigated" are listed.[40] The rules can and should state the policies that govern the grant or denial of applications. An annual report makes one general statement that has meaning: "It can never be in the public interest to protect banks against competitors who are either more efficient or more responsive to public demands. There are, moreover, positive public benefits to be derived through the periodic introduction into the banking industry of new competitive forces with fresh ideas and fresh talents."[41] Such a statement is all to the good as far as it goes, but it does not go nearly far enough.

Of course, now that reasoned opinions are available, the open policies should gradually emerge. Ideally, formal rules or policy statements should go about as far as feasible in providing the needed clarification, and then opinions in individual cases should develop further refinements, which in turn should lead to a reworking of the formal rules or policy statements. One may assume that some movement in this direction is probable, even if it falls short of an ideal system.

Another continuing failure is the lack of published procedural regulations. The new regulations issued in 1967 [42] do not reflect the significant procedural changes, even though the Administrative Procedure Act in clear terms requires the publication of procedural regulations.[43]

Altogether, despite the deficiencies, the cumulative effect of the

40 12 CFR § 4.2 (e) (1967) , unchanged since 1964.
41 Annual Report (1964) , 3.
42 32 F.R. 9513 (1967) .
43 5 U.S.C. § 552.
The comptroller's explanation of his failure to publish procedural regulations is that the new procedural system is still experimental and is still developing. The answer to the explanation is that even experimental regulations must be published in order to comply with the Administrative Procedure Act.

structuring is very considerable. Before the changes, the comptroller's discretionary power was clearly excessive, for he could act on secret evidence, without stating findings, without reasoned opinions, without a system of open precedents, and usually without any effective check upon possible arbitrariness. After the changes, the chances of arbitrariness or other abuse, though not eliminated, are substantially reduced, for the evidence is normally open for all to see, the comptroller must state his findings openly, he must write reasoned opinions, and the writing of opinions should gradually grow into a system of open precedents. Ample discretionary power continues. No substantial disadvantage from the structuring, either to private parties or to the comptroller, is discernible. Even though availability and scope of judicial review remain about the same,[44] *the basic shift that has been successfully accomplished is essentially from uncontrolled discretion to controlled discretion. The best of it is that such a shift from unstructured to structured discretion is possible for many functions of many administrators, with a resulting increase in the quality of justice.*

We need extensive studies that will locate the unstructured discretion and that will determine how far it can and should be structured.

9. *The United States Parole Board.* An outstanding example of completely unstructured discretionary power that can and should be at least partially structured is that of the United States Parole Board. In granting or denying parole, the board makes no attempt to structure its discretionary power through rules, policy statements, or guidelines; it does not structure through statements of findings and reasons; it has no system of precedents; the degree of openness of proceedings and records is about the least possible; and procedural safeguards are almost totally absent. Moreover, checking of discretion is minimal; board members do not check each other by deliberating together about decisions; administrative check of board decisions is almost nonexistent; and judicial review is customarily unavailable.

---

44 Reviewability and the theoretical scope of review remain the same, but the structuring means as a practical matter a more effective review, for the judges are better able to understand what the administrators have done.

The board makes about fifteen thousand decisions per year granting or denying parole—an average of about fifty per working day. The board also fixes eligibility dates in some cases, prescribes conditions of parole, issues warrants for retaking parolees, and revokes parole. This discussion is limited to the main function of granting and denying parole.

The board has never announced rules, standards, or guides. The most specific standard is the statutory provision, repeated by the board's regulations, that the board "may in its discretion" release a prisoner on parole if the board finds "a reasonable probability that such prisoner will live and remain at liberty without violating the laws" and that "such release is not incompatible with the welfare of society." [45] The board has never publicly stated any substantive principles that guide it in determining the probability that a prisoner will commit another crime or whether his release will be compatible with the welfare of society. The board has not publicly listed the criteria that are considered.[46] Nor has it even tried to state the characteristics of cases in which parole will obviously be granted or will obviously be denied. It has not indicated its position with respect to major patterns of cases that are most frequently recurring.

The board makes no attempt to evolve principles through case-to-case adjudication.[47] It does not select specific cases raising basic questions of policy for especially intensive consideration with a view to creating a useful precedent.

The board's system is the same for easy cases as for hard cases, the same for application of old ideas as for development of new

---

45   18 U.S.C. § 4203.

46   But a former chairman has listed the criteria as follows: "Gravity of the offense . . . Prior criminal record . . . The use made by the inmate of the various programs of the institution . . . The strength of the parole plan . . . Health condition—both physical and mental . . . Attitude of the offender toward his crime, his associates and himself . . . Conduct record in confinement . . . The impression made by the offender on the hearing member, his keeper, and others." Richard A. Chappell, "Federal Parole," 37 F.R.D. 207, 210 (1965). Such a list is at least a beginning.

47   Of course, for all I know, the board may have a highly developed system it keeps entirely secret. For instance, it could be especially skillful in handling the few well-publicized prisoners and in calculating political advantages and disadvantages of various moves. It could have policies that would not stand the light of day, such as extra caution in paroling a prisoner whose violation of parole would be widely publicized.

ideas. Each member votes in his own office without discussing the decision with his colleagues. Troublesome problems are never made the subject of board meetings. Board members never deliberate together. They do not write memoranda discussing pros and cons. They think separately. They vote separately. No board member knows the reasons for his colleagues' votes.

What has just been said seems hard to believe. But the board not only admits the facts stated; it proclaims them in print. The board in 1964 published a pamphlet entitled "Functions of the United States Board of Parole," in which it explained:

Voting is done on an individual basis by each member and the Board does not sit as a group for this purpose. Each member studies the prisoner's file and places his name on the official order form to signify whether he wishes to grant or deny parole. The reasoning and thought which led to his vote are not made a part of the order, and it is therefore impossible to state precisely why a particular prisoner was or was not granted parole.

Because no one ever knows the reason for any decision of the board, no prisoner is ever told why the board has denied parole. A prisoner who is sentenced to fifteen years and becomes eligible for parole after five years usually believes that the court has disposed of five years of his life and that the board has power over ten years. After waiting five years, he is notified that his parole has been denied, he asks why, and he is told that the board never gives reasons. If he presses far enough, he may learn that the board itself does not know the reason. But the board keeps asserting that its purpose is to rehabilitate prisoners. I wonder whether the board has ever inquired into the effect on a prisoner's rehabilitation of the board's refusal to give him any reason for denying him parole.[48]

The failure to state reasons has additional consequences. Even the most flagrant abuse of discretion is likely to go uncorrected. If

48 "In Michigan and Wisconsin, the parole boards are careful to explain to the inmate the reason for the decision reached. They are especially careful to explain parole denials and to suggest what, if anything, the inmate can do to improve his chances for parole later." Robert O. Dawson, "The Decision to Grant or Deny Parole: A Study of Parole Criteria in Law and Practice," 1966 Wash. Univ. L. Q. 243, 302.

a board member is in such a hurry to get to his golf game that he votes in sixteen cases without looking inside the files, no one under the board's system can ever know the difference, even though the personal liberty of sixteen men may be at stake. How could a board member have less incentive to avoid prejudice or undue haste than by a system in which his decision can never be reviewed and in which no one, not even his colleagues, can ever know why he voted as he did? Even complete irrationality of a vote can never be discovered. Should any men, even good men, be unnecessarily trusted with such uncontrolled discretionary power?

The Administrative Procedure Act, fully applicable to the board, provides: "Prompt notice shall be given of the denial in whole or in part of any written application, petition, or other request of any interested person made in connection with any agency proceeding. Except in affirming a prior denial or where the denial is self-explanatory, the notice shall be accompanied by a brief statement of the grounds for denial." [49] Prisoners make written applications for parole. I think that the board's failure to state "grounds" for denying applications is a clear violation of the act. The board has been violating the act ever since it was enacted in 1946.

The board has no regard for the advantages of openness. Except for specified items that the board "may in its discretion" disclose or that it "will" disclose to a "party in interest," all parole records are "strictly confidential." [50] Especially interesting is the explicit provision that the date of a sentence, which is available to the public in court records, will be disclosed only to a party in interest. The contrast between the courts and the board is striking: Courts' records, including transcripts of evidence, are open to all;

---

49   5 U.S.C. § 555 (e). The legislative history fully supports the literal words of the statute. Both the Senate committee and the House committee said: "This subsection affords the parties in any agency proceeding, whether or not formal or upon hearing, the right to prompt action upon their requests, immediate notice of such action, and a statement of the actual grounds therefore. The latter should in any case be sufficient to apprise the party of the basis of the denial." Senate Documents, No. 248, 79th Cong., 2d Sess. (1946) 206, 265. This plainly means that a prisoner who makes written application for parole is entitled to have "a statement of actual grounds" of the denial, "whether or not the proceeding is formal or upon hearing."

50   28 CFR § 2.48.

the board's records are almost entirely closed. The Constitution expressly guarantees a right to a "public" trial, so that courts will have incentive to avoid arbitrariness, even though other safeguards are so plentiful; the board operates in secret, where its arbitrariness cannot be observed or criticized, even though other safeguards are almost totally absent. Facts bearing on details of crimes committed, especially damaging to the individual's privacy and his chances for future adjustment, are open to the public in court records; facts about his prison record, disclosure of which may have little effect on his privacy and may not at all damage his future adjustment, are kept "strictly confidential."

The board's system is without either safeguards or check. What the board calls "hearings" are brief interviews and disputes of fact are resolved without trials. The board denies interviews in some cases. The staff is insufficient, says the chairman of the board, but he acknowledges that the board has never asked for an appropriation that will permit interviews in all cases. Board members cannot check each other because they do not know each other's reasons. Administrative review is theoretically possible but almost never occurs. And because parole is deemed only a privilege, the courts refuse to review for abuse of discretion.

The board in my opinion should (a) develop open standards, as specific as feasible, to guide its decisions, (b) state findings and reasons when parole is denied, and when it is granted on the basis of a policy determination that may have value as a precedent, (c) open proceedings and records to the public except to the extent that confidentiality is essential, (d) develop a system of open precedents, and (e) move toward group decisions made by members who deliberate together. In addition, (f) courts should review parole denials for errors of law, unfair procedure, or abuse of discretion.

(a) Although discretion obviously cannot be supplanted with rules for granting or denying parole, much can be done to move in the direction of rules. Criteria can be stated to govern extreme cases either way—those in which parole clearly should be granted or denied. Guides can be formulated for some of the most usual factual patterns. A pamphlet published in 1963 by the Advisory Council on Parole of the National Council on Crime and Delinquency, entitled "Guides for Parole Selection," demonstrates the feasibility of guides, and I think a good agency over a period of time could push that thinking a good deal further.[51]

(b) I think that justice requires that a prisoner be told the reasons for a denial of parole, with rare exceptions, as when a psychiatric condition otherwise requires. Withholding reasons is likely to harm the rehabilitation process. Statement of findings and reasons will not assure fairness of the decision, but it will pull in that direction. A member who merely votes yes or no, with no findings or reasons, may in human fashion give in to emotions or whims. Subjecting his findings and reasons to the view of outside critics—and inside critics—may cause him to try to make his action appear rational, and the easiest way to appear rational is usually to be rational. Furthermore, equal justice will be more likely if cases can be compared.

(c) Openness alone could have a great effect upon the quality of the board's performance. The board is almost completely immune to criticism by anyone; it should not be. Openness should serve as a protection against administrative arbitrariness, in the same way that the constitutional guarantee of a "public" trial is designed as a protection against judicial arbitrariness. The board should no longer assume that all processes and all records should be closed unless a special reason calls for opening them; it should assume that all processes and all records should be open unless a special reason calls for closing them. The Information Act,[52] after all, so requires with respect to records. The problem of specifically what information and processes should be open or closed is a large one; some facets of it may perhaps be solved by a system of using numbers instead of names for some classes of information.

(d) In a good system, the board's efforts to develop standards and guides should interact with its efforts to establish precedents through giving special consideration to cases which raise basic or

---

51 See *The Challenge of Crime in a Free Society*, 12: "Just as carefully formulated and clearly stated law enforcement policies would help policemen, charge policies would help prosecutors and sentencing policies would help judges, so parole policies would help parole boards perform their delicate and important duties."
See also Dawson, "The Decision to Grant or Deny Parole," 243.
52 5 U.S.C. §552.

recurring problems. But even apart from such special cases, equal justice requires the board to strive for consistency. The system of secret and unexplained decisions neither rewards the mental effort required for such striving nor penalizes the lack of such effort. Open precedents, perhaps with numbers instead of names, can supply the needed incentive. Prisoners should have a right to know the law that so vitally affects them: "It is an essential element of justice that the rules and processes for measuring parole readiness be made known to the inmate. . . . One can imagine nothing more cruel, inhuman, and frustrating than serving a prison term without knowledge of what will be measured and the rules determining whether one is ready for release." [53] The board's standards, guides, and precedent cases should all be available to any prisoner who wants to see them, although the individuals involved need not be identified.

(e) Obviously, for all cases that present problems, as distinguished from routine cases that quickly produce unanimity through separate voting, board members should deliberate together. The decision in each problem case should be the product of group thinking. The findings and reasons in such cases should be those of a majority unless a majority fails to find a common position. If the case load so requires, board members should sit in panels; if necessary in order to secure the advantages of group decisions, panels should include staff members. For problem cases, group decisions made possible through subdelegation are clearly preferable to decisions by board members without group deliberation.[54]

(f) The courts should reexamine their long-standing position that parole is only a privilege and that therefore parole decisions are not reviewable for abuse of discretion.[55] The principal test of reviewability should be the need or lack of need for what the

---

53 Porter, *Criteria for Parole Selection,* Proceedings of American Correctional Association (1958) , 227.

54 As of mid-1968 the board has changed from five-man decisions in adult cases to two-man decisions, so that each member decides twenty cases per day instead of fifty. This change seems encouraging. But reasons are not yet stated for denials.

55 The traditional doctrine is embodied in such cases as Richardson v. Rivers, 335 F.2d 996 (D.C. Cir., 1964) , and Peterson v. Rivers, 350 F.2d 457 (D.C. Cir., 1965) , denying review on the ground that, as stated in 350 F.2d at 458, "the power to grant parole is committed to the judgment of the Parole Board."

judges have to offer. Because parole cases involve vital interests of individuals, and because the performance of the Parole Board seems on the whole about as low in quality as anything I have seen in the federal government, I think a judicial check is much needed. Judges are especially well equipped to determine whether administrative discretion has been abused. The mere knowledge of board members and staff that an abuse of discretion can be brought to the attention of a reviewing court can provide new incentives for better administrative behavior.

The Parole Board can easily enhance the quality of justice it administers if it will move toward open standards and guides, open findings and reasons, open proceedings and records, open precedents, and group decisions.

10. *Sentencing.* The power of judges to sentence criminal defendants is one of the best examples of unstructured discretionary power that can and should be structured. The degree of disparity from one judge to another is widely regarded as a disgrace to the legal system. All the elements of structuring are needed—open plans, policy statements and rules, findings and reasons, and open precedents. Application to sentencing of what I have learned about structuring of other discretionary power leads me to believe that structuring the sentencing power is feasible, and I am happy to say that the specialized thinking about sentencing that is reflected in recent literature confirms that conclusion, although most of the recently developed understanding about how to structure the sentencing power is yet to be carried into operation.

A Senate Committee reported in 1958:

The Bureau of Prisons has advised the committee that an examination of case histories and court statistics indicate[s] that widespread disparities characterize the sentences now imposed by Federal judges. During 1957 average sentences to imprisonment for all types of crimes varied from 8.9 months in New Hampshire to 54.6 months in western Oklahoma. The Bureau's study of case histories indicates that the disparities are even more extreme than the statistics reveal. A postal law violator and drug addict . . . received a 6-month sentence, while another postal law violator whose crime and background were much less serious received a 3-year sentence. In 2 similar cases of check forgery, 1 defendant received a 3-year sentence, while the other received a 24-year sentence. . . . Even the proportion of convicted offenders placed on probation for all types of crimes varies widely, ranging from 15.3 percent in western Texas to 68.8 percent in Vermont. . . . The existence of wide disparities casts doubt upon the evenhandedness of justice and discourages a respect for the law.[56]

The same report contains a statement from the Administrative Office of the United States Courts:

Time and again there were cases in which offenses were similar and in which offenders had substantially the same background but in which the defendants received widely disparate sentences. . . . No matter how one looked at these cases and no matter whether one believed that a light sentence or a heavy sentence was proper, the presence of inequality, disparity, and consequent unfairness and injustice was plainly apparent.

A leading student of the subject has written: "Some judges use probation in 10 per cent or less of their cases, while others are up to 70 or 80 per cent, and there are all the variations in between." [57]

A 1958 federal statute, recommended by the Judicial Conference, has laid the groundwork for structuring of the sentencing power by federal judges.[58] The statute authorizes institutes and joint councils on sentencing "for the purpose of studying, discussing, and formulating the objectives, policies, standards, and criteria for sentencing." The statute even specifies that agenda may include "the formulation of sentencing principles and criteria."

The 1958 statute is splendid but the accomplishment under it through more than fifteen institutes seems somewhat disappointing. Judge Edward J. Devitt said at a 1966 institute:

Unjustified disparity is the main complaint, and it seems that regardless of how many sentencing institutes we have and how often we get together to discuss consensus among ourselves, the facts, supported by dependable statistics, continue to reflect unjustified disparity between the sentences imposed for the same crime upon persons in like circumstances and with similar histories and backgrounds. . . . It would appear that our present sentencing machinery does not provide an effective

56 Senate Reports, No. 2013, 85th Cong.
57 Sol Rubin, "Disparity and Equality of Sentences," 40 F.R.D. 55, 56 (1967).
58 28 U.S.C. § 334.

method by which we can do away with, or appreciably minimize, disparate treatment of offenders.[59]

Judge Devitt accordingly concludes:

I suggest that the problem of unjustified disparity of sentence must be met in some way through the placing of a limitation upon the exercise of discretion by judges. It is impractical to reason that 341 Federal District Judges with diverse backgrounds, experiences and viewpoints about crime and punishment, can ever be expected to impose like sentences in similar cases.[60]

Even so, the first step in reducing disparity may have to be from unguided discretion to guided discretion, and the education of the judges at the institutes is surely a part of that first step. California, New York, and Pennsylvania have inaugurated sentencing institutes, and other states should follow.

More successful, according to the judges' appraisals, are the sentencing councils in the Eastern District of Michigan, the Eastern District of New York, and the Northern District of Illinois. A panel of three or more judges meets from time to time to consider each other's cases before sentences are imposed. Each judge has studied each presentence report prepared by probation officers, and each has filled out a Sentencing Council Recommendation Chart, indicating his recommended disposition and his reasons. The judges of the panel discuss each case, each judge leading the discussion about his own cases. Judge Theodore Levin says:

We have found that the Council tends to create consensus among the judges on which factors are most relevant in sentencing and the weight to be accorded to each of them. . . . We are getting closer in the development of a uniform philosophy. . . . The range of the varying recommendations has become increasingly narrow. We have particularly experienced a substantial decrease in the frequency with which the Council is confronted by disagreement about the type, rather than the quantum, of the sentence. . . . The Council has tended to produce sentences more closely conforming to modern correctional theory. Prison terms in general are shorter.[61]

59   42 F.R.D. 218, 220 (1967) .
60   Id. at 225.
61   Theodore Levin, "Toward a More Enlightened Sentencing Procedure," 45 Neb. L. Rev. 499, 505, 507 (1966) .

Judge Joseph C. Zavatt relates his five-year experience with a sentencing panel:

These conferences have tended to create a consensus as to what factors have greater relevance in sentencing and as to the weight to be accorded to each. . . . Whereas, back in 1962, there was much disagreement as to which defendants should receive probation and which should receive jail sentences, today the panel is usually unanimous. . . . And in the process we have steadily increased the percentage of defendants placed on probation. . . . Today there is not as great a spread between the length of terms of imprisonment recommended by the conferees and that tentatively arrived at by the sentencing judge. . . . It has been my observation over the past five years that our so-called "tough" judges have become less tough and our so-called "lenient" judges have become less lenient. What has really happened is that all of our judges have become more reasonable.[62]

Significant structuring of the sentencing power is accomplished through the Model Sentencing Act, prepared by fifty judges of the Advisory Council of Judges of the National Council on Crime and Delinquency,[63] and by the Model Penal Code of the American Law Institute. On the question whether the substantive policies are wise or unwise I take no position, but, assuming the validity of those policies, I do admire the techniques by which both the Model Act and the Penal Code structure discretion in at least seven ways: (1) By setting forth the overall planning of a system for exercise of discretion; (2) by expressing a basic philosophy in the direction of more probation and less severe sentences, as in the Model Act's provision that offenders not "dangerous" "shall be dealt with by probation, suspended sentence, or fine whenever such disposition appears practicable and not detrimental to the needs of public safety and the welfare of the offender, or shall be committed for a limited period", and as in the Penal Code's listing of eleven grounds to be accorded weight in favor of withholding sentence of imprisonment; (3) by making presentence investigations mandatory in specified cases; (4) by allowing defendants

62 41 F.R.D. 469, 480 (1967). See also an account by Judge Talbot Smith, "The Sentencing Council and the Problem of Disproportionate Sentences," 11 The Practical Lawyer 12 (Feb. 1965).
63 9 Crime and Delinquency 339–69 (1963).

opportunity to challenge investigation reports, with some qualifications; (5) by establishing major new categories, such as "dangerous offenders" and "atrocious crimes" in the Model Act, and
"a persistent offender," "a professional criminal," "a dangerous,
mentally abnormal person," and "a multiple offender" in the Penal Code; (6) by elaborately defining such terms; and (7) by requiring that severe sentences be supported by findings of specified
facts, to be incorporated in the record. Furthermore, the Model
Act (but not the Penal Code) provides: "The sentencing judge
shall, in addition to making the findings required by this Act,
make a brief statement of the basic reasons for the sentence he
imposes." [64]

The structuring that is done by the Model Act and the Penal
Code is so considerable that adoption of either measure would unquestionably result in a substantial reduction in the disparity of
sentences. Yet rather extreme disparity is still possible, for judges
must still exercise broad discretion to fix sentences at or below the
prescribed maxima, to decide whether the facts fit a particular
category, and to make such choices as those between imprisonment and probation. After all, judges in the sentencing councils
have been discovering that they often have wide differences even
about interpreting presentence reports.

To appreciate the accomplishment of the two recommended
statutes, let us contemplate the traditional system under which the
judge has no guide except a statutory mandate, such as not less
than one year nor more than fifteen years. He can do as he pleases
within the limits. If he chooses, he can focus on the crime alone,
without considering the criminal. He can act without a presentence investigation. He can be guided by a theory of retribution,
by a theory of deterrence, or by a theory of rehabilitation—or by
no theory. He can give a wholly emotional response and get approving headlines in the newspapers by expressing indignation
against the crime, without making any effort to find a rational basis for any facet of his decision. He can announce his decision
without findings, without reasons, without relating what he does
with what he has done before, and without relating his decision to
the relevant decisions of other judges. His discretionary power is

64   § 10.

so much at large that review by an appellate court would usually be futile.

Is it surprising that under such a system the degree of disparity is so great?

The structured discretion under the Model Sentencing Act and the Model Penal Code stands in contrast to the traditional unstructured discretion of the usual sentencing judge, and the result of the structuring is movement toward increased rationality and toward mechanisms that make possible a check by outside observers and by an appellate court. Having a presentence investigation report in the record means a good deal more than having a better factual foundation for the decision; it also means that an obligation automatically arises to make a decision that will be rationally guided by the facts brought out by that report. And as soon as something appears to which rationality is supposed to attach, an appellate court, as well as independent critics, have something to take hold of in appraising the decision. Furthermore, as soon as the judge is required to make specified findings in order to classify the defendant, for instance, as a "dangerous offender," a goodly portion of what was previously wide-open discretion becomes fact-finding, and the findings must be supported by evidence in the record, including the investigation report. The judge's emotions inevitably yield, at least in some degree, to the structuring: No longer can a severe sentence rest on nothing more than an expression of moral indignation, for the facts in the record must support the findings, and the findings must support the severe sentence. Under the Model Sentencing Act, for instance, unless the judge can make the findings required for first degree murder, for "dangerous offender," or for "atrocious crime," the sentence cannot exceed five years. And the judge has to prefer probation, suspended sentence, or fine to imprisonment if "practicable and not detrimental to the needs of public safety and the welfare of the offender."

Altogether, the structuring is very substantial, even though much discretionary power remains.

Although one of the leading writers on sentencing has asserted that "Disparity can be alleviated only by the imposition of controls such as those written into the Model Sentencing Act," [65] I believe that the institutes and the sentencing councils tend to alleviate disparity, and that other methods can also contribute. Here we approach virgin territory which existing literature has not entered. Experience with other discretionary power leads the way. The two largely unused tools that seem appropriate are policy statements and precedents.

Should not one primary objective of the sentencing institutes be to reach a consensus on some of the basic questions of sentencing philosophy? Statements by large groups of judges could provide helpful guidance to all judges on such questions as whether a refusal to plead guilty should mean a heavier sentence (as it may more often than not) ; whether a heavy sentence should ever be imposed without a presentence investigation; whether one guide should be the provision of the Swiss Criminal Code that "The judge measures the punishment in proportion to the guilt of the wrongdoer"; whether such an approach involves retribution and whether all reliance on retribution as a factor in a sentencing judge's thinking should be minimized; whether probation should be allowed in 20 percent of felony cases or in 50 percent or in 80 percent; whether the characteristics of cases suitable for probation can be identified; whether in some types of cases, such as embezzlement by executives, general deterrence should override the usual guides for selecting individuals for probation; whether or when to send a corporate executive to jail for violating the Sherman Act. Surely Congress was right in authorizing the institutes to attempt "the formulation of sentencing principles and criteria." [66]

In two ways precedents can be usefully developed on sentencing problems. Perhaps the sentencing institutes—and others—can take some of the main recurring problems, not merely from the standpoint of types of crimes but also from the standpoint of types of personalities and of circumstantial settings, and prepare elaborate precedent opinions, which all judges will be free to use as guides. Even a half dozen such opinions, if elaborately formulated and if supported by a strong vote of a large number of judges, would pro-

---

65   Sol Rubin, "The Model Sentencing Act," 39 N.Y.U. L. Rev. 251, 260 (1964).
66   28 U.S.C. § 334.

vide extremely useful guidance. Although many problems about sentencing probably cannot yet be dealt with by such means, simply because of lack of sufficient understanding and lack of sufficient agreement, many such problems can be. Some aspects of sentencing philosophy can be better developed through discussions of a set of detailed facts than through efforts to make generalized statements.

The other way that precedents can be useful is through the appellate review that seems sure to grow out of adoption of either the Model Sentencing Act or the Model Penal Code. The structuring required by those measures will give reviewing courts something that is intrinsically reviewable, for they can require findings that respond to the record and sentences that respond to the findings. The inevitable movement will be away from the view that "Where the sentences imposed are within the limits fixed by law, we will not inquire into the court's reasons for the penalties imposed." [67] Courts do review when they find something appropriate for review.[68] *One major reason our legal system has failed to produce meaningful guides for sentencing is the absence of a satisfactory system of reasoned opinions and precedents.* Even in the dozen states that provide for appellate review of sentences, the opinions of reviewing courts are too often limited to statements of facts and conclusions. This is true, for instance, of Connecticut's Sentence Review Division, whose opinions had so little value that publication was discontinued; even the selected opinions now published lack reasoning that is related to the purposes of criminal sanctions.[69]

67   Liscio v. Liscio, 203 Pa. Super. 83, 198 A.2d 645 (1964).

68   E.g., Yates v. United States, 356 U.S. 363 (1958); United States v. Wiley, 278 F.2d 500 (7th Cir., 1960).

69   See, for instance, the dozen sentencing opinions in 24 Conn. Supp. For an excellent discussion of the earlier opinions, see "Comment," 69 Yale L. J. 1453 (1960). See also Thomas, "Theories of Punishment in the Court of Criminal Appeal," 27 Mod. L. Rev. 546 (1964).

A Norwegian legal scholar expresses surprise at the American lack of uniformity in sentencing, and he says that in Norway, "The trial court is under an obligation to state its reasons for the choice of punishment, and even a sentence of an ordinary city or county court can be appealed to the Supreme Court, both by the defendant and by the prosecution." Johannes Andenaes, "The Legal Framework," in 2 Scandinavian Studies in Criminology (1968), 9, 13.

From other countries we Americans can learn a good deal about how to prevent excessive disparity in sentencing. See Mueller and LePoole, "Appellate Review of Legal but Excessive Sentences: A Comparative Study, 21 Vand. L. Rev. 411 (1968).

Of course, the main reason that judicial opinions on sentencing are not more meaningful is that judgments are still so largely based on primitive guesswork about such key factors as deterrence and rehabilitation. The long-term structuring of the discretionary power of sentencing must reflect research and more research.

V

Checking
Discretion

1. *The principle of check.* The American idea of "checks and balances," primarily a constitutional doctrine involving the interrelation of the three departments of government, is also a practical idea that applies all the way down the line to the lowest clerks. What may be called "the principle of check" means simply that one officer should check another, as a protection against arbitrariness. The most usual checking authority is a superior of the officer who acts initially, who in turn may be checked by his superior in a hierarchical organization. But checking may also be effective when it is by a colleague on the same level, by one or more subordinates, by legislators to whom interested parties petition, by legislative committees or their staffs, by an official critic known as an ombudsman, by private organizations, by the press, by an administrative appellate tribunal, or by a reviewing court.

Paradoxically, the principle of check is often at its best when it is limited to correction of arbitrariness or illegality, and it may be relatively ineffective when it includes de novo review. This is because of the important fact, sometimes overlooked, that a de novo determination may itself introduce arbitrariness or illegality for the first time and not be checked, whereas a check may be limited to the one objective of eliminating arbitrariness or illegality, so that almost all final action is subject to a check for arbitrariness or illegality. The recognized superiority of a check to a de novo determination is one of the main reasons that the mainstay of judicial review of administrative action is a review of limited scope, not de novo review, although in some circumstances de novo review may be desirable.

Institutional decisions intrinsically involve the principle of check. A jury of twelve is better than a jury of one because the twelve check each other's weaknesses, emotions, and idiosyncracies; a nine-judge court or a three-judge court is better than a one-judge court for the same reason. The National Labor Relations Board of five members may be better geared to dispensing discretionary justice than the Secretary of Labor—unless the secretary shares his deliberation with members of his staff, as he is likely to do; indeed, the secretary may assign a problem to a five-man group for deliberation and decision, subject to his review, and the protection against arbitrariness may be stronger than that provided by the NLRB's system of five-man decision without independent executive review. Institutional decisions at their best draw much strength from their built-in systems of checks and balances. For instance, institutional decisions by a federal regulatory agency may draw from staff specialists of various kinds, with initial review by chiefs of the specialists; then more generalized staffs may integrate the reports from various specialist staffs, with review by their chief; the whole product may then be put through the minds of the agency's top officers, who usually supply the broader perspective, including political considerations. The machinery for institutional decisions may thus invoke the principle of check at many points.

2. *Supervision and review by superior officers.* Possibly the most important check of discretionary action is simply the normal supervision of subordinates by superiors. Supervision may include advance instructions, checking of random samples, the subordinate's reference of difficult problems to the superior, and appeals by the affected party from the subordinate to the superior. Obviously, sufficient supervision can be a good protection against arbitrary exercise of discretion.

An evil that commonly grows up in any government office which handles a large volume of small cases involving individuals who are typically unrepresented by counsel is the systematic effort of officers to discourage aggrieved parties from taking their cases to superior officers. Even when the agency's published rules provide for review, parties are often given the impression that the initial decision is final. Even when the practice borders on falsification, superiors sometimes purposefully manage not to know about it; appeals to them add to their work loads. Whenever a party is thus discouraged from appealing, administrative arbitrariness may remain unchecked even when check is especially needed.

I think the quality of discretionary justice in many agencies throughout the government can be vastly improved by systematically informing every party aggrieved by an informal decision of his right to reconsideration by a higher officer. This can be easily accomplished. The Administrative Procedure Act, which now requires a statement of "grounds" for denying any written application made in connection with any agency proceeding,[1] should be amended by adding a requirement that every such denial should be accompanied by a written statement of the prescribed procedure for any reconsideration or review that the law allows.

Because supervision is so clearly desirable, somewhat surprising is the complete absence of supervisory power over some of the most vital discretionary power in our legal system, such as the power to prosecute or not to prosecute. The American system, in contrast with that of the continental European countries, usually leaves the city and county prosecutors largely unsupervised,[2] with the result that the enormous power to prosecute or not to prosecute is typically (1) unchecked by higher authorities, (2) secretly exercised, (3) often influenced by political or other considerations extraneous to justice, and (4) without findings, without reasoned opinions, and without a system of open precedents. Is such an atrocious combination of the four factors the best system we can devise for controlling discretionary power which vitally affects the quality of justice?

3. *Administrative appeals.* The term "administrative appeals" usually signifies review by an independent officer or tribunal at the instance of the aggrieved party, although sometimes the term means review by a superior. The difference can be a vital one: A superior officer has a continuing relation with each subordinate and often has official, psychological, or personal reasons for protecting that relation, so that his review of a subordinate's deci-

1 5 U.S.C. § 555 (e).
2 See pages 191–95, below.

sion is often affected by and even controlled by considerations other than its merits. A superior usually is not independent of a subordinate. Even though efficiency often impels review by superiors instead of review by independent officers, a check by an independent officer rather than by a superior is often what justice requires.

Throughout federal, state, and local governments, many gains in the quality of justice could easily be made by creating more independent officers to take over the reviewing functions now performed by superior officers.

Administrative appellate tribunals are typically highly successful in providing a needed check. They are numerous, but one may wonder why they are not still more numerous. By and large, administrative appeals are in many aspects preferable to judicial review, especially for small cases, because they are less expensive, because in many of them a party need not be represented by counsel, and because they usually reach the merits of cases without becoming enmeshed in legal technicalities that plague reviewing courts, such as standing, ripeness, forms of proceedings, sovereign immunity, and unreviewability. I think a full study would uncover many kinds of business now reviewed by the courts that could be better reviewed by an administrative appeals tribunal.

Administrative appellate agencies are quite diverse. Some imitate the procedure of appellate courts; others are as informal as conversation. Some review records of trial-type hearings; others take their own evidence. The scope of review is limited in some and de novo in others. The decisions of some are reviewable by higher authorities, some not; some are judicially reviewable and some not. Decisions of some, such as the Board of Veterans Appeals, are reviewable neither administratively nor judicially. Some appeals agencies are independent and carefully immunized from off-the-record influences either by administrators or by parties, as are the Social Security Administration's hearing examiners and its Appeals Council, but others, such as the Board of Immigration Appeals, are subordinate to an executive authority who wields prosecuting power—an obviously undesirable arrangement. State and local appellate agencies, such as boards of zoning appeals, likewise have widely differing characteristics.

Despite the usual success of systems of administrative appeals, some such systems do not seem to be planned to maximize justice.

For instance, the Visa Office of the State Department handles annually from seven to ten thousand cases of refusals of visas by consular officers. Top officers insist that their discretion is largely controlled by the large body of precedents, which they say they normally follow. But the precedents are generally unavailable to affected parties. The system is an outstanding example of secret law, which continues despite the Information Act.[3]

4. *Check by legislators and by legislative committees.* Legislative supervision of administration appears on the surface to be a mass of confusion—appropriations committees pulling administrative policies in one direction and substantive committees in some other direction, individual members of both kinds of committees helping constituents to pull agencies in still another direction in particular cases, lobbying directed to key legislators in order to influence policies made by bureaucrats, legislative enactments designed to reverse or to modify administrative positions, legislative investigations for the purpose of reaching business pending before agencies including both rule-making and adjudication, committee chairmen pressuring agency chairmen and committee staffs pressuring agency staffs, administrative action notably in defiance of the will of legislative committees.

The obvious answer to the question whether the legislative impact on administration is beneficial or harmful is that it is mixed—some is helpful, some is innocuous, some is pernicious. Whether the net effect is a plus or a minus I do not know; my impressions are that the net effect of legislative supervision of major administrative policies may be beneficial, and that the net effect of legislative supervision of administrative justice in particular cases may be harmful. (Of course, the two categories overlap, because major policies are often made in particular cases involving administrative justice.) The surprise here is that the results of attempted legislative supervision of administration have been so little studied; the literature is plentiful but almost all of it is from the standpoint of legislators—how much of their time such super-

---

3   8 U.S.C. § 1202 (f) provides that "records . . . pertaining to the issuance or refusal of visas or permits to enter the United States shall be considered confidential. . . ." The records are thus exempt from required disclosure under the Information Act, because of 5 U.S.C. § 552 (b) (3) . That the nondisclosure of precedents may be legal does not mean that it is sound.

vision consumes, how and why they choose subjects for investigation, and how the tasks of supervision fit into their other duties.
Studies are needed of legislative supervision from the standpoint
of administrators—whether the legislative inquiries and pressures
help or hinder good administration, how much of their time is di-
verted from their main functions, and how far the legislators seem
to abuse their powers.[4]

Some of the philosophical questions about legislative supervision of administration evoke divided opinion. When in 1963 a
Senate appropriations committee directed in its report "that no
funds appropriated in this bill be expended by the SEC" for regulation of banks offering interests in a pooled investment, the
chairman of the Banking and Currency Committee protested on
the Senate floor. Professor William L. Cary, who served for four
years as chairman of the SEC, says in his splendid book *Politics
and the Regulatory Agencies,* with reference to control by an appropriations committee of specific purposes for which funds should be
used:

Certainly in theory this is a development which should not be permitted to grow. It is an interference with the prerogatives of the substantive committee. As a "bureaucrat" I resisted it to the utmost. Yet when
one realizes the numerous agencies and departments which any one
committee is charged with overseeing, there is some logic in favor of
multiple supervision. Furthermore, the details of administration of statutes written in broad language seem to come before appropriations
committees. Can Congress really exercise detailed supervision except in
the course of the process of appropriating? It is clear that this committee maintains the most systematic and continuous examination of an
agency's activities.[5]

The quoted passage seems to begin with opposition and to wind
up with approval; perhaps the first two sentences were written by
Chairman Cary of the SEC and the rest of the passage by Philosopher Cary of Columbia University! The thoughtful philosopher
seems to win the tussle with the perceptive administrator.

4 An excellent article is Frank Newman and Harry Keaton, "Congress and the
Faithful Execution of Laws—Should Legislators Supervise Administrators?" 41 Calif.
L. Rev. 565 (1953–54).
5 *Politics and the Regulatory Agencies* (1967), 40–41.

When major policy under a statute containing no meaningful guides on the question is worked out through cooperation between a legislative committee and an agency, the governmental machinery may be operating as it should. Even when lobbyists are influencing the committeemen to oppose the agency's effort to protect the public interest as the agency sees it, the system may be sound; to condemn responsiveness of administrative policies to the strongest pressures would in some circumstances mean condemning the heart of democratic government. That policies are sometimes determined by segments of Congress rather than by the whole Congress is not always objectionable.

Often legislative review of individual cases effectively corrects administrative misbehavior. This may have been so, for instance, of the Streulens case in 1962. Streulens was a Belgian who came to the United States as director of the Katanga Information Service; the State Department revoked his visa when he criticized the State Department. The fifteen members of the Subcommittee of the Senate Judiciary Committee rendered a unanimous and persuasive 72-page report finding "a glaring abuse of the visa power and a performance unworthy of the government of a great nation." [6] Another example is the effective review by the House Select Committee on Small Business in 1963 of a Federal Trade Commission advisory opinion that retail druggists in various neighborhoods of a city would violate the antitrust laws by inserting joint ads in newspapers including prices.[7]

Day-to-day influences may be more important than committee hearings, even though most of what goes on without hearings seldom comes to public attention. For instance, the chairman of the House Committee on Interstate and Foreign Commerce spent many hours with the chairman of the Federal Communications Commission in working over the CATV regulations before they were issued by the commission, but I have never seen a public report of that fact. A good deal of this kind of constant supervision is responsible government.

6 Committee Print, 87th Cong., 2d Sess., "Visa Procedure of the Department of State, The Struelens Case, Report to the Senate Committee on the Judiciary" (1962) , 72.

7 See FTC Advisory Opinion on Joint Ads, Hearing before the Select Committee on Small Business, H.R., 88th Cong., 1st Sess., Pursuant to H. Res. 13 (1963) .

Even so, the main impact of legislative supervision of administration may be from what legislators regard as their "casework"—helping constituents in their dealings with administrators—which is not always responsible government. The casework does provide a check, it keeps bureaucrats on their toes, it corrects some injustices, and it sometimes means better administration. But the harms may be greater. Some legislators put pressure on administrators for favorable action irrespective of the merits. One careful student of the subject has found that "legislators, singly and collectively, are often the generators of rather than the guardians against maladministration." [8]

Casework should be understood not only from the standpoint of legislators who help constituents but also from the standpoint of an administrator. I recall interviewing an executive who presided over 750 federal employees, after I had already formed a tentative opinion that applicants helped by Congressmen were favored over other applicants. He seemed to me completely candid. He said he personally looked at any case when a Congressman asked him to, that his staff handled more than two thousand cases a month, that he had about twenty congressional requests a month, and that by reason of his thirty-five years' experience he could often find ways that the staff had not found to decide for an applicant. He said with feeling that that result was clearly unsatisfactory and then he asked: "What would you do?"

The particular officer seems to me powerless to correct the injustice. His superiors, less conscientious than he, cannot bring about immediate correction, although they could probably do so over a period of time if they had the needed incentive. An especially important fact about interference by Congressmen in administrative adjudication is that it happens almost never in some agencies, such as the Securities and Exchange Commission, and that it happens very frequently in some other agencies, such as the Immigration Service. In other words, even though Congressmen are the actors, each agency can build its own tradition, to which Congressmen usually (but not always) conform. The encouraging fact is: If the SEC can do it, other agencies can.

Obviously, Congressmen should reform their own practices. Yet

8 Walter Gellhorn, *When Americans Complain* (1966), 136.

a remark by Senator Dirksen unquestionably represents the majority attitude: "I have been calling agencies for 25 years. . . . Are we to be put on the carpet because we represent our constituents, make inquiries, and find out what the status of matters is, and so serve our constituents?" [9] Of course, status inquiries may be harmless or may involve subtle pressure, as no one knows better than Senator Dirksen.

A partial correction of improper behavior of Congressmen could possibly come from the Information Act, which opens to public inspection all written communications between Congressmen and administrators and probably opens to public inspection any notes of oral communications. A more likely partial correction may be transfer of some of the casework to an independent ombudsman, discussed in the next section.

5. *Check by ombudsmen.* An ombudsman is a high-level officer whose main function is to receive complaints from citizens who are aggrieved by official action or inaction, to investigate, to criticize, and to publicize findings. An ombudsman has no power to correct injustice or maladministration, except by criticizing and persuading. Experience in other countries, especially the Scandinavian countries, New Zealand, and since 1966 Britain, shows that the mere existence of an ombudsman gives administrators added incentives to avoid injustice and to correct maladministration. An ombudsman's criticisms often provide effective relief to aggrieved citizens, and other protections may be inadequate, as they usually are when administrative appeal and judicial review are either unavailable or too expensive for the circumstances.

As of this writing, an ombudsman system has been adopted by the State of Hawaii and by several American cities. I think the idea can and should be adapted to most American state and city governments. Yet an ombudsman system cannot be a substitute for competent administration, for conscientious personnel, for adequate supervision of public employees by superiors, for administrative appeals, or for judicial review of administrative action. An ombudsman system should be added to such protections and should not be regarded as a substitute for them.

9   105 Congressional Record 14057 (1959).

The federal government already has an officer who is authorized by statute to play the role of an ombudsman. The Administrative Conference Act[10] authorizes the chairman of the conference to "make inquiries into matters he considers important for Conference consideration, including matters proposed by individuals inside or outside the Federal Government." Perhaps the Administrative Conference will be wise to experiment by constituting itself an ombudsman for only limited areas of federal activity, and to encourage and study experimentation with the idea by particular agencies, rather than trying to move at once to a government-wide ombudsman system. An office to serve the entire federal government might require from two thousand to four thousand employees, and such a large bureaucracy may prove ill-suited to check the rest of the bureaucracy.

Another idea that has been strongly promoted is establishment of a central office to help Congressmen with their casework. That the vast mass of more than 200,000 complaints annually could be more efficiently handled by a central office than by the staffs attached to the office of each Congressman seems clear. But, as pointed out in the preceding section, congressional casework results not only in correction of bad administration but also on occasion in interference in good administration, because some Congressmen and their staffs are more interested in winning credit from complaining constituents than in assuring that the merits of cases will be judiciously considered. The long-term objective should be effective criticism of administrators by independent officers who have no stake, direct or indirect, in any particular results.

One may hope that the Administrative Conference will locate the areas of federal administration in which an ombudsman system can usefully supplement other methods of protecting against administrative arbitrariness.[11]

6. *Absolute discretion—why not judicial review?* Absolute dis-

---

10 5 U.S.C. §§ 573–76.
11 Literature about the ombudsman is voluminous. The two books that seem clearly outstanding are Walter Gellhorn, *Ombudsmen and Others* (1966) (a systematic treatment of official critics in nine countries), and Gellhorn, *When Americans Complain* (the cream of the thinking about ombudsmen, plus its application to American governments).

cretion means unchecked and unreviewable discretion. When no other authority can reverse the choice made, even if it is arbitrary and unreasonable, discretion is absolute. Assertions are common that absolute discretion is an evil that should not be tolerated, and condemnations of absolute discretion come not only from politicians and polemicists but also from our most distinguished judges and scholars. For instance, Mr. Justice Douglas has declared: "Law has reached its finest moments when it has freed man from the unlimited discretion of some ruler, some civil or military official, some bureaucrat. Where discretion is absolute, man has always suffered. . . . Absolute discretion . . . is more destructive of freedom than any of man's other inventions." [12] In another opinion, Mr. Justice Douglas has said: "Absolute discretion, like corruption, marks the beginning of the end of liberty." [13]

Rare is the individual whose emotional response is not wholly favorable to the main thrust of Mr. Justice Douglas' remarks. By every test, absolute discretion seems undesirable; the courts should not be cut off from correcting injustice. Even so, the Douglas remarks state an ideal that has not been realized and that probably can never be realized. The reality is that absolute discretion is often inevitable, and whenever it is, its continued existence does not mark the beginning of the end of liberty. The idea stated by Mr. Justice Douglas has to be cut down to what is possible, and sometimes it has to be further cut down to what is practicable. Even when absolute discretion is not inevitable—even when we are able to eliminate it—we often prefer to keep it, because the price for eliminating it is too high.

A few illustrations will show that absolute discretion is not *always* an evil.

A district court renders a decision, relying on Supreme Court decisions, and the court of appeals affirms. The Supreme Court holds the opposite, explicitly overruling its earlier decisions. No other authority can review the decision. The power the court has exercised is clearly discretionary and it is clearly absolute. "Where discretion is absolute, man has always suffered."

—The power of pardon is absolute. When the President or a gov-

---

12   United States v. Wunderlich, 342 U.S. 98, 101 (1951).
13   New York v. United States, 342 U.S. 882, 884 (1951).

ernor grants a pardon, no other authority may review. Similarly, when the executive refuses a pardon, no other authority may review, no matter how outrageous the determination may be. Does the absoluteness of the power mark the beginning of the end of liberty?

The policeman is uncertain whether a motorist has gone through a red light, stops him, listens to what he has to say, disbelieves his version of the facts, and writes a ticket. The fine is fifteen dollars. In time alone, going to court would cost the motorist at least a hundred dollars, and the chances that the court would not accept the policeman's word are one in a thousand. If the practicality is what counts, the policeman's discretionary power is absolute.

Two domestic air carriers seek certificates for an overseas route. The President grants a certificate to one but not the other. The other seeks judicial review under a statute unequivocally providing for such review, but the Supreme Court holds the determination unreviewable, on the ground that a decision that may be based upon "intelligence services whose reports are not and ought not to be published to the world" is a decision "for which the Judiciary has neither aptitude, facilities, nor responsibility and which has long been held to belong in the domain of political power not subject to judicial intrusion or inquiry." [14] The President's decision, no matter how arbitrary or unfair, is absolute.

A parolee admits that he has violated the terms of his parole, but his excuses are appealing, and the parole officer wonders whether leniency is better than revocation, since the parolee has been making progress. If the officer nevertheless decides in favor of revocation, no other authority can or will review; the officer's discretionary power is absolute. Indeed, throughout our legal system, officers often have unreviewable discretionary power to be lenient. And a discretionary power to be lenient *always* means a discretionary power not to be lenient. Is the absolute power of an officer to determine in each individual case how lenient to be the beginning of the end of liberty, even when long-term imprisonment is at stake?

When children almost die from eating paint from the walls, a

14   Chicago & So. Airlines v. Waterman S. Corp., 333 U.S. 103, 111 (1948).

family court orders the children permanently taken away from the mother, who is mentally retarded. Then state officers make a discretionary determination to sterilize her, over her objection. She has neither the means nor the understanding to hire her own lawyer, but she manages to bring the case to a lawyer in the government-supported program of legal services for the poor. The lawyer exercises a discretionary power to decline her case on its merits and because he is too busy with other cases. Whatever her theoretical right of review, the practical fact is that absolute discretionary power is exercised through the order to sterilize her and the lawyer's refusal to help.

Examples of discretionary power which is in fact tolerated and deliberately continued could easily be multiplied. In many instances, I think, the absolute power is either inevitable or justifiable. Although a good deal of discretionary justice that is not now judicially reviewable probably should be, a goal of trying to eliminate *all* absolute discretion is unrealistic, as the illustrations seem to me to show.

Professors Hart and Sacks, in their excellent work *The Legal Process*,[15] assert:

In a government under law, it seems, there can be no such thing as an official discretion which is absolute. Every official who holds office under the Government of the United States, for example, is bound at the very least to try to exercise his powers in such a way as to further the principles and policies set forth in the Preamble to the Constitution of the United States and in relevant and valid Acts of Congress. So of state officials with respect to state constitutions and statutes.

This seems to me quite unreal. When the executive is deciding whether to pardon or the policeman whether to write a ticket or the President whether to grant a certificate to one or both airlines or the parole officer whether to be lenient or the welfare lawyer whether he is too busy with other cases, I think no such officer will or should think of the Preamble to the Constitution. In what we call government under law, we do in fact have a good deal of official discretion which is absolute.

Although absolute discretion is sometimes inevitable, although

15   *The Legal Process* (Tentative ed., 1958), 171.

we sometimes prefer absolute discretion to whatever may be the practical alternative, and although we therefore should not aim at eliminating all absolute discretion, we surely can and should do far more than we have done to eliminate the absolute discretion that we find to be unnecessary or unjustified.

7. *A new tribunal to review small cases.* The American system of judicial review of administrative action has evolved in response to pressures from representatives of parties with large interests, and the system frequently fails to take care of parties with small interests. Judicial review in some other countries, among which West Germany may be outstanding, has been planned in the interest of all litigants—large, medium, and small. We Americans need to learn from other countries how to provide effective review for small cases.

In our federal courts, for example (to which the present discussion is limited because of the diversity of state systems), litigation expense makes much administrative action unreviewable from a practical standpoint. A long-term practitioner in Washington, in a context of review of federal administrative action by federal courts, has estimated that "an issue of average complexity cannot adequately be carried to the courts except at a cost which will range upward from $5,000." [16] Inquiries of other Washington practitioners confirm this and add that even for the simplest cases the minimum may be about $1,500, although occasionally an enterprising nonlawyer gets his case before a federal court without counsel.

An aggrieved party with four or five thousand at stake is often well advised not to seek judicial review, no matter how clear the bureaucrat's injustice to him, and seldom is judicial review feasible for a case involving a thousand or two.

The reality is that whatever the statutes may provide and whatever the judicial decisions may hold, judicial review for small cases is often unavailable because of high litigation costs.

The largest expense is usually an attorney's fee, which a federal court, in absence of special statute, can never order the government to pay on behalf of a private litigant, even if the court finds

---

16 Warner Gardner, "The Administrative Process," in *Legal Institutions Today and Tomorrow*, ed. M. G. Paulsen (1959), 140.

that the officer's behavior giving rise to the litigation was outrageous. A 1966 statute has at last corrected a previous imbalance by providing that a court may award other costs to either a private litigant or the government, but not an attorney's fees.[17]

Availability of judicial review of small cases in the Administrative Court of West Germany is not defeated by litigation expenses. The usual expense to a party who is unrepresented by counsel is under $25. Eighty per cent of complainants are in fact unrepresented by counsel. Clerks or lawyers attached to the court help parties to prepare their written complaints. No transcripts are ever prepared at parties' expense. Furthermore, a party who wins against the government is reimbursed for costs, including his attorney's fee, if any.[18]

The vital fact is that judicial review of small cases is generally available to Germans and not to Americans.

S. 18, 90th Congress, was introduced by fifty-nine Senators to extablish a Small Tax Division within the Tax Court of the United States, to review asserted tax deficiencies not exceeding $2,500, and providing that a taxpayer may represent himself before the division. My opinion is that the general thinking behind S. 18 is sound but that the proposed reform should not be limited to the tax field. Indeed, because the machinery for administrative appeals is relatively good in the Internal Revenue Service but is either nonexistent or unsatisfactory in many other agencies, the need for a small claims tribunal is much greater in many other parts of the government than it is in the tax field.

I propose that Congress should establish a government-wide Appeals Tribunal, manned by commissioners whose qualifications are like those of examiners under the Administrative Procedure Act, with jurisdiction to review federal administrative action for which judicial review is now provided either by statute or by common-law remedy but which as a practical matter is unreview-

---

17   28 U.S.C. § 2412.
18   The facts stated have been obtained from Dr. Ernst Pakuscher, a judge of the West German Supreme Administrative Court. The facts seem somewhat more favorable to small litigants than the corresponding facts about the better-known French Conseil d'État. Winning parties in the French tribunal are not reimbursed for counsel fees.

able because litigation expense equals or exceeds the interests at stake. A maximum jurisdictional limit, such as $4,000, should be prescribed, and jurisdiction should extend to designated classes of administrative action affecting interests not readily measurable in money. The tribunal's personnel should assist parties who are without counsel but parties should be free to be represented by their own counsel. The Appeals Tribunal should consider agency materials without transcripts and should use informal procedure of the kind that is customary in small claims courts. The tribunal should have power to set aside administrative action unsupported by the evidence, contrary to law, or involving abuse of discretion, but should have no power to substitute judgment on questions of policy or discretion. Existing appeals boards now operating satisfactorily probably should be undisturbed, and a full study may show the desirability of new such boards with specialized jurisdiction. A full study also is likely to identify many classes of administrative action throughout the government that are not now judicially reviewable but that should be reviewable by the Appeals Tribunal. The internal organization of the Appeals Tribunal should resemble that of the United States Tax Court. The tribunal's personnel should be insulated from the personnel of agencies whose action is reviewed. The tribunal should state findings and write opinions but the precedential value of its decisions should be regarded as weak. Probably its decisions should be judicially reviewable at the instance of an agency which certifies that review of a question of law or policy is vital to the agency.

The gap that results from theoretical availability but practical unavailability of judicial review can be only partially filled by government-supported legal aid, which may have a large future. Legal aid is not a protection for a party who is willing and able to pay his own expenses but who foregoes the only remedy the system provides because it costs as much as he is entitled to recover.

8. *Needless obstacles to judicial review*. When a private party goes to court to get relief from what he believes to be injustice inflicted on him by a government officer, the government might
(1) do what it can to facilitate a judicial decision on the merits,
(2) go to the opposite extreme and spend taxpayers' money by

having government lawyers place obstacles in the way of a judicial decision on the merits, or (3) follow some middle course. My opinion is that the first course is the sound one, and that the second is inexcusable. Yet the United States Government generally follows the second, with rare exceptions.

Among the government's legal staffs are many specialists in the technicalities of such doctrines as ripeness, standing, forms of proceedings, government and officer immunity from liability, and unreviewability. Year in and year out these government lawyers keep concocting intricacies within intricacies, trying to persuade courts to adopt them, and often succeeding. The doctrines just listed are truly complex—so much so that discussion of them fills 770 pages of my Administrative Law Treatise and its Supplement. No comparable quantity of law exists in other legal systems, so far as I can find. I agree that something in the nature of such doctrines is essential for an orderly system and to limit courts to tasks appropriate for them. But from the standpoint of a good system of justice, the extreme complexity is much more harmful than it is helpful.

Such an experience as the following is commonplace in the federal courts: A private party thinks that a bureaucrat's determination of a question involving ten thousand dollars is unjust, he decides to risk about five thousand in legal expenses to take the case to court, his lawyer is competent but is no match for the government specialists in the technical defenses, the government lawyers manage to take the case to a higher court by interposing technical defenses, the litigating expenses mount and no end is in sight, and the party finally follows his lawyer's advice to drop the case even though the court has not even begun to consider the merits. The party has lost his ten thousand, he thinks unjustly, and he has lost perhaps an additional ten thousand in legal expenses, and he has no forum open to him in which he can feasibly seek justice. In the present climate of opinion in the legal profession, neither judges nor government officers nor private practitioners nor government lawyers nor legislators seem concerned about numerous cases of this kind.

Can we not do better?

I think we can, and I propose: (1) That the doctrines of standing[19] and ripeness[20] be simplified in the direction of opening judicial doors that are now often closed; (2) that the forms of proceedings be simplified, especially by abolishing mandamus and relief in the nature of mandamus and substituting the mandatory injunction;[21] (3) that sovereign immunity be abolished and that to fill the resulting vacuum a new body of law be developed around the concept "issues appropriate for judicial determination;" [22] (4) that the presumption of reviewability be strengthened so that a good deal of administrative action not now reviewable will be;[23] and (5) *above all, that the system of constant pressure from government lawyers to increase the legal complexities and to close the judicial doors to determinations on the merits should be relaxed.*

Although my first four recommendations for surgical operations on the technical defenses seem to me promising, I should like to emphasize the fifth proposal. No one has malevolently planned our system so that private parties who go to court for relief against administrative injustice will often be forced to litigate technical defenses instead of litigating the merits of their cases. Our system is the result of long-term, rudderless drift, and the main wind that has blown has been the constant ingenuity of government lawyers to win their cases. Private lawyers, even the ablest, have

19   The Supreme Court has called the law of standing a "complicated specialty of federal jurisdiction." United States ex rel. Chapman v. FPC, 345 U.S. 153, 156 (1953). I think the remark is entirely accurate. Yet the state courts, too, have to answer any and all questions about standing, and they have built much less complicated law. The state law of standing is probably sounder than the federal law. State courts often open the judicial doors when federal courts close them, and the reason may be that the specialists in the employ of the federal government so skilfully keep hammering away for closing the federal judicial doors, using each victory as a basis for a new victory. The result, in my opinion, is often injustice, because the courts too often fail to reach the merits of controversies.

Reform of federal law of standing should be easy, for all that is needed is application of the Administrative Procedure Act, 5 U.S.C. § 702, which confers standing upon a person who is "adversely affected or aggrieved by agency action within the meaning of a relevant statute." Committees of both House and Senate said that this provision "confers a right of review upon any person adversely affected in fact by agency action or aggrieved within the meaning of any statute." The federal courts should, in my opinion, recognize the standing of "any person adversely affected in fact by agency action."

See 3 Davis, *Administrative Law Treatise* Chap. 22 (1958).

20   Id., Chap. 21.

21   Id., §§ 23.09–23.12.

22   Id., Chap. 27. See especially the proposed draft of statute, set forth in § 27.10 (1965 Supp.)

23   Id., Chap. 28.

often been outwitted by the extreme of specialization in the technical defenses by the government lawyers, and the system has gradually become warped accordingly. The intricacies of the technical remedies have grown, the need for litigating them has increased correspondingly, and the intricacies grow still further. Someone needs to find an escape from the vicious circle.

The needed escape, I think, has to be from the tendency of government lawyers, like any other lawyers, to use all available tricks to win for their client. That government lawyers use all legal and ethical means to win their cases is, of course, only natural. But I think they can and should rise to a slightly higher degree of sophistication. Uncle Sam is not an ordinary client. Uncle Sam always wins when justice is done. This means he may lose when judgment is entered for him, and he may win when judgment is entered against him. That this is so is not merely an idealist's dream but a hard-headed reality. It has *sometimes* been the basis on which government lawyers have exercised their important discretionary power.

For instance, in Ceballos v. Shaughnessy,[24] government lawyers made a concession on a point which they had won in both lower courts. Without the concession, they might have won a judgment in the Supreme Court, as they had in both lower courts. Because they made the concession, the Supreme Court entered judgment against them. They thought justice was thus done, and I agree.

Should not the spirit behind this concession more frequently actuate government lawyers?

What I am suggesting is that the role of government lawyers in defending suits against the government does and should involve a semi-judicial function. Even when they can win by interposing a technical defense, I think that sometimes they should help the court to reach the merits. When their conscientious appraisal of a case leads them to believe that the chances are substantial that a court may find that the aggrieved party has suffered injustice at the hands of a government officer, I think they should refrain from interposing a technical defense unless the policy reasons behind the defense are strong as applied to the case.

24   352 U.S. 599 (1957).

If Congress, the President, or top legal officers were to direct that lawyers defending suits against the government are not to interpose technical defenses in cases that seem meritorious unless the policy behind the technical defense is important as applied, the total amount of uncorrected injustice from governmental action would unquestionably be drastically reduced, with no offsetting disadvantage. The result would not be the payment of taxpayers' money to undeserving plaintiffs. The worst that could happen from a mistake of a government lawyer in failing to use a technical defense would be that a court would decide the case on its merits.[25]

On one kind of technical defense, the British Government, instead of spending taxpayers' money to place technical obstacles in the way of plaintiffs who sue the government, helps such plaintiffs. The Crown Proceedings Act[26] provides that if the plaintiff "has any reasonable doubt whether any and if so which of those departments is appropriate" as defendant, he may name the Attorney General, who then has the whole responsibility for naming the proper department as defendant. The British Government thus bears the burden of locating the proper defendant in a suit against the government.

When citizens bring their actions against the West German Government in the Administrative Court, the government pays a staff of lawyers and clerks to help the citizens to prepare their cases, including the drafting of the complaints.

The British and the German systems of helping citizens who sue the governments seem to me preferable to the American system of spending taxpayers' money to increase the burden on plaintiffs who sue the United States Government or one of its officers. I think we should adopt the basic idea of the British and the Germans—and develop it further.

25 Of course, deciding on the merits could sometimes mean that the litigation would delay the effectiveness of an agency's program. But courts are quite capable of appropriately deciding whether a program should be enjoined or not enjoined during protracted litigation.

26 10 & 11 Geo. VI, c. 44, § 17 (3) (1947).

VI

The Practice of Selective Enforcement
Interlocked with the Theory of Privilege

1. *The nature of selective enforcement.* An outstanding characteristic of the American legal system, especially in contrast with European systems, is the prevalence of the discretionary power of law enforcement officers to refrain from enforcement even when enforcement is clearly appropriate. This discretionary power involves enforcement of laws of all kinds, regulatory as well as criminal law. A policeman usually assumes he has discretionary power to arrest or not to arrest a violator. A prosecutor normally assumes he has discretionary power to refrain from prosecuting even when the facts and the law clearly justify prosecution. A licensing agency may usually refrain from initiating a proceeding for suspension or revocation of a license even though initiation of such a proceeding is clearly appropriate. A regulatory agency usually has discretionary power to do nothing about rates that it thinks unreasonable, even though its main job may be to protect against unreasonable rates.[1] The Antitrust Division and the Federal Trade Commission have discretionary power aggressively to enforce the antitrust laws by prosecuting, by threatening to prosecute, by investigating and warning, by policy statements, by persuasion, and they also have discretionary power to refrain from enforcing, to do nothing, to enter into liberal consent arrangements, to give assurances that prosecutions will not be brought, or even to grant formal or informal clearances for action

1 The mandatory jurisdiction of the Interstate Commerce Commission is exceptional.

that might be deemed illegal. In general, almost all agencies and officers with power to act to protect the public interest normally have a discretionary power to refrain from acting even in a case in which action is clearly appropriate.

When an enforcement agency or officer has discretionary power to do nothing about a case in which enforcement would be clearly justified, the result is a power of selective enforcement. Such power goes to selection of parties against whom the law is enforced and selection of the occasions when the law is enforced. Selective enforcement may also mean selection of the law that will be enforced and of the law that will not be enforced; an officer may enforce one statute fully, never enforce another, and pick and choose in enforcing a third.

2. *The system of selective enforcement is unplanned.* Even though the system of selective enforcement has become a dominant feature of our legal system, no one planned it, and it has grown up in the face of planning against it. Statutes and ordinances generally provide that agencies or officers "shall" take action against violators, and the word "shall" represents the thinking of the planners. The system of selective enforcement thus seems to be clearly at variance with the only planning that has been done.

Could anyone reasonably plan a system of selective enforcement? Take, for instance, the common phenomenon of complete nonenforcement of some statutes by the police; should the policy of the community be determined by its elected representatives or by the police? Add the further fact that only 24 percent of patrolmen and 31 percent of top-level police have attended college and that even smaller percentages of each have graduated,[2] and what is the answer? As for agencies other than the police, could any sane planner conceivably have concocted the non-delegation doctrine as spun by the courts during the first half of the twentieth century and at the same time have planned a system of selective enforcement under which discretionary departures from clear statutes are not only unguided by legislative standards but are commonly contrary to the clear legislative intent?

2 *Crime Commission Task Force Report: The Police,* 10.

Selective enforcement is seldom disapproved. If all rational reasons concerning the presecution of A and B are equal and if the statute calls for prosecution of both, but A is prosecuted and B is not, A may not defend on the ground of irrationality and illegality of the decision not to prosecute B, unless A can show that he is the victim of systematic or intentional discrimination, and the difficulty of proving such discrimination with sufficient evidence is almost always insurmountable.[3] The important reality is that the system of selective enforcement has long endured without successful challenge and with unthinking but general acceptance by courts, by legislative bodies, and by the society.

3. *Is selective enforcement inevitable?* By examining other systems of law, one can prove conclusively that selective enforcement is not inevitable. More precisely, probably well over 90 percent of selective enforcement practices in the American system clearly *can* be abolished; somewhat less than 10 percent—perhaps much less than 10 percent—is intrinsic to the governmental task of law enforcement.[4]

A viable legal system can be developed in which substantially

3 In Yick Wo v. Hopkins, 118 U.S. 356 (1886), systematic racial discrimination by licensing officers was held to violate the equal protection clause. But the theory of the Yick Wo case does not apply to capricious enforcement. Although short of a holding on the crucial question, Edelman v. California, 344 U.S. 357 (1953), has a good deal of significance. One who spoke in a public park against the police was convicted of vagrancy. He contended in the Supreme Court that he had been denied equal protection by "discriminatory law enforcement." The court said: "The evidence adduced on trial showed at most that the vagrancy statute is not used by the Los Angeles authorities in all of the cases in which it might be applicable. Doubtless recognizing the necessity of showing systematic or intentional discrimination, petitioner made an offer of proof. . . ." The state court, however, had quashed his subpoena for police records, and the Supreme Court held that state law governed.

LaFave (*Arrest,* 161–63) says that "about half the appellate courts which have considered the problem have concluded that the equal protection clause is not applicable to discriminatory penal enforcement," that some courts hold that only classifications based upon "race, religion, color, or the like" violate the constitutional guarantee, that some courts hold that a defendant must show that he would be in a better position if others were prosecuted. "Thus," he concludes, "it is evident that the equal protection clause does not constitute an adequate basis for a court to consider the propriety or impropriety of the exercise of police discretion."

For a good collection of authorities and a skillful analysis, see "Comment," 61 Col. L. Rev. 1103 (1961).

4 Of course, reform of existing criminal statutes is an obvious prerequisite to substantially full enforcement. Anything approaching full enforcement of present statutes would be unthinkable. See pages 90–96, especially 91, above.

all law is enforced according to its terms, in which every violation known to enforcement officers is prosecuted, and in which the discretionary power of enforcement officers is minimal, except, perhaps, in a few unusual areas where substantial discretionary power is inevitable.

I assume that nearly all American readers of what has just been said will be highly skeptical, for the beliefs are deepseated and widespread that (a) statutes must overshoot but must be cut down to what is practical by enforcement officers who are in close touch with detailed realities, (b) the community should go on expressing its ideals through statutory prohibitions, with reliance on officers to fit the prohibitions to what is feasible, (c) a cushion of discretionary power not to enforce is essential in order to produce justice, (d) full enforcement would be intolerable, for everybody is guilty of violating many technical provisions, and (e) appropriations committees can never be persuaded to support enforcement against more than a small portion of all violators.

My response to these five beliefs is that (a) the legislative habit of writing statutes that overshoot is an unfortunate habit that can be gradually changed, and until it is changed enforcement officers should through their rule-making power cut down the statutes to what is practical; the rule-making power is preferable to case-to-case decisions because it tends to promote, not to undermine, evenhanded justice; (b) the community ought to express ideals but statutory prohibitions which cannot feasibly be enforced are the wrong vehicle for such expression; (c) a cushion of discretionary power may often be desirable to ease the sharpness of precise prohibitions, but a cushion one inch thick—not one hundred inches—may suffice, and the openly exercised discretion of a tribunal is preferable to the secretly exercised discretion of prosecuting officers; (d) full enforcement of present statutes would truly be intolerable, but this proves that the statutes should be revised, and that, pending revision, enforcement officers should clarify their policies through use of rule-making power; and (e) in the present climate of opinion appropriations committees will withhold funds for full enforcement and this proves the need for better education of the committee members, who reflect the false assumptions made by the entire community.

The false assumptions underlying typical American attitudes about the inevitability of selective enforcement may long endure and may long guide our practices, but the assumptions are nonetheless false. Lawyers in France, Germany, Italy, and Scandinavia do not share the American assumptions; their systems are built on the opposite assumptions. Discretionary power, relatively, is carefully limited and controlled in those countries, and nowhere is the contrast greater than that between the American assumption that selective enforcement is necessary and the continental assumption that it is not. A description of the German prosecuting power, from which most discretion is squeezed out, is presented below.[5]

4. *The quantitative importance of selective enforcement.* Because quantitative considerations need to be taken into account in the thinking that is done about discretionary justice, and because we have no studies based on measuring or counting, some estimates based on nothing better than general impressions may have some usefulness. I think that selective enforcement may account for about half of all the discretionary power that is exercised in individual cases in our entire legal system, and I think it is more likely to be more than half than less than half. (The three main ways of creating discretionary power are by legislative delegation, by legislative use of vague or undefined terms to which administrators must give meaning, and by administrative assumption of power of selective enforcement of clear law; the three overlap and are often mixed up together. I think the third probably involves more power than the other two combined.) In the potential for cutting back discretionary power, the estimate that counts is not of all discretionary power exercised in individual cases but is of all *unnecessary* such power. Using my subjective notion of what discretionary power is necessary or unnecessary, I think that probably more than nine-tenths of the discretionary power of selective enforcement is unnecessary but that not more than half of other discretionary power in individual cases is unnecessary. This means that I estimate that of all unnecessary discretionary power in individual cases in our entire legal system, about two-thirds is the power of selective enforcement.

5   See pages 191–95, below.

5. *Is selective enforcement unjust?* Selective enforcement obviously may be just or unjust, depending upon how the selections are made. Theoretically possible is a system of enforcement in only a fraction of the cases in which enforcement would be appropriate, with discretionary selections made in such a way that all the cases prosecuted are more deserving of prosecution than any of the cases not prosecuted.

The degree of probability of such an achievement is, I think, the same as the degree of probability that all public administrators will act with 100 percent integrity, will never be influenced by political considerations, will never tend to favor their friends, will never take into account their own advantage or disadvantage in exercising discretionary power, will always eschew ethically doubtful positions, will always subordinate their own social values to those adopted by the legislative body, and will make every decision on a strictly rational basis.

In estimating how often these conditions will be met, we must bear in mind that administrative choices to enforce or not to enforce are often made by a single officer, usually unsupervised, usually unchecked, almost always without a systematic statement of findings, almost always without a reasoned opinion, usually without any reporting to anyone of pressures or extraneous influences, and almost always without opportunity for the public to observe what is done or undone or with what motivations.

A cross section of normal administrators combined with a typical arrangement for selective enforcement seems to me very likely to mean that out of a number of cases equally deserving of prosecution, some will be prosecuted and some not, and also that many cases that are prosecuted will be less deserving of prosecution than many others that are not prosecuted. Furthermore, almost any enforcement agency or officer will confirm that this conclusion is borne out by experience.

But is such a result unjust? I think it is, and I propose to explain why I think so. On some of the philosophical considerations some minds may differ.

The central question about justice is this: If A and B are equally deserving of prosecution, or if A is more deserving of prosecution than B, is a decision to prosecute B but not A unjust?

Before considering the choices of officers at the level of initiating or prosecuting, let us first consider the choices of a tribunal (administrative or judicial) at the level of making a final decision after hearing. I think everyone will readily agree that the result is unjust if the tribunal imposes a penalty on B but not on A or if B's penalty is greater than A's, even though A and B are equally deserving of penalty or A is more deserving of penalty. The injustice would be aggravated by adding a further fact that the motivation of the tribunal stems from considerations extraneous to justice, such as a personal dislike of a member of the tribunal for B, a personal attachment to A, a political advantage to a member of the tribunal from favoring A, or the intervention of an influential person on A's behalf.

Now if the question remains the same in all respects except that it is shifted from the level of the deciding tribunal to the level of the initiating or prosecuting agency or officer, is the decision to prosecute B but not A unjust? I think the answer has to be the same; the result is unjust. And the injustice would be aggravated if the further fact is added that the motivation for prosecuting B but not A stems from considerations extraneous to justice.

Yet the prevailing belief within the American society, including the legal profession, has unquestionably been that greater care must be taken to safeguard justice at the level of making decisions after hearings, and that legislative bodies may appropriately delegate uncontrolled discretionary power to prosecuting agencies and officers. What accounts for this prevailing belief?

The answer is a complex mixture of factors, but much the most important factor is this reasoning: Intrinsic both to the criminal law and to other governmental restraints on private activities is the escape of some violators from effective enforcement. The escape of some violators is unavoidable and therefore is not unjust. The proper objective of an enforcement program is not the unrealistic one of penalizing all violators but the practical one of penalizing enough violators to induce a satisfactory degree of compliance. Therefore the prime requirement of justice is not to penalize all violators but is to avoid penalizing the innocent. The conclusion of this line of reasoning usually is: Justice is done as long as only the guilty are penalized.

The line of reasoning just presented is important because it is probably the principal prop for our system of selective enforcement, but the reasoning nevertheless may be unsound. The precise point where I think it goes wrong is its failure to distinguish between unevenness from unavoidable imperfections in detection systems and unevenness in conscious choices made by officers who are administering justice. Failures of detection are usually as impersonal as the lightning which hits X and not Y, but unevenness in officers' conscious choices involve the quality of justice the officers are administering.

Accepting the reasoning that justice is done as long as only the guilty are penalized would mean that even though A and B are equally deserving of penalty, justice is done by penalizing B and withholding prosecution of A, even though the prosecutor's reason for withholding prosecution of A is to further his own interests by yielding to the intervention of a politically influential person. The reasoning that justice is done as long as only the guilty are penalized thus proves too much.

Another common line of reasoning that seeks to justify discrimination between A and B is that A has no just cause for complaint because he goes free, and that B has no just cause for complaint because he is guilty and deserves to be penalized; therefore neither has been unjustly treated. This argument has enough merit that every American court will readily accept it, but we may still inquire whether it is sound.

Although I agree with the courts that nonprosecution of A is an insufficient reason to release B, I think that question is different from the one that primarily concerns us. Our question is not whether to release B but is whether the goal of the system of justice should include more than avoiding the imposition of penalties on the innocent. Should we be content with not punishing the innocent, or should we also strive for equal justice? My opinion is that we should strive for equal justice except when doing so will unduly sacrifice other values.

The ideal engraved on the Supreme Court building—"equal justice under law"—should apply not only to the Supreme Court and to other courts and tribunals but also to decisions made by agencies and officers that initiate or prosecute.

One consequence of this conclusion—a consequence that must be brought into bold relief even though for some minds it may detract from the conclusion—is that the question of what is justice in any particular case may not be determined by considering only the one case but must be determined in the light of what is done in comparable cases. If equality of treatment is one ingredient of justice, one cannot know whether penalizing B is just without looking at A's case—and C's and D's.

Accepting this proposition is a gigantic step, because mere leniency, which is otherwise only a negative factor, takes on affirmative importance, as we shall see in the next section.

6. *Injustice from leniency in enforcing.* In any system of selective enforcement one of the most frequent reasons for refraining from enforcement is leniency. The regulatory agency allows the utility to raise rates without challenge, the Trade Commission overlooks the small violation, the manager of public housing ignores the family income that exceeds the permissible limit, the social worker knows of the man in the house but chooses not to report him, or the policeman gives the boy a fatherly talk instead of arresting him. In talking with administrators, I find a prevailing attitude that leniency is a tool for relieving against possible injustice but that it is never a cause of injustice. I think this attitude is based upon a rather important misunderstanding. The discretionary power to be lenient has a deceptive quality that is dangerous to justice.

A fundamental fact about the discretionary power to be lenient is extremely simple and entirely clear and yet is usually overlooked: *The discretionary power to be lenient is an impossibility without a concomitant discretionary power not to be lenient, and injustice from the discretionary power not to be lenient is especially frequent;*[6] *the power to be lenient is the power to discriminate.*

During 1965 some civil rights demonstrators in Washington all pleaded guilty to the same offense, for which all were sen-

---

6 Leniency raises issues not only of justice to the accused but also of justice to victims and potential victims. Too much leniency of police in the ghetto, with better protection elsewhere, is a primary complaint of Negro groups. See *Report of the National Advisory Commission on Civil Disorders* (1968), 307–309.

tenced by two judges. One judge imposed heavy sentences, but the other judge was much more lenient. The newspapers and broadcasters prominently reported the case, with expressions of consternation that the offenses were identical but the penalties were disparate. The judge who imposed the heavy sentences then called a press conference to say that he was administering justice in his own court and that it was none of his concern that some other judge in another court was doing something different. The expressions of consternation in the press were then all the more vigorous. Who was right—the judge or the press? I think the denial of equal justice was clear. The discretionary power not to be lenient had been exercised in such a way as to produce injustice that was readily discernible to the whole community.

The power of pardon includes the power to be lenient even to those who have been lawfully convicted. Since it is discretionary it is also necessarily a power not to be lenient. If a governor of a southern state—or of a northern state—pardons white men more liberally than colored men, the injustice is obvious. The argument that the colored man has been justly treated because he has been found guilty after a fair trial fails to reach the injustice of discrimination in exercise of the pardoning power.

Enforcement officers (1) often illegally assume a discretionary power to be lenient, (2) use the power as an affirmative weapon to coerce conduct, (3) thereby produce discriminatory and unjust results, and (4) justify to themselves what they do by the unsound reasoning that punishing some violators cannot be unfair if all violators are supposed to be punished. A good illustration which brings out all four of these elements appears in the excellent book by Jerome Skolnick, *Justice without Trial.*[7] An Oakland ordinance, as interpreted officially by the district attorney, required holding every woman arrested for prostitution for eight days in jail for venereal testing. The ordinance conferred no discretionary power on the police. Even so, the police illegally assumed a discretionary power to be lenient to the girls who cooperated; only 38 percent of those arrested were held for venereal testing. One officer explained: "If a girl gives us a hard time . . . we'll put

7   *Justice Without Trial* (1966) , 108.

a hold on her. I guess we're actually supposed to put a hold on everybody, so there's nothing wrong in putting a hold on her . . . but you know how it is, you get to know some of the girls, and you don't want to give them extra trouble." (1) The ordinance required holding "every" arrested woman; the police illegally assumed the power to be lenient. (2) The police converted the power to be lenient into an affirmative weapon: "if a girl gives us a hard time . . . we'll put a hold on her." (3) The innocent girl is more likely to resist and therefore more likely to be held; the experienced girl is more likely to cooperate and therefore less likely to be held. The discrimination seems clearly unjust. And the personal element as a part of the motivation is even acknowledged: "you get to know some of the girls. . . ." (4) The usual specious reasoning that leniency for some is not unjust comes out with great clarity: "we're actually supposed to put a hold on everybody, so there's nothing wrong in putting a hold on her."

The widespread belief among judges, legislators, administrators, and lawyers that discretionary power to be lenient need not be protected against abuse rests on the supposition that withholding enforcement cannot hurt anyone. The supposition is unsound, both logically and practically. Logically, discretionary power to favor an individual cannot exist without discretionary power not to favor him. Practically, discretionary power to favor one individual means power to discriminate, power to refuse evenhanded justice. That discretionary power of enforcement officers is largely to subtract from the law's requirements does not justify failure to confine, to structure, and to check.

7. *The theory of privilege and government gratuity.* Favors from enforcement officers are only one form of privileges or government gratuities. An enormous area of discretionary power is affected by the theory that safeguards are somehow less needed for administration of privileges or gratuities than for administration of legal rights. The theory of privilege accounts for a large portion of the total failure adequately to confine, structure, and check discretionary power. The central question here that calls for full consideration is: To what extent, if at all, should discretionary power affecting privileges or gratuities be exempt from

the protections designed for discretionary power affecting legal rights?

The proportion of private interests that are regarded as privileges or gratuities is probably growing. Professor Charles A. Reich, in an especially stimulating article, has presented an impressive catalog of the growth of government largess.[8] Yet the direction of law development is, happily, (1) to classify as rights some items formerly regarded as privileges and (2) to give added legal protection to interests formerly called privileges, whether or not the term "rights" is applied.

Welfare benefits, including general assistance in some states and most of the benefits under the poverty program, are regarded as privileges or gratuities and not as rights; yet social insurance under the Social Security Act and public assistance in federally aided programs are rights.[9] Becoming or remaining a public employee has been held a privilege; yet courts have been finding ways to provide legal protections. Selling goods to the government has been held a privilege; yet a court has given legal protection to a seller, declaring: "Use of such terms as 'right' or 'privilege' tends to confuse the issues." [10] Continuing to live in public housing has been often treated as a privilege; yet the movement is away from the privilege idea, as shown by the recently imposed requirement that reasons for eviction be stated.[11] Most state courts have long held some occupational licenses, such as those for taverns, theaters, dance halls, and pool rooms, to be privileges, even though licenses for lawyers, doctors, and architects are legal rights; yet the movement is clearly toward treating all licenses as rights.[12] Use of streets and highways has been often branded a privilege, so that drivers' licenses could be revoked without hearings; yet the opposite view is taken in nearly all recent cases.[13] Attending public schools, once a privilege, has become a right.[14]

8 *Charles Reich*, "The New Property", 73 Yale L. J. 733 (1964) .
9 See pages 180–87, below.
10 Gonazalez v. Freeman, 334 F.2d 570, 574 (D.C. Cir., 1964) .
11 See pages 77–80, above.
12 E.g., Milligan v. Board of Registration, 348 Mass. 491, 204 NE.2d 504 (1965) .
13 E.g., Hannah v. Hults, 53 Misc.2d 921, 280 N.Y.S.2d 41 (1967) .
14 Madera v. Board of Education, 267 F. Supp. 356 (S.D.N.Y, 1967) .

A New York court in a recent opinion seems fully justified in saying that the privilege doctrine "is in process of being eroded by the courts." [15] The courts resort to many techniques in assisting the erosion. One that has appeal was used by Mr. Justice Brandeis a half century ago in discussing the second-class mailing privilege: "The fact that it is largely gratuitous makes clearer its position as a right; for it is paid for by taxation." [16] One of the simplest techniques is this: "Valuable privileges . . . are . . . entitled to the protection of law." [17] A recent opinion brands public employment as a privilege and then recognizes that its mixture with an interest in reputation is a legal right.[18] An especially good technique is to skip the labeling and to go directly to what is involved, after the manner of the Oregon court: "Whether the advantages of continued freedom on probation are deemed to be 'rights' or 'privileges,' . . . decision on the continued liberty of an individual should be made . . . with adequate procedural safeguards." [19] A remark of a federal court is both sound and intriguing: "One may not have a constitutional right to go to Baghdad, but the Government may not prohibit one from going there unless by means consonant with due process of law." [20] This thought can easily be rounded out into the tremendous proposition that discretion about privileges and gratuities should be properly confined, structured, and checked.

The privilege doctrine, however, still has a great deal of life in it. In absence of judicial clarification, both private parties and administrators tend to adopt the attitude that subsidies, for instance, are matters of privilege and not of right, and this attitude affects airline subsidies, ship subsidies, agriculture subsidies, housing subsidies, research grants to corporations and to universities, grants to institutions and to students for education, use of public lands for grazing and mining, use of rivers for hydroelectric power, use of nuclear materials and facilities, use of expensively developed

15   Bay Towing v. Broderick, 49 Misc.2d 657, 268 N.Y.S.2d 108, 111 (1966).
16   Milwaukee Social Dem. Pub. Co. v. Burleson, 255 U.S. 407, 433 (1921), dissenting opinion.
17   Albert v. Board, 286 App. Div. 542, 145 N.Y.S2d 534, 538 (1955).
18   Birnbaum v. Trussell, 371 F.2d 672 (2d Cir., 1966).
19   Perry v. Williard, Or. P.2d 1020, 1022 (1967).
20   Homer v. Richmond, 292 F.2d 719, 722 (D.C. Cir., 1961).

nuclear know-how, use of ports, use of airports, use of communications satellites, and the subsidy for second-class mail.

Parole and probation are still usually regarded as privileges, even to such an extent that a federal court, announcing that "probation and parole are matters of legislative grace," refused to inquire into an allegation that parole was denied with "prejudice, malice, and discrimination, and with having a personal dislike for negroes," and that white inmates with similar records were granted parole.[21] Remission of penalties and forfeitures is only a privilege and therefore not judicially reviewable for abuse of discretion.[22] The Supreme Court has held that a hearing may be denied to the wife of an American soldier who was seeking to enter the United States; the court said that "we are dealing here with a matter of *privilege*. Petitioner had no vested *right* of entry." [23]

The privilege doctrine at its worst can be monstrous, and it was at its worst in a recent case in the District of Columbia. An action was brought by mothers receiving assistance under the program of aid to families with dependent children, to enjoin oppressive investigations involving unreasonable entry of plaintiffs' premises. The plaintiffs sought a court order that no home be entered except with a search warrant or with uncoerced consent, and that assistance payments be no longer used as a club to exact an unwilling consent. The court denied relief, partly on the ground: "Payments of relief funds are grants and gratuities. Their disbursement does not constitute payment of legal obligations that the government owes. Being absolutely discretionary, there is no judicial review of the manner in which that discretion is exercised." [24] If in exercising their discretion the officers commit torts and crimes, legal remedies must be denied because the payments the officers make are gratuities!

A note of caution is necessary, however, for the privilege doctrine is not always totally without merit. For instance, the privi-

---

21 Richardson v. Rivers, 335 F.2d 996 (D.C. Cir., 1964) ; Peterson v. Rivers, 350 F.2d 457 (D.C. Cir., 1965) .

22 United States v. One 1961 Cadillac, 337 F.2d 730 (6th Cir., 1964) .

23 Court's italics. United States ex rel. Knauff v. Shaughnessy, 338 U.S. 537, 544 (1950) .

24 Smith v. Board of Commissioners, 259 F. Supp. 423 (D.D.C., 1966) , aff'd on other grounds 380 F.2d 632 (D.C. Cir., 1967) .

lege doctrine may properly apply to the President's decision to cut out an item of foreign aid to another government, to the President's denial of a pardon, and to the President's discharge of a cabinet officer. Similarly, when a public employee accepts his position with the understanding that he has a probationary status, his protections against discharge may properly be somewhat less than those accorded to an employee who does not have a probationary status.

Even though the privilege doctrine should not be condemned in all its applications, its use has generally been unfortunate in furthering the development of discretionary power that is inadequately confined, structured, and checked.

8. *Should discretion about privileges and gratuities be uncontrolled?* If X owns property worth a thousand dollars and Y has a subsidy worth a million, should X's legal protection against illegal or arbitrary exercise of discretionary power be more than Y's, less than Y's, or the same?

A businessman's answer to this question is likely to be the opposite of a lawyer's answer. The businessman is likely to say that the extent of the legal protection should depend upon the magnitude of the interest at stake, that the subsidy is worth a thousand times as much as the property, and therefore that it deserves more legal protection.

The lawyer is likely to say that the property deserves more protection because the subsidy is in the nature of a gratuity. When pressed, the lawyer may have some difficulty explaining to the businessman why the gratuity idea justifies discretionary power which is less confined, less structured, and less checked. Probably the best argument the lawyer can make is something like this: When Uncle Sam, the tall gentleman dressed in stars and stripes, is distributing handouts, to which no one has a legal right, he ought to be free to do as he chooses, in the same way that a private philanthropist is free to make a gift to one college and not to another. Therefore, one who wants a government subsidy is no more entitled to legal protection than the disappointed college.

The argument of the lawyer has enough persuasiveness that most courts, including the Supreme Court of the United States, go along with it. But I think it is demonstrably unsound. The argument is heavily based on the false assumption that Uncle Sam is a single human being. Uncle Sam—the United States Government—is not a single individual, but is partly a Congress which fixes basic policies, partly administrators who are supposed to carry out congressional policies and who may abuse their discretion in the process, and partly a system of courts which must decide whether or not to check the administrative abuses. A court that might properly refuse to check the old gentleman in stars and stripes, if he were a single human being, might well check Uncle Sam's agents when they depart from what Uncle Sam through Congress has directed them to do. *A court that checks Uncle Sam's agents is not limiting Uncle Sam's will but is helping to carry out his will.* Indeed, experience proves that courts are needed to check administrative abuses, that a court of judges is especially well qualified to do this kind of checking, and that abuses in administering a program of gratuities are as much in need of checking as abuses in administering any other program.

Let us look closely at a real case in which I think the Supreme Court went wrong. The case itself may be unimportant because the holding was later legislatively reversed, but the faulty reasoning, widely shared, is of great consequence. The level of justice in America can be substantially raised if this kind of unfortunate reasoning can be extracted from the thinking of judges, legislators, and administrators. The case is Perkins v. Lukens Steel Co.[25] The Public Contracts Act required sellers to the government to comply with certain minimum wage requirements, which the Secretary of Labor interpreted to be more extensive than the steel company thought justified by the statute. The company, whose continued existence probably depended on selling steel for defense purposes, asserted that the Secretary had "acted arbitrarily and capriciously and wholly without warrant or authority in law." The Court of Appeals for the District of Columbia held the Secretary's interpretation "so far beyond any possible proper application of the words as to . . . constitute an attempt arbitrarily to disregard the statutory mandate." The Supreme Court approached

25 310 U.S. 113 (1940).

the problem as one requiring "marking of boundaries of permissible judicial inquiry into administrative and executive responsibilities." The question was thus highly crystallized whether the courts should or should not check what the Court of Appeals had found to be administrative arbitrariness in interpreting the statute.

The Supreme Court, after observing that "no legal rights" of the company had been invaded, declared:

Like private individuals and businesses, the Government enjoys the unrestricted power to . . . determine those with whom it will deal, and to fix the terms and conditions upon which it will make needed purchases. . . . Courts have never reviewed or supervised the administration of such an executive responsibility even where executive duties "require an interpretation of the law." . . . The case before us makes it fitting to remember that "The interference of the Courts with the performance of the ordinary duties of the executive departments of the Government, would be productive of nothing but mischief."

The court accordingly held that federal courts were barred from deciding whether the administrators had erroneously interpreted the statute.

My opinion is that the decision was unsound in three separate respects: (1) Instead of saying that the administrators had invaded "no legal rights" of the company, the court should have said that the company had a large business interest at stake, that the result turned upon a question of statutory interpretation, that no one in the entire society is better qualified to resolve a controversy about statutory interpretation than the courts, that courts are needed to confine administrative discretion in accordance with statutory enactments, that officers who misinterpret a statute so as to apply sanctions against a company for doing what the statute if properly interpreted allows it to do are invading the company's legal rights, and that therefore the Supreme Court should decide the question of statutory interpretation.

Conceptualism which prevents judges from deciding a question of statutory interpretation on which large business interests depend is seriously faulty.

(2) The second way the court went wrong was in saying that

the power of the government to make purchases was "unrestricted." The government is still the government even when it acts in a proprietary capacity, and the Constitution imposes many restrictions on the government. If the administrators had adopted a policy of buying only from companies which coerce their employees to vote the Democratic ticket, one may be sure that the Supreme Court would say that the purchasing power is not "unrestricted." The Constitution obviously prevents the officers from buying from Baptists and not from Methodists or from whites and not from Negroes. The court later recovered its bearings and acknowledged that the government in its proprietary capacity is subject to constitutional restrictions.[26]

(3) The third way the Supreme Court went wrong is the one I want to emphasize in the present context, because the faulty reasoning is so widespread and because a correction of it is needed in order to develop a better system of confining, structuring, and checking administrative discretion. The idea at the heart of the court's decision was that *the government* had unrestricted power to deal or not to deal with the steel company on particular terms. The Court said "the Government enjoys the unrestricted power. . . ." But the question was not whether *the government* had misinterpreted the statute; the question was whether *the officers* were abusing their power by misinterpreting the statute. If we think of Uncle Sam as having spoken through Congress, as I think we should, the question was whether Uncle Sam's agents were departing from the instructions Uncle Sam had given them.

The Supreme Court, instead of saying that *the government* enjoys unrestricted power in buying steel, should have said that *the officers* obviously do not enjoy unrestricted power, for *officers of the government are always restricted by the limits of the power conferred on them by statute, as well as by constitutional limitations.*[27]

---

26 United Public Workers v. Mitchell, 330 U.S. 75, 100 (1947).

27 The court stressed in the Lukens opinion that the litigation caused the act to be "inoperative for more than a year." The answer to that is easy; the court explained in Abbott Laboratories v. Gardner, 387 U.S. 136, 156 (1967): "It is scarcely to be doubted that a court would refuse to postpone the effective date of an agency action if the Government could show, as it made no effort to do here, that delay would be detrimental to the public health or safety."

Now, on this background, let us return to the disagreement between the businessman and the lawyer, discussed at the beginning of this section. The businessman says the million-dollar subsidy is entitled to more legal protection than the thousand-dollar property because it is worth a thousand times as much. The lawyer says the old gentleman in stars and stripes can do as he pleases with his gratuities. I think the businessman is right and the lawyer is wrong. In deciding whether to provide legal protections, we should not be misled by the false image of the beneficent old gentleman; we should be guided by the hard-headed view that human beings in official positions may abuse their discretionary powers, that protection against such abuse is needed about as much for administration of gratuities as for administration of property rights, and that the courts are well equipped to correct abuses.

Even though circumstances can be found when some weight should be given to the concept of privilege or gratuity, my conclusion is that that concept has usually been harmful. With rare exceptions, when we know how to confine, to structure, and to check discretionary power, that knowledge should be the basis for our action, whether the subject matter is legal rights or privileges and gratuities.

9. *Discretion of officers and the "right" to welfare benefits.* Hardly any field of administration, except those of police and prosecutors, involves so much uncontrolled and illegal discretionary power as welfare administration. The field seems peculiarly in need of attention because, although the need for reform is widely understood, the developing consensus about the means of reform may be founded upon misunderstanding. Widespread opinion seems to support the view that what is needed is to convert benefits into "rights." Yet I believe—and I shall try to demonstrate—that in the 90 percent of public assistance programs that are federally assisted no significant progress toward better protection of the interests of beneficiaries can be made by a stronger emphasis on "rights."

The road to reform, in my opinion, is better confining, structuring, and checking of discretion of administrators: Discretion should be more fully guided by rules (clarified statutes, regulations, and instruction manuals), and superior officers should more strictly enforce the rules against their subordinates. Above all, federal officials should more diligently require state officials to conform to the federal requirements which are beautifully spelled out in the Handbook of Public Assistance Administration of the Department of Health, Education and Welfare.

The degree of lawlessness of welfare administrators is widely recognized. A report designated as "probably the most extensive and searching study ever undertaken of a local welfare problem in the United States" found that in Cook County, Illinois, 32 percent of decisions to withhold or terminate aid to dependent children were either "unlawful" or "questionable." [28] As of today, one can quickly find by interviewing intake workers in Cook County that applications are often rejected for clearly illegal reasons. For instance, a regulation provides in clear terms that aid may be denied to an applicant who refuses to cooperate in the effort to find her missing husband; aid is often denied to applicants who fully cooperate, and the reason given is that finding the husband is required. The applicant typically does not know what the regulation provides. Aid is often illegally denied for such a reason as failure of a mother to keep an appointment—even when the cause of missing the appointment was that a sick child needed the mother's care. Beneficiaries often fail to receive emergency relief, or allotments for furniture, clothing, and equipment because of their failure to make requests; no one ever informs them of their rights. Another kind of illegality involves forcing on beneficiaries "services" (including workers' moral standards) that are unwanted; beneficiaries seldom realize that they are entitled to refuse "services." According to workers in the county office, the state office, which is supposed to supervise to assure legality of practices, is itself the source of a good deal of the illegality. Appeals are taken from less than one-third of 1 percent of unfavorable decisions; the victims of illegal denials seldom know of their right to appeal.

The National Conference of Lawyers and Social Workers, speaking of individual substantive and procedural rights to public assistance, has said, "It has become increasingly clear that these rights are not universally observed and that, covertly or

28 Greenleigh Associates, *Facts, Fallacies and Future*, 56.

overtly, individuals are being denied the protection of these rights and, indeed, perhaps the enjoyment of their basic constitutional rights as well." [29] The conference proposed legal services: "Without the active intervention of the bar and the availability of legal services to assure equitable enforcement of the law the intent and meaning and purpose of the rights established under the Social Security Act are without value and it is the law as well as a democratic society which is demeaned thereby." [30]

I cannot agree that rights established by the act are without value in absence of intervention by the bar; of the eight million who depend upon public assistance as their primary income, only a handful have had legal services. If millions who are entitled to public assistance are denied it, a wholesale job has to be done through more effective federal enforcement against state administrators; the expensive and awkward remedy through legal services should be exceptional, not a mainstay for the millions of cases.

The most serious misunderstanding about public assistance involves the idea that abuses by welfare workers can be corrected if benefits are changed from gratuities or privileges to "rights." Protests seem to be building up in both legal literature and social work literature against the supposed failure to recognize that public assistance is a "right." To try to correct what seems to me confusion about fundamentals concerning "rights" and discretion in welfare programs, I shall advance ten propositions.

(1) "Rights" to welfare benefits do not exist unless they are created by or pursuant to legislation. Natural law ideas, such as the assertion in a legal periodical that "Fundamental human rights, it must be understood, are not mere property rights," may guide legislatures but cannot themselves be the source of rights. The statement in the "Universal Declaration of Human Rights" that "Everyone, as a member of society, has the right to social security" is a statement of an ideal that cannot be legally enforced.

(2) A legislative body, within constitutional limits, may condition welfare payments as it chooses, *whether the payments are*

---

29 *Rights of Public Assistance Recipients* (Jan., 1967, Publication No. 3), 6.
30 Id. at 8.

rights or gratuities. Numerous statements such as the following are based on misunderstanding: "If a 'right' is involved, it will no longer be subject to the governmental power to withhold . . . or to grant it subject to any terms or conditions whatever." [31] Whether a right should be granted, withheld, or granted conditionally is for the legislative body to determine, except that controls which would be unconstitutional if directly imposed may also be unconstitutional if imposed as conditions to benefits.[32] One view is that welfare beneficiaries should be as free as other citizens, a second view is that behavior that may increase the state's burden should be prohibited or discouraged, and a third view is that the morals of the beneficiaries should be controlled; the choice among the three views is for legislative policy-making, *whether benefits are rights or gratuities.*

(3) Existence of a "right" is often a matter of degree. A "right" is a legally protected interest. An "interest" is anything one wants, such as food, clothing, shelter, and luxuries. Various interests are given various degrees of legal protection. Even the best-protected "rights" are often qualified. A young man having a "right" to live may be drafted and ordered into enemy fire. A property owner's "right" may be taken for public use through discretionary action of an officer.

(4) The "right" to old-age *insurance* benefits is a strong one but is qualified. In the key case, Nestor and his employers had paid taxes into the old-age security fund, he had reached sixty-five, and the benefit payments had begun, but the Supreme Court upheld legislation authorizing termination of Nestor's benefits.[33] Yet the court declared that Nestor's interest was "of sufficient substance to fall within the protection from arbitrary governmental action afforded by the Due Process Clause." A critic of the Nestor case has written that "a man or a woman, after a lifetime of work, has no rights which may not be taken to serve some public policy." [34] More accurate would be a statement that such a man

31 Bernard Schwartz, "Crucial Areas in Administrative Law," 34 G. Wash. L. Rev. 401, 438-39 (1966).
32 Sherbert v. Verner, 374 U.S. 398 (1963).
33 Flemming v. Nestor, 363 U.S. 603 (1960).
34 Reich, "The New Property," 733, 775.

or woman, like the owner of land, has rights which are protected by the due process clause against some kinds of infringement and not against others, and that the meaning of due process depends upon judicial interpretation, whether the subject matter is old-age insurance or land.

(5) The right-gratuity dichotomy should not be confused with the rule-discretion dichotomy. A right may be wholly dependent upon discretion. A gratuity may be governed wholly by rules and not at all by discretion. In a determination of what is a right or a gratuity, discretion may be one factor pulling toward gratuity but may be more than offset by other factors, including statutory words of entitlement, availability of hearing procedure, and judicial review. A right of a farmer to use his land may be cut off by the discretion of a highway engineer, and then the farmer may have a right to money, but the amount may depend on discretion. One injured by a negligent driver may have a right to recover but realization of the right may depend upon discretion of a jury in applying the test of the reasonably prudent man. An alien who seeks to enter the United States has only a privilege, because the Supreme Court has so interpreted the Immigration Act, but the extent of the privilege is governed largely by rules and is susceptible of being governed almost entirely by rules.

(6) Because interests become rights when they are given sufficient legal protection, a claimant who is entitled to a hearing and entitled to judicial review may usually be deemed to have a "right," and a claimant for public assistance in a federally aided program is so entitled, as shown by the next two propositions.

(7) Judged by procedural protections, public assistance benefits in federally aided programs are clearly "rights." The Social Security Act provides that state plans, to win federal grants, must "provide for granting an opportunity for a fair hearing before the State agency to any individual whose claim for assistance under the plan is denied or is not acted upon with reasonable promptness." [35] Such a provision governs all public assistance programs under the act, including old age, medical, families of dependent children, the blind, the permanently and totally disabled. The

---

[35] Subsection (a) (4) of 42 U.S.C. §§ 302, 602, 1202, 1352, and 1382.

Handbook of Public Assistance Administration, containing the Health, Education, and Welfare Department's regulations to guide federal and state officers, prescribes *procedural protection that equals or exceeds that given by federal regulatory agencies to business interests of the greatest magnitude.* Fundamental procedural protection is prescribed for informal handling, as well as for hearings with determinations on the record. A claimant is entitled to an interview, to reliance on his statements and on public records as the primary sources of facts, to written notice of decisions, to a statement of reasons for denial, and to use of case records containing information needed for an appeal. A claimant who takes an appeal is entitled to a hearing conducted by an impartial official, adequate notice and information about hearing procedure, publication of hearing procedure, a right to be represented by counsel, information about counsel and fees if counsel is provided, opportunity to examine all documents and records used at the hearing and to question or refute any evidence, a decision on the record, a verbatim transcript, and notice of right to judicial review. The *Handbook* in § 6333 requires state officers to "emphasize that there is 'due process' in program administration affecting the 'right' to public assistance."

The prescribed procedure seems to me to create a well protected "right." I see no substantial deficiency in the prescribed procedure, although of course some questions are debatable, such as whether a claimant should be furnished free counsel and whether benefits may be terminated pending hearings. The deficiencies in the whole picture seem to me very grave, but the deficiencies have nothing to do with lack of "right." The failure is almost wholly the lack of clarity of substantive rules and the lack of enforcement against the administrators. *The correction that is needed is clarification of substantive rules, and full administrative compliance with those rules. Superior officers must enforce more strictly against subordinates; federal officials must enforce more strictly against state officials.*

A distinguished advocate of better protection for welfare claimants argues that "full adjudicatory procedures are far more appropriate in welfare cases than in most of the areas of administrative procedure" such as "regulation of economic affairs, or dispensation of benefits such as airline routes or television licenses." [36] He creates the impression that full adjudicatory procedures are not available in welfare cases. Although his meaning is somewhat unclear, my view differs drastically from his. I believe that (1) no significant deficiency exists in the adjudicatory procedure prescribed for public assistance involving federal funds, (2) in both business regulation and in welfare administration the procedural mainstay is not and ought not to be the adjudicatory hearing but is and should be the informal conference, and (3) whatever the subject matter, adjudicatory procedure is inappropriate until informal procedure has failed to produce agreement.[37]

(8) From the standpoint of judicial enforcement, a "right" to public assistance under a federally aided program exists, for some state statutes provide for judicial review and such review is generally available as a matter of common law. An example is Collins v. State Board of Social Welfare,[38] in which parents were given a declaratory judgment that a classification system for aid to dependent children was unconstitutional. The court assumed reviewability, and it explicitly rejected an argument founded on sovereign immunity. Of course, judicial review does not mean that a court takes over administration of benefits; it usually means that a court may decide issues of law, review the findings to determine whether they are supported by substantial evidence, and determine whether administrative discretion has been abused.

(9) Because "rights" in all federally aided programs can be administratively enforced through hearing procedure that is as adequate as any hearing procedure accorded business interests of the greatest magnitude, and because "rights" in all such programs are judicially enforceable, the road to reform is not more emphasis on "rights." The road to reform is better systems of confining, structuring, and checking the discretion of officers. The confinement most needed is reduced discretion to deny benefits and to attach conditions to payments. Although amendment of statutes is

36 Charles Reich, "Individual Rights and Social Welfare: The Emerging Legal Issues," 74 Yale L. J. 1245, 1252–53 (1965).
37 See the scholarly criticism of the Reich position in Joel Handler, "Controlling Official Behavior in Welfare Administration," 54 Calif. L. Rev. 479, 488 (1966).
38 248 Ia. 369, 81 N.W.2d 4 (1957).

desirable, much of the needed confinement can and should be brought about by administrative rule-making. Probably the authors of the excellent *Handbook of Public Assistance Administration* should consider requiring such rule-making. The checking that needs to be improved is not only closer supervision by superiors over subordinates, to eliminate illegal practices,[39] but is especially a more vigorous federal enforcement against state officers of federal requirements.[40]

(10) In programs of general assistance administered by state and local governments without federal funds, involving less than 10 percent of all public assistance, the degree of legal protection accorded claimants varies from one end of the scale to another. In many such programs, claimants have no "right" to benefits. They should have. It is here that many voices are quite properly crying for recognition of "rights." [41]

39 An extra-legal check that has significant effectiveness in Cook County, Illinois, is a handbook, in simplified language, prepared by the Independent Union of Public Aid Employees. The handbook informs applicants of their rights, with the result that officers' illegality tends to be checked. Furthermore, the union sometimes goes into action to help applicants.

40 Another needed reform may be a new classification of personnel; the time will surely come when counseling services will be provided by personnel better qualified than workers primarily concerned with administering money payments.

41 Reform of general assistance can be readily achieved by bringing it under the federal cover, as recommended by the 1966 report of the Advisory Council on Public Welfare.

VII

Confining, Structuring, and Checking the Prosecuting Power

1. *Must the prosecutor's discretionary power be uncontrolled?* Viewed in broad perspective, the American legal system seems to be shot through with many excessive and uncontrolled discretionary powers but the one that stands out above all others is the power to prosecute or not to prosecute. The affirmative power to prosecute is enormous, but the negative power to withhold prosecution may be even greater, because it is less protected against abuse.

The prosecuting power is not limited to those who are called prosecutors; to an extent that varies in different localities the prosecuting power may be exercised by the police, and a goodly portion of it is exercised by regulatory agencies, licensing agencies, and other agencies and officers. The prosecuting power is not limited to the criminal law; it extends as far as law enforcement extends, including initiation of proceedings for license suspension or revocation, and even to enforcement of such provisions as those requiring that rates or charges be reasonable.

Even though the many prosecuting powers at all levels of government obviously vary widely in the extent and manner of confining, structuring, and checking, the major outlines are almost always governed by a single set of universally accepted assumptions. The principal assumptions are that the prosecuting power must of course be discretionary, that statutory provisions as to what enforcement officers "shall" do may be freely violated without disapproval from the public or from other officials, that determinations to prosecute or not to prosecute may be made secretly without any statement of findings or reasons, that such decisions by a top prosecutor of a city or county or state usually need not be reviewable by any other administrative authority, and that decisions to prosecute or not to prosecute are not judicially reviewable for abuse of discretion.

Why these various assumptions are made is not easy to discover; the best short answer seems to be that no one has done any systematic thinking to produce the assumptions, but that the customs about prosecuting, like most other customs, are the product of unplanned evolution. Whatever caused the assumptions to grow as they did, prosecutors usually assert that everybody knows that they are necessary.

But I wonder: Why should a prosecutor—say, a county prosecutor—have discretionary power to decide not to prosecute even when the evidence of guilt is clear, perhaps partly on the basis of political influence, without ever having to state to anyone what evidence was brought to light by his investigation and without having to explain to anyone why he interprets a statute as he does or why he chooses a particular position on a difficult question of policy? Why should the discretionary power be so unconfined that, of half a dozen potential defendants he can prove guilty, he can select any one for prosecution and let the other five go, making his decision, if he chooses, on the basis of considerations extraneous to justice? If he finds that A and B are equally guilty of felony and equally deserving of prosecution, why should he be permitted to prosecute B for felony but to let A off with a plea of guilty to a misdemeanor, unless he has a rational and legal basis for his choice, stated on an open record? Why should the vital decisions he makes be immune to review by other officials and immune to review by the courts, even though our legal and governmental system elsewhere generally assumes the need for checking human frailties? Why should he have a complete power to decide that one statute duly enacted by the people's representatives shall not be enforced at all, that another statute will be fully enforced, and that a third will be enforced only if, as, and when he thinks that it should be enforced in a particular case? Even if we assume that a prosecutor has to have a power of selective enforcement, why do

we not require him to state publicly his general policies and require him to follow those policies in individual cases in order to
protect evenhanded justice? Why not subject prosecutors' decisions to a simple and general requirement of open findings, open
reasons, and open precedents, except when special reason for confidentiality exists? Why not strive to protect prosecutors' decisions
from political or other ulterior influence in the same way we
strive to protect judges' decisions?

The unthinking answer to such questions as these is that the
prosecutor's function is merely to do the preliminary screening
and to present the cases, and that the decisions that count are
made on the basis of the trial. But public accusation and trial often
leave scars which are not removed by proof of innocence. Mr. Justice Jackson was talking realism when he said, as Attorney General:

> The prosecutor has more control over life, liberty, and reputation than
> any other person in America. His discretion is tremendous. He can have
> citizens investigated and, if he is that kind of person, he can have this
> done to the tune of public statements and veiled or unveiled intima-
> tions. Or the prosecutor may choose a more subtle course and simply
> have a citizen's friends interviewed. . . . He may dismiss the case be-
> fore trial, in which case the defense never has a chance to be heard.
> . . . If the prosecutor is obliged to choose his cases, it follows that he
> can choose his defendants. . . . [A] prosecutor stands a fair chance of
> finding at least a technical violation of some act on the part of almost
> anyone. . . . It is in this realm—in which the prosecutor picks some
> person whom he dislikes or desires to embarrass, or selects some group
> of unpopular persons and then looks for an offense, that the greatest
> danger of abuse of prosecuting power lies. It is here that law enforce-
> ment becomes personal. . . .[1]

Mr. Justice Jackson was discussing what a prosecutor does af-
firmatively; the damage done by public accusation may be permanent even when innocence is proved in a later proceeding. What a
prosecutor does negatively is almost always final and even less
protected—withholding prosecution, nol pros of a case, acceptance of a plea of guilty to a lesser offense—even when such decisions are irrational or improperly motivated and even when the

1   24 J. Amer. Jud. Soc. 18–19 (1940) .

result is unjust discrimination against those who are not similarly favored. The notion that the tribunal that holds the trial corrects abuses of the prosecuting power is obviously without merit.[2]

Nor will the other usual justification for uncontrolled discretionary power of prosecutors stand analysis—that the intrinsic nature of the prosecuting function is such that the only workable system is uncontrolled discretion. True, the habit of assuming that *of course* the prosecutor's discretion must be uncontrolled is so deeply embedded that the usual implied response to questions as to whether the prosecuting power can be confined or structured or checked is that the questioner must be totally without understanding. Inability of those who are responsible for administering the system to answer the most elementary questions as to the reasons behind the system is itself a reason to reexamine.

Lawyers all over the continent of Europe know that a prosecuting system can be viable without uncontrolled discretion. A quick look at a prosecuting system in one such country will show that the basic assumptions Americans have long made about the prosecuting power are not the only possible ones.

2. The prosecuting system in West Germany. Some knowledge of continental attitudes about the prosecuting power is useful, not because those attitudes should be transplanted to America, but because Americans need to realize that the assumptions on which our system is built are not inevitable.

Alexander Pekelis, who, with a European background, examined in depth both European and American legal institutions, observed that

. . . under the American system criminal prosecution is simply a right and never a duty of the federal or state attorney. Its exercise is wholly within the discretion of the prosecuting officers and the grand jury. In Italy . . . prosecution [is] a duty of the attorney general; in France and in Germany the prosecuting agency had but a slight degree of discretion, and this pertained to minor offenses and was subject to review by the court. . . . Thus the practical administration of criminal justice [in

2 Perhaps nine-tenths of the abuses of the prosecuting power involve failure to prosecute, and courts normally have no occasion to review such cases. Even when an abuse is affirmative, a court is unlikely to review the exercise of the prosecutor's discretionary power. For a discussion of judicial review of prosecutors' discretion, see pages 209–14, below.

the United States], at least in its negative aspect, becomes an administrative rather than a judicial activity. . . . In brief, then, comparative investigations thus far seem to reveal that in the administration of justice the common-law countries have traditionally relied upon a wide exercise of discretionary power to an incomparably greater extent than any civil-law country in Europe.[3]

Although no two continental systems of prosecuting are the same, all stand in contrast with the Anglo-American systems in the fundamental attitude about discretionary power of prosecutors. The continental countries seem in general to reflect the Pekelis background remark that "the European Rechtsstaat was planned and organized with the very purpose of reducing the human element in the administration of justice to its imaginable minimum. . . . The less discretion, the more justice." [4] British and American attitudes seem the opposite: Uncontrolled discretionary power of prosecutors is simply assumed.

American assumptions that a prosecutor must in the nature of things have a broad and largely uncontrolled discretionary power run so deep that I have found extreme skepticism on the part of any Americans to whom I have tried to explain the European attitudes about prosecuting. The almost universal reaction is along this line: "The prosecuting power intrinsically involves broad discretion because (1) in the nature of things all law can't be enforced, (2) the prosecutor has to interpret uncertain statuto-

---

3   Alexander Pekelis, *Law and Social Action* (1950) , 81–83.

4   Id. at 80. Although some major features of the prosecuting systems of the continental countries stand in contrast with those of the English-speaking nations, still some differences from one continental country to another are significant. For instance, prosecutors in Denmark and Norway have a very wide discretion to waive prosecution, but such waivers are generally limited to less serious offenses and are exceptional for serious crimes. In Sweden and Finland, the "principle of legality" means that prosecutors have a legal duty to prosecute if they find guilt sufficiently established; the main exceptions relate to young offenders. See Andenaes, *The Legal Framework*, 9, 10.

The contrast between England and the continent is brought out by a British writer, Glanville Williams, "Discretion in Prosecuting," [1956] Crim. L. Rev. 222: "It is completely wrong to suppose (as is sometimes done) that the institution of prosecution is an automatic or mechanical matter. This is, indeed, the theory in some Continental countries, such as Germany, where the rule is that the public prosecutor must take proceedings for all crimes that come to his notice for which there is sufficient evidence, unless they fall within an exception for petty offences, in respect of which he is given discretion. In England, however, there is discretion in prosecuting in respect of all crimes."

ry provisions, and (3) the prosecutor has to exercise discretion in deciding whether the evidence is sufficient." But the plain fact is that viable systems exist in which prosecutors have almost no discretionary power. Let us look more closely at one of them, that of West Germany.

Like the realities of the American prosecuting power, the realities of the German prosecuting power are beyond the statutes and the published reports of cases. The crucial element is the customary practices of prosecutors. To get the facts, I have sought help from five informants, all of whom have a German legal education and experience in the German system, and two of whom have had experience in prosecuting German cases: A distinguished legal scholar in comparative law who has worked in America since 1933, [5] a judge of the Supreme Administrative Court,[6] a young legal scholar in a German university who has taught as a visiting professor in two American law schools,[7] and two younger legal scholars who have come to America from Germany.[8] In the facts I am about to relate, the five are unanimous; omitted from my description is one facet about which they are not unanimous.

A German lawyer who is asked whether or not a German prosecutor has discretionary power is likely instinctively to say no. This is because students in German law schools are taught that prosecutors do not have discretionary power. The practice for the most part conforms to the theory that is taught, although some deviations from the theory can be found.

The American will immediately ask: "How on earth can a prosecutor interpret vague or ambiguous statutes and pass upon sufficiency of evidence without exercising discretionary power?" The German answer to that question is one that deserves to be understood by Americans. A crucial part of the answer is that some of the discretion exercised by American prosecutors is exercised by German judges.

5 Professor Max Rheinstein of the University of Chicago.
6 Dr. Ernst K. Pakuscher.
7 Professor Fritz Scharpf of the University of Constance, who was visiting professor at the Yale Law School 1964–66 and at the University of Chicago during 1966.
8 Associate Professor Gerhard Casper and Assistant Professor Peter Schlechtriem, both currently teaching at the University of Chicago Law School.

The most important difference between the German system and the American system is this: *Whenever the evidence that the defendant has committed a serious crime[9] is reasonably clear and the law is not in doubt, the German prosecutor, unlike the American prosecutor, is without discretionary power to withhold prosecution. This means that selective enforcement, a major feature of the American system, is almost wholly absent from the German system.* The German prosecutor does not withhold prosecution for such reasons as that he thinks the statute overreaches, that justice requires withholding enforcement because of special circumstances, that the statute ought to be enforced against some violators and not others, that he lacks time for bringing a marginal prosecution, or that he finds political advantage in not prosecuting. Hence the German prosecutor never has discretionary power to engage in plea bargaining.

The German and American systems also differ when the evidence or the law or both seem to the prosecutor to be doubtful. When a doubt seems to require a discretionary choice, the German prosecutor does not resolve the doubt; he almost always presents a doubtful case to the judge, who determines the sufficiency of the evidence and the proper interpretation of the law. Of course, in America the prosecutor makes a discretionary determination in every doubtful case, either to prosecute or not to prosecute.

Even when the prosecutor finds prosecution of a suspect clearly inappropriate, the German system, unlike the American system, provides protection against abuse of power. When a crime is reported by the police or by a private party, a file is opened and registered; the file can be traced at any time. A German prosecutor can never simply forget about the case as his American counterpart may do. The file cannot be closed without a statement of written reasons, which in important cases must be approved by the prosecutor's superior, and which must be reported to any victim of the crime and to any suspect who was interrogated. Every prosecutor is supervised by a superior in a hierarchical system

9 With respect to certain small misdemeanors, including traffic offenses, both the police and the prosecutors in Germany have a substantial power of selective enforcement. This exception is explicitly recognized in the statutes.

headed by the Minister of Justice, who is himself responsible to the cabinet. The supervision is real, not merely a threat; files are in fact often reviewed. Availability to victims of crimes of procedure to compel prosecution constitutes still another check.

Departures from the theory that prosecutors lack discretionary power in Germany are few and slight. Determining whether to make an investigation of a suspect, or whether to investigate further, or whether innocence is so clear that the case should not be presented to the judge may involve some element of discretion. And a little play in the joints is probably inevitable. One of my German informants has the impression, for instance, that the statute against homosexual practices is not fully enforced in Hamburg, but he thinks that the method of withholding prosecution is usually by finding the evidence insufficient; if his impression is correct, some discretionary power even about policy may in fact be exercised. During the Weimar Republic the Minister of Justice, with Cabinet approval but in violation of the statutes, openly refused to prosecute for certain political crimes. Although a statute makes it a crime not only to perform an abortion but for a woman to have one performed, women are seldom prosecuted for having abortions performed. But these examples of deviations from the theory are highly exceptional. With respect to the great bulk of crimes, the German prosecutor ordinarily has no power of selective enforcement. In this he stands in contrast with his American counterpart, who, with respect to the great bulk of crimes, ordinarily has a power of selective enforcement.[10]

3. *Criminal prosecutions—federal tax fraud as an example.* In exercising their enormous discretionary power, prosecutors in criminal cases can make an ad hoc decision of every question, or they can in any degree confine and structure their discretionary power; they can also provide checks and procedural protections.

---

10 A case which is not typical of German attitudes shows how extreme the German theory can be when carried into practice. A judge found a woman guilty of stealing four diapers. The statute required a severe penalty because of a prior conviction of theft. The judge by strained interpretation imposed a lighter sentence, as he thought justice required. The judge was then prosecuted for violating the statute requiring the severe sentence! The answer to my question whether the prosecutor of the judge had discretionary power to withhold prosecution was, "None whatsoever."

The law seems to be that prosecutors may, if they choose, do nothing in the direction of confining or structuring or checking or providing procedural protections. The prevailing habit seems to be to do little or nothing more than the law requires. And the community seems to be largely indifferent to the uncontrolled discretion. Even so, I think major studies should be made to discover how far the uncontrolled discretion can and should be brought under control.

Because the power to bring criminal prosecutions is too multifarious to look at all of it at once, and because the problems of finding the degree of control of discretion are often difficult and often interlocked with considerations of substantive policy, the nature of some of the problems of moving from uncontrolled discretion toward controlled discretion will be suggested through a series of illustrative questions about prosecution of federal tax fraud:[11]

If an embezzler is convicted and sentenced, in what circumstances should he be prosecuted for not reporting income from his embezzlement? Should a general policy be stated as to whether and when two prosecutions will be brought for a criminal act which yields unreported income, or should each case be dealt with on an ad hoc basis? What should the prosecuting policy be for tax cheating involving less than ten dollars, less than a hundred dollars, less than a thousand dollars? Should internal rules try to keep the policy consistent? Should any of the rules be announced? Should some classes of falsity which have a large impact on the revenue, such as false dependency claims, be more frequently prosecuted than other classes of falsity, and should such prosecutions be more widely publicized? What should the policy be about settling or compromising criminal tax cases, should the policy be kept consistent through detailed guides for enforcement officers, or should decisions be made by subordinate officers on an ad hoc basis? If detailed guides are used, should they be announced? Should dismissal of felony charges be ex-

11 See Charles S. Lyon, "The Crime of Income Tax Fraud," 53 Col. L. Rev. 476 (1953), which has inspired most of the questions here stated about income tax fraud.

changed for pleas of guilty to misdemeanors, should the policy be clear and consistent, and should it be announced? Should a taxpayer's voluntary disclosure of his fraud be rewarded by less aggressive prosecution; if so, what should the reward be, and should a consistent policy be announced? Should payment of the full tax have some effect upon the prosecutors' choices; if so, what effect, and should a consistent policy be announced? Should the prosecutors follow a set of consistent policies about making recommendations to the court about sentencing, and should the policies be announced? Should promises of immunity be given in return for disclosures of information that may be valuable to the prosecutors, and should the policy about such promises be clarified and announced? What other kinds of cooperation by alleged tax evaders with enforcement officers should be rewarded, what should the rewards be, in what degree should the policies be clarified, and should they be announced? What should be the policy about prosecuting one who is critically ill and whose death may be caused or hastened by a prosecution; should the policy be clarified and announced?

As for structuring, when a position is taken on a question of policy or law in deciding whether or not to prosecute, should the facts be summarized and a reasoned opinion written? Should the accumulation of such findings and opinions be regarded as a body of precedents to guide decisions in other cases, subject to the usual processes of distinguishing or occasionally overruling? Should all the materials be open to public inspection, except when confidentiality is essential, so that the exercise of discretion by the prosecutors will reflect the potentiality of criticism?

As for procedural safeguards, should the underlying policy be to avoid serious damage to any party through either investigation or prosecution until he has had a chance to know the main charge against him and to confer with a deciding officer about it? For instance, if a practicing lawyer is likely to be adversely affected if tax officials systematically interview his clients to ascertain whether he is guilty of tax fraud, should he have opportunity for a conference about the question before the investigation is instituted? If the taxpayer's status or activity is such that institution of a prosecution, even if followed immediately by a finding of not guilty, may cause great harm, should the opportunity for an advance conference be allowed? Should procedural rules governing opportunity for such a conference be announced?

Whenever sensitivity to publicity is an especially important factor, should the court provide by procedural rule for a motion by the defendant for a closed hearing, and should such a motion be granted whenever significant harm to the defendant would remain after a finding of not guilty?

As for checking discretion, whenever investigation or prosecution may cause special harm to an individual, should subordinates' decisions to take action require approval by top officers, and when top officers are the initial actors, should they always make their decisions known to their staffs, with invitations to criticize? Should courts enlarge the area of judicial review of prosecutors' decisions for abuse of discretion?

These questions are only illustrative of the types of questions that need to be considered, just as tax fraud is only illustrative of the many kinds of prosecutions for crime. A thorough inquiry might locate ten or twenty times as many significant questions. My opinion is emphatic that such an inquiry is long overdue—that the assumptions on which prosecutors' uncontrolled discretion is founded are in need of reexamination. I am also inclined to believe—but I leave the question open—that a full study of the prosecuting power is likely to produce movement in the direction of greater control of discretion, through more confinement, more structuring, more checks, and more procedural protections. The specific answers here depend upon complex considerations that can be weighed only through studies far more extensive and intensive than the present preliminary inquiry.

4. *Antitrust guidelines.* An outstanding example of the need for confinement of prosecutors' discretion through rule-making is antitrust law, involving both criminal prosecutions and suits in equity. The idea that the Department of Justice should announce guidelines to indicate its prosecuting policies is not a new one, although the further idea that rule-making procedure is desirable seems to be.

In the 1938 annual report of the United States Attorney General, Mr. Thurman Arnold said on behalf of the Antitrust Division:

An important part of our task is to facilitate compliance with the laws by helping conscientious business men to understand them. . . . Not only judicial policy but prosecution policy must be developed by precedent and on publicly stated grounds if it is to clarify the law. . . . Business men are entitled to know what kinds of situations will lead to prosecution. . . . In consequence, on May 18, 1938, the policy was adopted of publishing explanatory statements in connection with each important step taken in the administration of the antitrust laws. These statements are intended cumulatively to formulate a consistent antitrust policy. . . .[12]

The appendix of that report commented:

The Department of Justice recently announced a policy under which there would be issued a series of public statements throwing light on the prosecution policy with respect to antitrust laws. . . . A guide to business men as to prosecution policy should be furnished by the Department wherever possible. . . . The statements will be issued in the form of announcements signed by the Assistant Attorney General in charge of the Antitrust Division, and approved by the Attorney General. . . . The aim of these statements in connection with any particular proceeding or investigation is to serve (1) as a guide to businessmen who seek information on the probable action of this Department in similar circumstances; (2) to aid the Department itself in formulating a consistent policy of antitrust law enforcement; (3) to serve as a warning to those engaged in similar illegal practices; and (4) to call the attention of the Congress to the interpretation and application of antitrust laws by the Attorney General, as they may have a bearing upon contemplated legislation.

Then follow thirty pages of fine print, devoted mainly to what are called "Statements of Grounds of Action" in particular cases. The thirty pages make a significant beginning toward clarification of prosecution policies.

The 1939 annual report of the Attorney General reiterated the intent "to formulate a consistent antitrust policy through the development of a body of explicit departmental precedents," and it

12 Pages 59–60.

said that the announcement of that intent "has been greeted by almost unanimous approval from businessmen and their advisers in their relations with the Department of Justice. It will, therefore, be continued." [13] But no policy statements were included in the Appendix. The 1940 and 1941 annual reports make no mention of the clarification program, even though Thurman Arnold continued in office. He now says that the program was discontinued because of the war, and he asserts his continued belief that such a program is needed and can be made to succeed.

The Attorney General announced May 8, 1965, that "we have already begun seeking to shape policy guidelines" for antitrust prosecutions and that the effort would be continued by the new Assistant Attorney General, Donald F. Turner. But as of this writing, Mr. Turner has not yet published guidelines, although guidelines on mergers have been drafted and may soon be issued.[14]

An especially persuasive reason why the Antitrust Division should announce some policy guidelines is that it has often taken the position that something in addition to law determines its prosecution policy. For instance, Mr. Turner has said several times that the division will bring only the cases it ought to win, not those it can win under existing law. He said in impromptu discourse in 1966 that in deciding what prosecutions to bring, "you have to draw on appropriate resources including economic reasoning, to the extent that it is available and helpful, and other special considerations of that sort." To the extent that the policy is based upon "economic reasoning" that differs from case law, surely those affected should be entitled to know what the economic reasoning is. Mr. Turner has specifically said that his judgment about economic wisdom, not the law, may be decisive. He was asked: "I assume there are some Supreme Court cases in recent years that you do not think represent sound social policy or sound economic policy. When you are coming to write your guidelines, and when you are coming to bring new cases, do you feel compelled to write into your guidelines or to bring new prosecutions because the law seems to be that way already, even

13   Page 39.
14   The merger guidelines were issued May 30, 1968.

though you think the law in that area is perhaps economically unwise? " His answer was: "No, I do not feel bound to do so." [15]

To the extent that the policy of the Antitrust Division differs from the law found in decided cases, something in the nature of guidelines seems essential to fairness, for otherwise businessmen are governed by policy or law that is inaccessible to them.

Not only does fairness require clarification of prosecution policy, but efficiency does. Litigation is the most expensive way to get the government's job done; rule-making is the least expensive way. One fundamental is that the typical businessman normally complies with law that is clear. Continuing uncertainty of law or policy is a needless barrier to voluntary compliance.

Of course, clarification and voluntary compliance have their limits. Probably a removal of all uncertainties—perhaps even of all major uncertainties—from antitrust law is an impossibility. The degree of clarification that is feasible varies widely from one area to another. No one doubts that cumbersome and expensive enforcement proceedings will still be necessary for a good many cases. But the important observation is that much can be done that has not been done to clarify antitrust prosecution policy and thereby to induce a greater proportion of voluntary compliance.

At one time the thinking within the division was that the contemplated guidelines would strive to state what is illegal but would avoid any assurance that specified practices are legal. The idea was that enforcement officers should take a fighting stance on every issue and should never give anything away; that idea has had strong support among staff members. But the later word is that the guidelines will indicate what is legal as well as what is illegal, as I think they should. Of course, clean lines between the prohibited and the permitted need not always be drawn. Nor must positions always be taken within zones of doubt. The three categories of the legal, the illegal, and the doubtful may often have to be acknowledged. But diligent effort should be made to locate the lines—not merely lines between the legal and the illegal but also the lines between the legal and the doubtful and between the doubtful and the illegal. Within the zone of the doubt-

15   30 A.B.A. Antitrust Section 111–12 (1966) .

ful, hypothetical cases may well be put and answered—both ways. The objective should be, as time goes on, to narrow the doubtful zone, and, as policy unfolds in particular action, to fill it in with concrete answers—both ways. The Treasury's tax regulations are useful and realistic because they state what is not taxable as well as what is taxable.

Of course, the task of clarifying antitrust law and policy is one that can never be finished. The idea that a set of definitive guidelines can be struck off at any one time is almost an absurdity. Like the common law, useful guidelines will be necessarily always in the process of becoming. Guidelines will necessarily yield to new judicial and administrative decisions and to new factual studies. Changeability will not destroy the guidelines' usefulness; changes that operate against private parties who have properly relied upon old guidelines should in general be limited to prospective operation.

Current thinking within the Antitrust Division is that the guidelines will be issued without following the rule-making procedure prescribed by the Administrative Procedure Act. The division contemplates issuance of the guidelines as a statement of its policies, along with a statement that criticisms and proposed amendments are invited and will be received at any time. My opinion is that the division has everything to gain and nothing to lose by following the APA procedure, even though the guidelines will be "interpretative rules" within the meaning of one main exemption from the required procedure. The division should first publish tentative guidelines for the purpose of inviting written comments, and then it should take into account the comments before publishing a final set. The probability is that the guidelines can be improved through that process, and even if they are not, giving affected parties a chance to express themselves *before the policies have become fixed* is a sound process of democracy.

An even more important reason for using a rule-making procedure for some of the guidelines is that to some extent facts about industry structures and practices must be found, and the most efficient method for finding such economic facts is rule-making procedure. Some portions of the guidelines program should respond to Commissioner Philip Elman's sound observa-

tion that "the basic need in the effective enforcement of the merger law is the development and formulation of standards of legality with reference to specific market and industry situations; and
this is essentially a problem of devising new and more adequate
means of factual inquiry." [16] That remark is as valid for the Antitrust Division as for the Trade Commission.

5. *Findings, reasons, and precedents in the Antitrust Division.*
Apart from the guidelines program—or as an extension of it—the
Antitrust Division can move toward greater clarification of its
prosecution policies by announcing findings and reasons whenever it takes action of any kind that is based upon significant policy. When it prosecutes a case, when it decides not to prosecute,
when it decides to dismiss or to nol pros, when it enters into a
consent arrangement, and when it grants a clearance, it can and
should state publicly the policy reasons for its action, and the policy statements should be treated as precedents which normally
will not be retroactively changed.

The division adopted this idea in part in 1938—to the extent
of publicly explaining the prosecutions it brought. In an article
of that year, Mr. Thurman Arnold said:

All complaints can not be prosecuted. A selection must be made.
Therefore, the grounds underlying that selection should be publicly
stated in each case to the end that a consistent and open policy of prosecution may gradually be derived from statements in connection with
individual cases. . . . If each important suit were prefaced by such a
statement of policy there would be built up gradually within the Department a reasonably consistent policy which would be a matter of
public record. . . . I propose to announce in connection with the particular cases or investigations which are instituted in the future enough
information so that the exercise of the discretion in selecting the cases
may be as consistent as public announcement and public criticism can
make it.[17]

As of this writing, my understanding is that the division has
decided to revive the system of explaining each prosecution, but
it has not yet decided to make public explanations of other policy

16 "Rulemaking Procedures in the FTC's Enforcement of the Merger Law," 78
Harv. L. Rev. 385, 391 (1964).
17 "Fair and Effective Use of Present Antitrust Procedure," 47 Yale L. J. 1294,
1300–1303 (1938).

determinations. Explaining decisions not to prosecute seems unlikely because of the division's basic reluctance to acknowledge that any practice is legal. Letters granting merger clearances have not been open to public inspection, and the tendency is away from the writing of such letters. Mr. Turner has made a public statement that he may abandon such formal letters in favor of mere termination of investigations.

Of course, many considerations that enter into a decision to prosecute or not to prosecute may properly be kept secret. When a prosecutor's objective with respect to law development seems to him attainable in three steps but not in one step, he may for reasons of strategy decline to prosecute a case raising the question whether the one step should be taken, but he need not disclose his strategy. When getting the evidence seems too expensive and the decision turns on budgetary factors, secrecy may be appropriate. When the key witness is recalcitrant but may not be in later circumstances, an announcement of the witness's attitude might be harmful. When deficiencies in the evidence may later be filled in, a public acknowledgment of the deficiencies is clearly undesirable. When a legal theory seems too weak to assert in one case, conceding the weakness might prejudice the use of the theory in another case in which the reasons for its adopttion are stronger.

Even though withholding the reasons for decisions to prosecute or not to prosecute may often be appropriate, public explanation can and should usually be made of determinations of substantive law or policy.

An excellent illustration is Mr. Turner's dismissal of a case brought by his predecessor against acquisition by Anheuser-Busch of the Rahr Malting Plant. No reasons were publicly announced at the time of the dismissal. But when a Congressman addressed a letter to the Attorney General requesting an explanation, Mr. Turner responded that the Anheuser-Rahr merger was vertical, that the Schlitz and Pabst cases involved horizontal acquisitions of competitors, that the Anheuser suit was filed "when it apparently was believed that that acquisition and similar acquisitions by other brewers would indeed threaten smaller competitors," that "it appeared to us fairly clear that there was no serious likelihood of this occurring," and that dismissal without prejudice meant that proceedings could be reinstituted if developments so required. That the explanation was finally made shows that it could have been made at the time of the dismissal. If it had been made at that time, the adverse criticism of the dismissal would have been less severe.

Although considerations of economy and efficiency must enter into the reckoning, as well as the interlocking of substantive policy with strategy factors that must be kept secret, I think that *the general practice should be to accompany all significant decisions of substantive policy with statements of findings and reasoned opinions.* Such findings and opinions should be open to public inspection and should guide the later determination of similar questions. At this time the Antitrust Division seems to be in the early stages of moving toward such findings and opinions.

6. *An example of a prosecutor's discretion that is fully structured.* One prosecutor in the United States—only one, so far as I have found—uses a system of fully structured discretion. That such a system not only exists but succeeds may be enough to prove that the idea of structuring the prosecuting power is something more than an academician's dream. The system is in full bloom not merely on the European continent but in a federal regulatory agency. The agency is the National Labor Relations Board, and the prosecutor is the Board's General Counsel. The system is very instructive.

The General Counsel's organization operates in Washington and in thirty-one regional offices. Charges are filed with regional directors, who assign them to field investigators. Most charges are of course disposed of by voluntary action—either agreement by the respondent, or withdrawal of the charge. When a charge is not disposed of by consent, the regional director and his staff either issue a complaint or refuse to do so. If a complaint is issued, the case goes to hearing and all the protections of a trial come into play. It is when a complaint is refused that the interesting and significant protections are afforded: The charging party is then entitled to (1) a statement of findings and reasons, (2) a decision which is fitted into the precedents and which itself becomes a precedent, and (3) a right to take an appeal to officers in Washington who are wholly independent of the officers in the regional office.

The disappointed charging party, as soon as he receives a written explanation for the refusal of the regional office to issue a complaint, may take his case to the Office of Appeals in the Washington office of the General Counsel. The seven supervisors and twenty attorneys in the Office of Appeals handled 1,350 cases in one recent year. An appeal goes first to an attorney who prepares a memorandum stating facts, issues, and recommendations. A supervisor works over the memorandum, and it then goes to the Appeals Committee, which makes the decision, subject to approval by the General Counsel. Unless a complaint is issued, a charging party is entitled to a reasoned opinion by the Office of Appeals. Since many problems get no further in the board's machinery than the Office of Appeals, opinions of that office are the only available precedents on some questions. They are indexed and freely used within the office, along with similar opinions given by the Advice Branch of the General Counsel's office in response to requests from regional officers for guidance on questions of law and policy. From the advice and appeal opinions, the General Counsel's office compiles a "book of digests" for the guidance of the staff on issues about which the General Counsel's decisions constitute the only relevant law. The digests that are thought especially significant, growing out of advice and appeals, are selected for publication in the General Counsel's "Quarterly Report on Case Developments." A previous practice of publishing all appeals cases through the Bureau of National Affairs was discontinued for lack of sufficient demand. Requests for inspection of unpublished opinions are so rare that the Director of the Office of Appeals remembers none, and the policy is therefore unclarified as to whether they are open to public inspection.

Although the formal rules do not so provide, either the charging party or the charged party may confer (separately) with a representative of the Office of Appeals. This opportunity for hearing is undercut, however, by availability of the full investigatory file to the Office of Appeals but not to the parties.

In view of the apparently unique success of the General Counsel in structuring his discretionary power to refuse to issue complaints, should he similarly structure his discretionary power to issue complaints? The argument for his doing so is that a trial is less than a complete protection against wrongful issuance of a complaint; the argument against his doing so is that appeals to the General Counsel from decisions of a regional office to issue a complaint might simply add to the onerous procedures that an innocent respondent must pursue before he is finally found not guilty. Perhaps the answer is that such appeals are desirable only in rare cases in which the impropriety of issuing the complaint can be quickly and conclusively shown. But that is permissible now, for 29 CFR § 102.33 authorizes the General Counsel to take control of any case at any time from a regional office, and a party in an appropriate case could surely request the General Counsel to exercise that authority.

The system of the NLRB General Counsel contains the major elements of a full structuring of discretionary power—findings, reasons, precedents, checks through appeals and through internal supervision, and procedural protections. The degree of openness may be adequate, as shown by lack of requests for unpublished opinions, but the lack of requests may be based on widespread assumption of lack of availability; the doubt could be removed by an announcement of availability of such opinions.

Altogether, the system of the NLRB General Counsel is deserving of admiration. It is surely worthy of study by other prosecutors.

7. *Administrative and judicial checking.* The top prosecutors of federal, state, and local governments are typically subject to little or no checking either by higher officers or by reviewing courts, no matter how seriously they have abused their powers and no matter how flagrant the injustice. This typical system may be in need of reexamination.

Especially unfortunate, in my opinion, is the complete lack of supervision of the typical city or county prosecutor. He is usually an elected official, and the theory is that he is responsible to the electorate. The reality is that nearly all his decisions to prosecute or not to prosecute, nearly all of the influences brought to bear upon such decisions, and nearly all his reasons for decisions are carefully kept secret, so that review by the electorate is nonexistent except for the occasional case that happens to be publicized. The plain fact is that more than nine-tenths of local prosecutors' decisions are supervised or reviewed by no one.

The American Bar Association's Commission on Organized Crime and Law Enforcement reported in 1952: "Apart from intervention in emergency situations the local prosecutor is usually left severely alone by the attorney general or the governor. . . . By and large throughout the country, the attorney general of the various states is not an important factor in connection with the ordinary processes of criminal justice." [18] That remark was made twenty-two years after the American Bar Association had sponsored a Model Department of Justice Act, which would centralize the prosecuting authority in the state attorney general.[19] At least seven states have adopted the idea,[20] but complete lack of supervision of local prosecutors continues in most states. Even when the state attorney general has the power of supervision, the elected subordinate usually manages to maintain a large degree of independence. I think the question is raised whether the prevailing system of electing local prosecutors is inconsistent with a sound system of discretionary justice.

When the prosecuting power is in an independent regulatory agency, no other officer of the government can review either a decision to prosecute or a decision not to prosecute. The White House has some control through the power of appointment and reappointment, but that control may be more likely to contribute to uneven enforcement than to relief from it. Congress in creating independent agencies probably lacks power to reduce the President's explicit constitutional power to "take Care that the Laws be faithfully executed," but the President normally refrains from interfering with the prosecuting power of the independent agencies. The practical fact is that that power, though enormous, is unsupervised. A check by Congress or its committees is always a possibility, and the mere potentiality of such a check may have

18   Report (1952) , 244.
19   59 A.B.A.R. 124 (1934) .
20   California, Iowa, Nebraska, New Mexico, North Carolina, Oregon, and Pennsylvania.

some effect, but legislative supervision of exercise of the prosecuting power is seldom, if ever, meaningful.

Judicial review of decisions to prosecute or not to prosecute is almost totally absent.[21] The law of the federal courts is well summarized in the 1967 opinion of the Court of Appeals for the District of Columbia. The defendant and A were indicted. Negotiations between A's counsel and an assistant United States attorney led to A's being allowed to plead guilty to misdemeanors, but the U.S. attorney declined to consent to the same plea for the defendant, who argued that he and A were equally guilty and that fairness required equal treatment. The court held that it could not review to determine whether the U.S. attorney had abused his discretion. The court reviewed the authorities and declared:

Few subjects are less adapted to judicial review than the exercise by the Executive of his discretion in deciding when and whether to institute criminal proceedings, or what precise charge shall be made, or whether to dismiss a proceeding once brought. . . . Two persons may have committed what is precisely the same legal offense but the prosecutor is not compelled by law, duty or tradition to treat them the same as to charges. . . . [N]o court has any jurisdiction to inquire into or review his decision. . . . [W]hile this discretion is subject to abuse or misuse just as is judicial discretion, deviations from his duty as an agent of the Executive are to be dealt with by his superiors. . . . [I]t is not the function of the judiciary to review the exercise of executive discretion whether it be that of the President himself or those to whom he has delegated certain of his powers.[22]

Although I agree that two persons who have committed the same offense need not be equally treated, because the treatment should depend upon factors in addition to the offense committed, everything else quoted from the court's opinion seems to me deeply unsound. Instead of saying that "few subjects are less adapted to judicial review" than prosecutors' discretion, I would say that few subjects are more adapted to judicial review than a protection

---

21 A judicial trial is an acceptance of a prosecutor's decision to prosecute, not a review of it. Even a quick finding of not guilty may leave untouched the harms that flow from the prosecution. Of course, the big power which can be discriminatorily exercised is the power not to prosecute. Of one thousand decisions not to prosecute, the usual number totally unknown to judges is probably one thousand.

22 Newman v. United States, 382 F.2d 479 (D.C. Cir., 1967) .

against abuse. Instead of saying that "it is not the function of the judiciary to review the exercise of executive discretion," I could cite a hundred Supreme Court decisions stating that it is the function of the judiciary to review the exercise of executive discretion;[23] after all, under the Administrative Procedure Act judicial review of the exercise of executive discretion is the rule and unreviewability is the exception. The court's opinion seems to me completely empty of valid reasons. Yet the authorities discussed in the opinion unquestionably support the result.

One main reason that seems to actuate federal courts in holding that discretion of prosecutors may not be reviewed to protect against abuse has been stated by the Fifth Circuit in a 1965 opinion: ". . . it is as an officer of the executive department that he [the U.S. Attorney] exercises a discretion as to whether or not there shall be a prosecution in a particular case. It follows, as an incident of the constitutional separation of powers, that the courts are not to interfere with the free exercise of the discretionary powers of the attorneys of the United States in their control over criminal prosecutions." [24] This reason is so clearly unsound as to be almost absurd. If separation of powers prevents review of discretion of executive officers, then more than a hundred Supreme Court decisions spread over a century and three-quarters will have to be found contrary to the Constitution! If courts could not interfere with abuse of discretion by executive officers, our fundamental institutions would be altogether different from what they are. If the statement just quoted from the Fifth Circuit were true, the courts would be powerless to interfere when executive officers, acting illegally, are about to execute an innocent person!

The most convincing passage I have found in support of unreviewability of prosecutor's discretion to protect against abuse of power appears in a 1949 opinion:

He [the prosecutor] must appraise the evidence on which an indictment may be demanded and the accused defendant tried, if he be indicted, and in that service must judge of its availability, competency

23 The case law is fully presented in Chap. 28 of my *Administrative Law Treatise.*
24 United States v. Cox, 342 F.2d 167, 171 (5th Cir.), certiorari denied 381 U.S. 935 (1965).

and probative significance. He must on occasion consider the public impact of criminal proceedings, or, again, balance the admonitory value of invariable and inflexible punishment against the greater impulse of the "quality of mercy." He must determine what offenses, and whom, to prosecute. . . . Into these and many others of the problems committed to his informed discretion it would be sheer impertinence for a court to intrude. And such intrusion is contrary to the settled judicial tradition.[25]

Yes, the court is surely right that judicial intrusion into the prosecuting function is contrary to the settled judicial tradition. But why is it? Is it because the tradition became settled during the nineteenth century when courts were generally assuming that judicial intrusion into any administration would be unfortunate? Is it because the tradition became settled while the Supreme Court was actuated by its 1840 remark that "The interference of the Courts with the performance of the ordinary duties of the executive departments of the government, would be productive of nothing but mischief"? [26] Is it because the tradition became settled before the courts made the twentieth-century discovery that the courts can interfere with executive action to protect against abuses but at the same time can avoid taking over the executive function? [27] Is it because the tradition became settled before the successes of the modern system of *limited* judicial review became fully recognized?

On the basis of what the courts know today about leaving administration to administrators but at the same time providing an effective check to protect against abuses, should the courts not take a fresh look at the tradition that prevents them from reviewing the prosecuting function? Throughout the governmental system, courts have found that other administrative or executive functions are in need of a judicial check, with a limited scope of review.[28] *The reasons for a judicial check of prosecutors' discre-*

25   Howell v. Brown, 85 F. Supp. 537, 540 (D. Neb. 1949).
26   Decatur v. Paulding, 39 U.S. (14 Pet.) 497, 516 (1840).
27   The turning point may have come in American School of Magnetic Healing v. McAnnulty, 187 U.S. 94 (1902). The action of the Postmaster General could be reviewed because: "Otherwise, the individual is left to the absolutely uncontrolled and arbitrary action of a public and administrative officer." 187 U.S. at 110.
28   The general federal rule, which has exceptions, is embodied in the Administrative Procedure Act, 5 U.S.C. § 701–706.

tion are stronger than for such a check of other administrative discretion that is now traditionally reviewable. Important interests are at stake. Abuses are common. The questions involved are appropriate for judicial determination. And much injustice could be corrected.

The usual assumption that the prosecuting power is inherently unsuitable for judicial review is contradicted by the experience in West Germany, and it is contradicted by a slight amount of American experience. We do have a bit of review of prosecutors' discretion around the edges. For more than a century Michigan has had a statute providing that when a prosecuting attorney investigates a case and decides not to prosecute he shall file with the court a written statement "containing his reasons in fact and in law" and that if the court is not satisfied with the statement it may direct that the case be prosecuted.[29] The Michigan system seems well designed to protect against discriminatory prosecuting policies and against abuses stemming from political influence. The Michigan idea seems worthy of full consideration elsewhere.

A federal court can review a decision to prosecute when the defendant shows an abuse of discretion in failing to prosecute his competitors. The Supreme Court declared in the key case: "If the [Federal Trade] Commission has decided the question [whether cease and desist orders should be withheld until respondents' competitors are proceeded against], its discretionary determination should not be overturned in the absence of a patent abuse of discretion." [30] The statement clearly implies that the discretionary determination can be overturned upon a showing of a patent abuse of discretion. The Seventh Circuit has specifically so held, in a case in which it found that the commission had "se-

29 Mich. Stat. § 28.981, dating from 1859 provides: "It shall be the duty of the prosecuting attorney of the proper county to inquire into and make full examination of all the facts and circumstances connected with any case of preliminary examination as provided by law, touching the commission of any offense whereon the offender shall be committed to jail . . . and if the prosecuting attorney shall determine in any case that an information ought not to be filed, he shall . . . file with the clerk of the court a statement, in writing, containing his reason in fact and in law, for not filing an information . . . such court may examine said statement, together with the evidence filed in the case and if, upon such examination, the court shall not be satisfied with said statement, the prosecuting attorney shall be directed by the court to file the proper information and bring the case to trial."
30 Moog Industries v. FTC, 355 U.S. 411, 414 (1958).

lected one whose share of the market is less than 6%, although the practice complained of is common to the industry." [31] The Supreme Court approved the view expressed by the Seventh Circuit by declaring that the commission "does not have unbridled power to institute proceedings which will arbitrarily destroy one of many law violators in an industry," but the Supreme Court found "no basis for a conclusion that the practice held illegal by the Commission was prevalent throughout the plumbing industry." [32]

If an abuse by the Federal Trade Commission in exercising its prosecuting power is thus judicially reviewable, why should not any abuse by any prosecuting officer or officers be likewise judicially reviewable? If some courts may review a prosecutor's nolle proseque, [33] why not all? If some courts may review deals made through plea bargaining and thereby correct some injustice, [34] why not all? If some courts review intentional discrimination by a prosecutor, [35] why not all? If some courts can compel prosecutors to take affirmative action, [36] despite the anachronistic theory that separation of powers forbids the judicial branch of the government to correct abuses by officers of the executive branch, [37] why not all? In general, if some abuses of some prosecutors are reviewable in some courts, why should not all abuses of all prosecutors be reviewable by some court?

Perhaps the law of the long-term future can be glimpsed in a dissenting opinion in the Supreme Court. A tax evader was prosecuted under a statute with a greater penalty, even though he could

31   Universal-Rundle Corp. v. FTC, 352 F.2d 831 (7th Cir., 1965).
32   FTC v. Universal-Rundle Corp., 387 U.S. 244, 250, 251 (1967).
33   E.g., State v. Ashby, 43 N.J. 273, 204 A.2d 1 (1964).
34   The Crime Commission's Task Force Report on The Courts said at page 9: "Although the participants and frequently the judge know that negotiation has taken place, the prosecutor and defendant must ordinarily go through a courtroom ritual in which they deny that the guilty plea is the result of any threat or promise. As a result there is no judicial review of the propriety of the bargain— no check on the amount of pressure put on the defendant to plead guilty. The judge, the public, and sometimes the defendant himself cannot know for certain who got what from whom in exchange for what."
35   E.g., People v. Utica Daws Drug Co., 16 App.Div.2d 12, 225 N.Y.S2d 128 (4th Dept. 1962).
36   See the Michigan statute set forth above in note 29.
37   See the 4–3 division of the court in four opinions in United States v. Cox, 342 F.2d 167, 171 (5th Cir.), certiorari denied 381 U.S. 935 (1965).

have been prosecuted under a statute with a lesser penalty. The trial judge refused to charge the jury that it could find him guilty of violating the statute with the lesser penalty, and the Supreme Court affirmed. The dissenters objected to what they found to be "unreviewable discretion of one individual"—the prosecutor. They asserted that such unreviewable discretion seemed to them "wholly incompatible with our system of justice." [38] I agree, except that I think our system of justice has been drifting too far toward unreviewable discretion of prosecutors. The attitude of the dissenters may be the harbinger of tomorrow's law. I think it should be.

The entire large problem of judicial check of prosecutors' discretion is in need of a full study—a study which will be free from the false assumptions that now dominate American thinking about the discretion of prosecutors.

38   Berra v. United States, 351 U.S. 131, 139, 140 (1956). The dissenters said: ". . . We should construe these sections so as not to place control over the liberty of citizens in the unreviewable discretion of one individual—a result which seems to me wholly incompatible with our system of justice. . . . Of course it is true that under our system Congress may vest the judge and jury with broad power to say how much punishment shall be imposed for a particular offense. But it is quite different to vest such powers in a prosecuting attorney. A judge and jury act under procedural rules carefully prescribed to protect the liberty of the individual. . . . No such protections are thrown around decisions by a prosecuting attorney. Substitution of the prosecutor's caprice for the adjudicatory process is an action I am not willing to attribute to Congress in the absence of clear command."

See also Bazelon, J., dissenting, in Henderson v. United States, 349 F.2d 712, 713–14 (D.C. Cir., 1965) : "At oral argument I asked Government counsel why this appellant, a non-addict found with large quantities of narcotics, was treated so much better than addicts accidentally found in possession of $40 worth of drugs, or persuaded into making a $10 sale to a police undercover agent or informer. Government counsel offered this explanation: the United States Attorney may have reason to think that such addicts are substantial operators, but may have no way to prove it. Such reasoning is at the heart of the tyranny in the invisible prosecutorial choice he is permitted to make. I am dismayed at the proposition that a prosecutor may sentence offenders to jail terms longer than appears to be warranted by the transaction with which they are charged, because he *thinks* they are involved in bigger stuff—and that this choice may never be reviewed."

See also the Bazelon opinion in Hutcherson v. United States, 345 F.2d 964, 974–75 (D.C. Cir., 1965) .

VIII

Summary and
Perspective

1. *The basic jurisprudential question.* In its largest dimension, the central question of this essay is a basic one that legal philosophers have pondered for thousands of years: In our entire legal and governmental system, how can we improve the quality of justice for individual parties; how can we reduce injustice? Over the centuries, the main answer has been to build a system of rules and principles to guide decisions in individual cases. That is a good answer, as good for the future as for the past. The continued development of rules and principles is both desirable and inevitable.

Yet something more is needed, something the philosophers over the centuries have not supplied. If we stay within the comfortable areas where jurisprudence scholars work and concern ourselves mostly with statutory and judge-made law, we can at best accomplish no more than to refine what is already tolerably good. To do more than that, we have to open our eyes to the reality that justice to individual parties is administered more outside courts than in them, and we have to penetrate the unpleasant areas of discretionary determinations by police and prosecutors and other administrators, where huge concentrations of injustice invite drastic reforms.

And even after we enter administrative territory, significant progress is unlikely if, along with the organized bar's administrative law committees, we focus only on the superior agencies that deal with large economic interests, such as the federal regulatory agencies and the Internal Revenue Service, where the quality of justice is usually reasonably high, and neglect the generally inferior agencies which deal with mixtures that seem more human than economic, such as police, prosecutors, welfare agencies, selective service boards, parole boards, prison administrators, and the Immigration Service, where the usual quality of justice is relatively low. Unlike the bar groups, we must dig into the kinds of injustice that can be neither cured nor alleviated by either formal hearings or judicial review.

The strongest need and the greatest promise for improving the quality of justice to individual parties in the entire legal and governmental system are in the areas where decisions necessarily depend more upon discretion than upon rules and principles and where formal hearings and judicial review are mostly irrelevant. We must try something that neither the legal philosophers down through the centuries nor our current study groups of the organized bar have tried—we must try to find ways to minimize discretionary injustice.

2. *The more specific question.* Probably nine-tenths of the basic question of how to reduce injustice to individual parties in our whole system of law and government is contained in the much narrower question: How can we reduce injustice to individual parties from the exercise of discretionary power? That is the central question of this essay.

3. *The framework of a suggested approach.* The broad framework of the approach I recommend is expressed in this one sentence: The vast quantities of unnecessary discretionary power that have grown up in our system should be cut back, and the discretionary power that is found to be necessary should be properly confined, structured, and checked.

4. *A government of laws and of men.* The starting point has to be a recognition that what we have and what we ought to have is a government of laws and of men. No legal system in world history has been without significant discretionary power. None can be.[1] Discretion is indispensable for individualized justice, for creative justice, for new programs in which no one yet knows how to

1   See pages 17–19, above.

formulate rules, and for old programs in which some aspects cannot be reduced to rules. Eliminating discretionary power would paralyze governmental processes and would stifle individualized justice. Those who would forbid governmental coercion except on the basis of rules previously announced seem to me to have misunderstood the elements of law and of government.[2]

5. *Cutting back unnecessary discretionary power.* The proper goal is to eliminate unnecessary discretionary power, not to eliminate all discretionary power. My observation is that all levels of American government—federal, state, and local—are shot through with unnecessary discretionary power. Such power far exceeds what is necessary for an industrialized society, as is conclusively shown by the relative success of the countries of Western Europe in limiting such power.[3] We can and we should cut back huge quantities of unnecessary discretionary power.

6. *Improved statutory standards largely a false hope.* The traditional proposal for limiting unnecessary discretionary power is to require more meaningful standards when power is delegated. That approach seems to me unpromising for three reasons: (1) Legislative bodies have neither the capacity nor the inclination to do substantially more through statutory drafting than they now do in providing policy guidance to administrators, and legislative bodies ought to be allowed to govern the extent of their own participation.[4] (2) The idea of requiring standards fails to reach the great bulk of discretionary power which has grown without legislative delegation. (3) The hope not only for development of meaningful standards but also for going beyond standards to rules lies in the use of administrative rule-making power. The second and third reasons are elaborated in the next two sections.

7. *The incongruity of the non-delegation doctrine alongside the huge ungranted power of selective enforcement.* The three sources of discretionary power of officers are purposeful legislative delegations, vague statutory terms to which administrators must give meaning, and public acquiescence in administrative assumption of ungranted power. The third probably involves more

2 See pages 28–44, above.
3 See pages 191–95, above.
4 See pages 44–51, above.

power than the first two in combination, and the second probably involves more than the first. Yet the non-delegation doctrine, requiring meaningful standards to guide the exercise of delegated power, is designed only for the first.

The non-delegation doctrine seems crazily incongruous when placed alongside realities of the commonplace power of selective enforcement, as exercised by police, prosecutors, regulatory agencies, and other administrators. Not only is the power of selective enforcement typically ungranted through legislative delegation, and not only is it completely unguided by statutory or other standards, but it is also unstructured and unchecked, and it includes the power to set aside legislation in whole or in part, no matter how clearly the legislative will has been expressed.[5] What is still worse, the power of selective enforcement is exercised by single officers in individual cases,[6] with no requirement of consistency, so that a statute is set aside in one case, enforced in the next case, and partially enforced in a third case. And no equal protection clause, no principle of equal justice, and no judicial review are ordinarily available to a victim of arbitrary exercise of the power of selective enforcement.[7]

Here is a simple example. A statute, an ordinance, and a police manual all provide that a policeman "shall" arrest all known violators of law. A policeman lectures a boy from a middle-class neighborhood, but he arrests a boy from the slums, although he knows that both are equally guilty of violating the same statute. Because the evidence against both boys is clear, the policeman's decision is the only one that counts, for the release of the first boy is permanent and the conviction of the second follows almost automatically. No standard, meaningful or otherwise, guides the policeman's decision. The policeman's release of the first boy is in contravention of the statute, the ordinance, and the police manual, but, if prevailing customs are followed, superiors in the department could know all the facts without disapproving. And the plain practicality is that in our whole legal system the second

5 See pages 162–66, above.
6 See pages 88–90, above.
7 See pages 209–19, above.

boy has no legal remedy, even though he has obviously been denied equal justice and equal protection of the laws.

The unplanned, ungranted power of selective enforcement has been assumed by the police, by prosecutors at all levels, and by many other administrators.[8] A regulatory agency may institute a rate reduction proceeding against one company but not against another. A licensing agency may look the other way when one licensee violates but quickly move to suspend or revoke the license of another.

The power of selective enforcement is so dominant that it may account for about two-thirds of all unnecessary discretionary power over individual parties in our entire governmental system.[9]

The courts go along with the huge ungranted and unguided system of selective enforcement, never murmuring a word about the lack of standards. At the same time many courts go on singing silly tunes about a requirement of standards when legislative bodies intentionally delegate!

8. *Administrative rule-making is a key.* The hope lies, I think, not in better statutory standards, but in earlier and more elaborate administrative rule-making and in better structuring and checking of discretionary power.

Administrative rule-making is the key to a large portion of all that needs to be done. To whatever extent is practical and consistent with the need for individualized justice, the discretion of officers in handling individual cases should be guided by administrative rules adopted through procedure like that prescribed by the federal Administrative Procedure Act.[10] Agencies through rule-making can often move from vague or absent statutory standards to reasonably definite standards, and then, as experience and understanding develop, to guiding principles, and finally, when the subject matter permits, to precise and detailed rules. The constant objective, when discretionary power is excessive, should be for earlier and more elaborate administrative rules.

---

8 Except in New Mexico, state legislation is uniform in imposing a duty on the police to enforce criminal statutes. See page 86, note 57, above.

9 See page 166, above.

10 5 U.S.C. § 553; pages 54–74, especially 65–68, above.

9. *Rules need not generalize.* The principal reason for inadequacy of administrative rules is inability of administrators to see all around a subject sufficiently to risk generalizations in rules. That is the state of mind of most administrators on most subjects, so that even when the need for rules is recognized, their issuance is long delayed. The way out of this common impasse is for administrators to recognize that *rules need not be in the form of generalizations.*[11] When an administrator knows the answer to a hypothetical case, he should issue a rule, stating the case, his position, and his reasons, without a generalization. When further hypothetical cases can be added, they should be. As this kind of rule-making interacts with decisions in particular cases, generalizations will usually emerge in due course.

10. *Rule-making power need not be separately granted.* Lack of a statutory provision which separately grants a rule-making power is not a justification for failure to issue rules. Whenever an officer has a discretionary power to decide what to do in a particular case, he necessarily has power to announce how he will exercise that power.[12] Such an announcement may be an interpretative rule, but it may have great value even though, for want of a statutory grant of power, it may lack force of law.

11. *The courts should consider the creation of a judicial requirement of rule-making.* The judicially created non-delegation doctrine, under which legislative bodies are supposed to be required to state meaningful standards to guide the exercise of discretionary power, is rapidly declining and retains little effectiveness, because legislative bodies have been unable or unwilling to provide meaningful guidance for administrative discretion. The courts are largely powerless in the face of continued assertions of the legislative will. If the courts are so inclined, I think they can save the non-delegation doctrine by pumping new life into it and at the same time making a slight shift in the doctrine: The courts can continue their requirement of meaningful standards, except that when the legislative body fails to prescribe the required standards the courts can allow the administrators to prescribe

11 See pages 59–64, above.
12 See pages 68–74, above.

them within a reasonable time. The idea that either the legislative body or the administrators through the exercise of their rule-making power can supply the needed standards can gradually become an affirmative judicial requirement that administrators having power that is unguided by meaningful statutory standards must within a reasonable time issue meaningful rules which will properly confine their discretionary power in individual cases.[13] Adoption of this proposal will involve the courts in an ambitious undertaking which will involve many difficulties, but the judicially-created non-delegation doctrine is increasingly rejected,[14] as it should be, and new controls are needed to fill the vacuum. The courts have often undertaken more difficult assignments and have seen them through. Looking backward, we ought to see clearly that if such a requirement of administrative rule-making had been enforced from the beginning of this century instead of the non-delegation doctrine, and if such an aspiration had taken the place of the extravagant version of the rule of law, much unnecessary and uncontrolled discretionary power—and hence much injustice—could have been avoided.

12. *Wide applicability of rule-making requirement.* The desirability of administrative rules extends as far as discretionary power extends. Whenever any agency or officer has discretionary power, rule-making is appropriate. The general objective should be to go as far as is feasible in making rules that will confine and guide discretion in individual cases.[15] For instance, the largely uncontrolled discretionary power of managers of public housing to evict tenants for being "undesirable" should, in the interest of discretionary justice, be governed by detailed rules.[16] Among the regulatory agencies, the Federal Trade Commission may be outstanding for the woeful inadequacy of its rules. Its trade regulation rules probably ought to be multiplied by about a hundred; when rules can do a job more efficiently and much less expensively, the easier but more cumbersome and far more expensive

13   See pages 57–59, above.
14   See pages 44–51, above.
15   Unfortunately, how far is feasible is a question that must be determined for each discretionary power in each particular context.
16   See pages 77–80, above.

method of adjudication is wasteful of taxpayers' money.[17] The Comptroller of the Currency, in granting and denying bank charters and in approving or disapproving branch banks, should state his basic policies in a set of elaborate rules.[18] The United States Parole Board, which never gives reasons in denying parole, should do the necessary thinking—which it seems to avoid—to state through rules the considerations that guide it in granting or denying parole.[19] Above all, police and prosecutors, discussed in the next two sections, should, to the extent feasible, work out their policies through rule-making proceedings.

13. *The police, the administrative process, and rule-making.* In our entire system of law and government, the greatest concentrations of unnecessary discretionary power over individual parties are not in the regulatory agencies but are in police and prosecutors. Unfortunately, our traditional legal classifications—"administrative law," "the administrative process," and "administrative agencies"—have customarily excluded police and prosecutors. The terminology as such is unimportant, but it has carried with it a failure to transfer know-how from advanced agencies, such as the federal regulatory agencies, to such backward agencies as the police departments of our cities. I think that both police and prosecutors, federal as well as state and local, should be governed by many principles that have been created by and for our best administrative agencies.

The police are among the most important policy-makers of our entire society.[20] And they make far more discretionary determinations in individual cases than any other class of administrators; I know of no close second. Comparing police decisions with regulatory agencies' decisions is as baffling as comparing murder with a million dollars, but the amount of governmental activity through the police, measured by man-hours, is more than forty times as much as the amount of governmental activity through all seven of the independent federal regulatory agencies; those agencies in the aggregate have about 10,000 employees but the

17 See pages 70–74, above.
18 See pages 120–26, above.
19 See pages 126–33, above.
20 See pages 80–84, above.

nation has about 420,000 policemen, exclusive of supporting personnel in the departments.

Our best administrative agencies do not allow subordinates to go in all directions in deciding multifarious cases; they pull toward uniformity by issuing precise and detailed rules. The Internal Revenue Service is outstanding (not typical) ; the 1968 version of its Federal Tax Regulations fills 4,400 double-column pages, a truly magnificent body of law. The problems of the police, at the level at which the police work on them, are much less complex; most of them (but not all of them) can and should be guided by detailed and meaningful rules—rules that will be realistic and enforced, not the kind of rules now in police manuals that all officers know they have to violate. Enforcement policies resting upon social values usually should be determined not primarily by individual patrolmen but by top officers of the departments, as well as by other officers of the local government. And the community should be informed and allowed to participate, except when confidentiality is necessary. Rules are needed to improve the quality of justice meted out by officers in individual cases, but something else is also especially needed—resort by the police to rule-making procedure. The public usually should know what policy problems are under consideration, and usually should have opportunity to participate, in accordance with rule-making procedure like that of federal agencies. Such rule-making procedure is one of the greatest inventions of modern government. The police should use it.[21]

One major byproduct of police rule-making, an especially important one, should be the awakening of legislative bodies to the need for basic reform of criminal statutes, especially those relating to crimes without victims, in order to narrow the gap between the statutory law and the law that is enforced. Our system of statutes reflecting the pretensions of the community and enforcement reflecting the realities of community practices is an atrocious system, for it is a major source of injustice. An officer should not have uncontrolled discretionary power to invoke a stat-

21 See pages 80–96, above.

ute against one violator out of a hundred, without explaining why, without check by a supervisor, and without judicial review even if his action is wholly capricious.[22]

14. *Prosecutors, selective enforcement, and rules.* The enormous and much abused power of prosecutors not to prosecute is almost completely uncontrolled, even though I can find no reason to believe that anyone planned it that way—or that anyone would. Prosecutions are often withheld, sometimes on the basis of political, personal, or other ulterior influence, without guiding rules as to what will or will not be prosecuted, without meaningful standards stemming from either legislative bodies or from prosecutors themselves, through decisions secretly made and free from criticism, without supporting findings of fact, unexplained by reasoned opinions, and free from any requirement that the decisions be related to precedents.[23] Furthermore, decisions of a top prosecutor are usually unsupervised by any other administrative authority, and decisions not to prosecute are customarily immune to judicial review. Even a capricious or politically induced decision to prosecute A but not B, when the evidence against B is stronger and B is otherwise more deserving of prosecution, is typically unreviewable either by a higher administrative authority[24] or by a court.[25]

The seeming unanimity of American prosecutors that their discretionary power must be completely uncontrolled is conclusively contradicted by the experience of West Germany, where the discretionary power of prosecutors is so slight as to be almost nonexistent, and where almost all they do is closely supervised.[26]

I think we Americans should learn from other nations that the huge discretionary power of prosecutors need not be unconfined, unstructured, and unchecked. We should reexamine the assumptions to which our drifting has led us—that a prosecutor should have uncontrolled discretion to choose one out of six cases to prosecute, without any requirement that the one most deserving

22 See pages 90–96, above.
23 See pages 188–91, above.
24 See pages 144, 188–91, above.
25 See pages 209–13, above.
26 See pages 191–95, above.

of prosecution be chosen, or to trade a lesser charge for a plea of guilty in one case but not in another, with no guiding rules or standards, without disclosing findings or reasons, without any requirement of consistency, without supervision or check, and without judicial review.[27]

Prosecutors, in my opinion, should be required to make and to announce rules that will guide their choices, stating as far as practicable what will and what will not be prosecuted, and they should be required otherwise to structure their discretion.[28] Even the Antitrust Division of the Department of Justice, whose subject matter is far more difficult than that of most prosecutors, can and should issue guidelines or rules to guide most of its enormous discretionary power.[29]

In the regulatory agencies, abuse of the power to prosecute or not to prosecute may be ten times as frequent as abuse of the power of formal adjudication and therefore may be ten times as damaging to justice. For instance, in agencies that regulate rates, the crucial decisions are less likely to be those made on the records of formal hearings than those made without procedural safeguards about initiating action—deciding whether and when to do nothing. What are the controls and safeguards for rate-making agencies' systems of continuing surveillance, resting on negotiation far more than on rule-making or adjudication, and what should they be?

15. *Interaction between rules and open precedents.* Administrative rules should be vastly multiplied both for confining discretion (fixing the boundaries)[30] and for structuring it (guiding its exercise within the boundaries).[31] In addition, systems of open precedents, interacting with rule-making, should contribute to the confining and structuring of discretion. The normal progression in dealing with new subject matter is from unguided discretion to some use of precedents, to clarification of standards,

27 See pages 188–91, above.
28 The words "as far as practicable" are a drastic limitation on the thought expressed, but they are essential. The problems of discovering what is practicable call for studies of major magnitude.
29 See pages 198–203, above.
30 See pages 54–57, above.
31 See pages 97–99, above.

to greater use of precedents, to discovery of broad principles, and finally to formulation of rules which answer most major questions and many minor ones. Throughout our governmental system this normal progression is often a stage or two behind the stage where it can feasibly be.[32] When the administrative lag is too much, the courts should refuse to uphold administrative action which has an inadequate basis in either rules or precedents.[33]

The prosecuting power everywhere, whether exercised by police, by prosecutors, by regulatory agencies, or by other administrators, can and should be highly structured by both rules and precedents. To the extent practicable, every such officer who decides a significant question of policy that may have value as a precedent should write a reasoned opinion which will guide later decisions and which should be open to public inspection except when confidentiality is essential.[34] This proposal obviously fits some circumstances and not others. I think it especially fits the Antitrust Division, the Federal Trade Commission, and most ordinary prosecutors; it is a misfit for some police activities.

16. *Other structuring—openness.* Other kinds of structuring which can help protect against uncontrolled discretionary power in individual cases include open plans, open policy statements, and open findings and reasons.[35] Openness is a natural enemy of arbitrariness, a natural ally in the fight against injustice. I think we need to reexamine fundamentally our seemingly unplanned tendency at all levels of government, in the courts as well as in the agencies, to close all informal processes and the accompanying papers but to open all formal hearings, transcripts of hearings, and related papers. The question worth considering is whether at both levels privacy and confidentiality should be appropriately protected and whether at both levels all else should

32 See pages 106–111, above.
33 See pages 57–59, above.
34 Determining "the extent practicable" and "when confidentiality is essential" must be done in each specific context. Despite the enactment in 1966 of the Information Act, 5 U.S.C. § 552, I think that in general our society is only in the primitive stages of answering the basic questions of what information should be open and what should be confidential.
35 See pages 99–111, above.

be open.[36] Earlier planning is needed to guide discretion, especially in the regulatory agencies, which, for want of planning, tend to be too much occupied with treating symptoms instead of underlying causes. A good system for forcing needed administrative planning is that of the SEC Special Study, 1961–63, which was singularly successful and deserves to be regarded as a model for use in other fields.[37] The widespread assumption that findings and reasons are suitable only for cases that have gone to hearing is all wrong; findings and reasons are often more important for informal discretionary action.[38]

The difference between unstructured and structured discretion can be easily appreciated in the banking agencies, especially in the changes recently made by the Comptroller of the Currency in approving or disapproving charters and branches. Before the recent changes, the outstanding features of the system were secret evidence, secret law, and secret policy. Applications and supporting materials were secret, the findings of investigators were secret, no findings were openly stated, no reasoned opinions were released to the public, no system of open precedents guided decisions, and no rules or policy statements clarified the relevant law and policy. Pursuant to the recent changes, applications and supporting materials are open except to the extent that confidentiality is essential, findings and reasons are openly stated, and open precedents are in process of development. By reason of the structuring, the chances of arbitrariness or other abuse, though not eliminated, are substantially reduced.[39] *The same sort of structuring can be applied to many functions of many administrators in federal, state, and local governments, with a great gain in the quality of justice.*

Inspiring lessons as to how to structure discretionary power can be learned from the provisions governing sentencing in the Model Sentencing Act and the Model Penal Code. The draftsmen were focused more on substance than on method, but they have beautifully demonstrated how, in an extraordinarily difficult area,

36 See pages 111–16, above.
37 See pages 99–102, above.
38 See pages 103–106, above.
39 See pages 120–26, above.

power which has to be discretionary can nevertheless be made to yield to structuring.[40]

17. *Fairness of informal procedure.* In both numbers of parties affected and amounts involved, fairness of informal procedure may be fifty or a hundred times as important as fairness of formal procedure, even though the focus of recent critics of the administrative process has been almost entirely on formal procedure. The prevailing assumption that the only choice is between providing a party the full panoply of procedural rights through a trial-type hearing and providing no procedural safeguards at all should be reexamined. Realization that the choice is not between all and none should open a whole vista for imaginative procedural thinking of the kind that has been almost totally absent.[41] For instance, even when a trial is inappropriate, a party may sometimes be entitled to know the general nature of the evidence against him and to be allowed five minutes to say what he wants to say. The Small Business Administration may properly deny loans of government money without hearings, but its nondisclosure to the applicant of information about him which it has obtained from the Federal Bureau of Information or from the House Un-American Affairs Committee seems to me unfair.

We need extensive and intensive studies of fairness of informal procedures.

18. *Checking discretion.* American government is stronger in checking discretion than in confining or structuring it. An outstanding need is for establishing a system of supervising decisions of local prosecutors, perhaps in each instance by a state attorney general.[42] The natural system of administrative appeals from subordinates to superiors is less desirable than appeals to independent officers, because of superiors' official, psychological, and personal relationships with their subordinates.[43] The excellent device of administrative appellate tribunals, manned by independent officers, should be used much more than it is. Checks by legislative

40 See pages 133–41, above.
41 See pages 116–20, above.
42 See pages 143–44, 188–91, and 207–209, above.
43 See pages 143–46, above.

committees and by legislators are both helpful and harmful to administration; in the aggregate, the net effects may be beneficial with respect to broad policies but injurious to individual justice.[44] An independent ombudsman, having no stake in results either through helping constituents or otherwise, usually can be a better critic of administration than a legislator.[45]

The American assumption that prosecutors' discretion should not be judicially reviewable developed when executive functions were generally unreviewable. The assumption is in need of re-examination in the light of the twentieth-century discovery that courts can review executive action to protect against abuses while at the same time avoiding judicial assumption of the executive power. The reasons for judicial review of prosecutors' discretion are stronger than for such review of much administrative discretion that is customarily reviewable. The whole problem of possible judicial review of prosecutors' discretion is in need of a full study.[46]

19. *A new tribunal for inexpensive review.* Litigation expense means that judicial review is unavailable for small cases, whatever the theory. We Americans need to learn from other countries that simplified review can be quite effective even though its cost is low. I recommend the establishment of a Federal Appeals Tribunal designed to provide inexpensive review of governmental action in cases involving less than $4,000.[47]

20. *Eliminating needless barriers to judicial review.* By and large, the American system of judicial review is excellent, with some exceptions, including its neglect of small cases, but one gradual development seems to me especially in need of correction. When citizens seek judicial review, a beneficent government should facilitate determinations on the merits, even though it may legitimately protect against improper use of judicial machinery. Specialist lawyers representing the federal government are tending to push beyond proper limits the technicalities of such doctrines as ripeness, standing, forms of proceedings, gov-

44 See pages 146–50, above.
45 See pages 150–51, above.
46 See pages 209–14, above.
47 See pages 155–57, above.

ernment and officer immunity, and unreviewability, and the resulting intricacies are becoming harmful barriers to determining cases on their merits. On rare occasions, government lawyers have assumed a semi-judicial role and have preferred justice to legal victories, and this is precisely what I think is needed. Government lawyers should be instructed not to interpose a technical defense in a case that seems meritorious without a finding that the policy behind the technical defense is essential as applied. The worst that can happen from opening the judicial doors in a doubtful case will be that a court will decide on the merits.[48]

21. *Philosophical underpinnings.* Punishing the innocent is unjust; is failing to punish the guilty also unjust? Since the escape of some violators is probably inevitable, the practical answer has to be that justice does not require the punishment of all who are guilty. But what if the reason for lack of punishment of one who is guilty is not failure of detection but is a deliberate choice of an officer? What if A and B are equally guilty, or A is more deserving of punishment than B, but an officer makes a deliberate choice to punish B but not A? In what circumstances, if at all, is a decision to release A unjust? And if prosecution is involved instead of punishment, this crucial question emerges: If A and B are equally deserving of prosecution, or if A is more deserving of prosecution than B, is a decision to prosecute B but not A unjust? [49]

In an affluent country, I think the legal system's answers to such questions as these should be based upon the most careful deliberation, not on considerations of convenience and economy, which gain support from habits and assumptions. Yet I doubt that our prevailing practices rest upon the best thinking of which our society is capable.

Our whole system of selective enforcement is built upon the assumption—and I think it is no more than an assumption—that justice does not require equal treatment by police, prosecutors, and other enforcement officers of those who are equally deserving of prosecution or of other governmental initiative.

This assumption, in my opinion, is in need of profound reex-

48   See pages 157–61, above.
49   See pages 167–72, above.

amination. The question that needs to be asked is whether our ideal of equal justice should be fully applicable to police, prosecutors, and other enforcement officers in their exercise of the prosecuting and initiating functions.

Another philosophical problem on which my view differs from the established one is this: If X has property worth a thousand dollars and Y has a subsidy worth a million, should X's legal protection against illegal or arbitrary exercise of discretionary power be more than Y's, less than Y's, or the same? The Supreme Court, along with many other courts, often reasons that the property is entitled to more legal protection, on the theory that Uncle Sam, like any other donor, can do as he chooses about making gifts. I think the subsidy deserves more protection because it is a thousand times as valuable. The reasoning about Uncle Sam seems to me specious, because the practical question about control of discretion is never whether the government should have power to be arbitrary; it is always whether particular officers should have such power. The philosophical problem is a vital one, because a large portion of discretionary power involves gratuities, privileges, or leniency.[50]

22. *Leniency and privilege.* One huge contributor to discretionary injustice is the idea that leniency and privilege should be exempt from protections we know how to provide. Our legal institutions seem to be largely constructed on the belief that protections are needed when government imposes obligations or restrictions on private parties but not when government confers gratuities or privileges or relieves private parties of obligations or restrictions. This idea is of crucial consequence; it is the foundation for our elaborate system of selective enforcement, which may account for two-thirds of unnecessary discretionary power. Even though the view that leniency and privilege are undeserving of a normal quota of protection is deeply embedded in case law and seems to have broad support of legislators, judges, administrators, and practitioners, I suggest that it is in need of reexamination. The inescapable reality, insufficiently appreciated, is that the discretionary power of public officers to confer privi-

50   See pages 176–80, above.

leges or to be lenient is always intrinsically a discretionary power not to confer a privilege or not to be lenient and is susceptible to many kinds of abuse, including the worst sort of discrimination, favoritism, or caprice, and may be extremely damaging to private interests.[51]

23. *The unfinished task.* The subtitle of this essay, "A Preliminary Inquiry," is precisely accurate. The aim is not to advance a set of definitive proposals. The three main purposes, as stated in the preface, are much more limited. The first one, the basic one on which all else depends, is to open the way into the jungle of discretionary power by demonstrating the falsity of the seemingly universal assumption that discretionary justice is too elusive for study. The second is to open up problems that call for further attention. And the third is to formulate an approach and to try to lay some of the foundations on which some answers can be constructed.

Even if my suggested approach is fully accepted, most of the thinking that has to be done to minimize injustice in the ways indicated is yet to be done. Cutting back unnecessary discretionary power means examining thousands of separate powers, discovering what cutting is feasible, and evaluating in each instance the wanted and unwanted results. The overall goal is properly to confine, to structure, and to check discretion, but that is always a matter of degree, and the optimum—not the maximum—has to be located for each power. The price to be paid for each step toward control of discretion has to be weighed. Frequently competing interests will and should prevail, or compromises will have to be worked out.

Not only must almost every proposal be examined in each of thousands of specific contexts of particular discretionary powers, but the first necessary step has to be to bring together for the first time a tremendous amount of information about the discretionary functions now performed within our federal, state, and local governments. Even though we live in a period of more governmental activity than ever before in world history, the information available about governmental processes seems to be at a low

51 See pages 170–72, above.

ebb. The need for more descriptive and critical studies of the realities about the administration of government programs seems to me urgent.[52]

We need not only empirical studies but also, I think, more philosophical digging. Our jurisprudence of statutes and of judge-made law is overdeveloped; our jurisprudence of administrative justice, of police justice, of prosecutor justice—of discretionary justice—is underdeveloped. *We need a new jurisprudence that will encompass all of justice, not just the easy half of it.*

Despite the magnitude of the task, I think we can and should provide a considerably better brand of discretionary justice to individual parties. Let us get on with the job of cutting back unnecessary discretionary power and finding better ways to confine, to structure, and to check necessary discretionary power.

52 Broadly speaking, political scientists of the present generation are so much preoccupied with science that they do not make descriptive *and critical* studies of government. I agree with the drive for science, but I think it is temporarily overriding other vital interests. My view can best be stated through this small sample: In Washington I lunched with a young political scientist who was writing a Ph.D. thesis on a particular unit of the government. His mastery of his subject was superb and I asked him many questions not only about facts but also about his opinions and impressions. He reminded me "You should understand that in my paper I don't express any opinions."

I think it exceedingly unfortunate that the political scientists under whom he was working had influenced him to withhold his critical judgments. To me the judgments of that perceptive and exceedingly well informed mind had great value. To the extent that attitudes of today's political scientists cut off the expression of such judgments, the result seems to me a barrier to development of better understanding and a barrier to improvement of governmental processes.